MOZ

MY STORY

To my mum, dad, Steve, Chris and Vicky, thanks for the fantastic start in life and for your continued unconditional love.

To Clare, I can't put into words how grateful I am for your constant love and support and for giving me the two most precious things on earth.

To Leo, whatever you do in life, I'll be the proudest dad ever. Make sure you always look after your mum and sister.

To my princess Maya, when you finally leave the nest and break daddy's heart, don't break it too hard.

Leo and Maya, to quote Bob Dylan, may you stay forever young.

In loving memory of Terry Newton. Rest in peace mate.

MOZ
MY STORY

ADRIAN MORLEY with PHIL WILKINSON

VSP

Published by Vision Sports Publishing in 2012

Vision Sports Publishing
19-23 High Street
Kingston upon Thames
Surrey
KT1 1LL

www.visionsp.co.uk

ISBN: 978-1-907637-57-5

Copy editor: Alex Morton
Cover design: Doug Cheeseman
Cover picture: SWpix
Back cover picture: Getty Images

Typeset by Palimpsest Book Production Limited, Falkirk, Stirlingshire

Printed and bound in the UK by TJ International, Padstow, Cornwall

A CIP Catalogue record for this book
is available from the British Library

CONTENTS

ACKNOWLEDGEMENTS

T hanks to Phil Wilkinson for his tireless work, and for making writing this book so enjoyable. To his wife Claire and their three children, for allowing my life to take up so much of theirs for the past year.

Thanks to everyone at Vision Sports Publishing, Andy Wilson, Rebecca Hutchings, Nick Walshaw at Sydney's *Daily Telegraph* and *Rugby League Week* for their help.

Thanks to those who provided tributes for this book – Ryan Giggs, Ellery Hanley, Ruben Wiki, Jamie Peacock, Ricky Stuart and Matt King.

Finally, thanks to all the coaches, team-mates and everyone else who have helped me enjoy a career which has exceeded my wildest dreams.

FOREWORD
BY RYAN GIGGS

I used to play in the same rugby league team as a lad called Morley, who was a tough, aggressive, no-nonsense forward. His name was Chris, and his 11-year-old brother, Adrian, used to come along to his games to cheer him on. Now, a quarter of a century on, I'm honoured to write a foreword for his autobiography.

I had to give up playing all other sports when I signed schoolboy forms with Man United when I was 14. For some reason, they weren't too keen on the idea of me playing rugby league at the same time!

A few years later, when I was in the United side, I was pleased to see Adrian break into the Leeds first team and go on to make a real mark in Super League. I took an interest in his career because I knew him and his brother, and because he was from the same area as I was. It's been great to see his career unfold the way it has. Not many British players have been out to Australia and made the same impact he has. He was, and is, regarded as one of the world's best players, and in the area where we grew up people are extremely proud of him.

Quite a few of the United boys are rugby league fans. Wayne Rooney, Rio Ferdinand, Michael Carrick and Paul Scholes all like the game. We stop over in a hotel the night before a Saturday match, and so we usually eat at 7.30pm and then gather around the TV to watch the Super League.

I've been a Wigan fan ever since my dad took me to a Test match at Central Park, and I saw Shaun Edwards and Martin Offiah play for Great Britain. But I love watching the sport, no matter who is playing and I'll of course look out for Moz whenever he is playing.

I sent him a text message to wish him well before the Challenge Cup Final in 2010, and was delighted when I saw him lift the famous trophy at Wembley Stadium.

He's always been fiery, tough and uncompromising – I can't help but love the way he plays the game. But the quality I really admire about him is his longevity. You don't see many rugby league players continuing into their mid-30s, especially not at such a high level, and it's a huge credit to Moz that he's been able to do that. I'm sure he has taken the best advice and been well looked after, like I have, but ultimately it comes down to his desire and his determination.

The older I get, the longer it takes me to recover from games. I feel tired the day after a game, sometimes two days after a game. I can only imagine what Moz feels like after a game with what he puts his body through! The fact he's played more than 400 games of top-level rugby league, still putting in the hits and making the yards for his team, is remarkable.

Rugby league has changed so much over the years. The players are all top athletes, and Moz has not only gone with that, he's led the way. He's never been picked for the Warrington team and the England team because of his name, but for his performances.

We live less than a mile apart, and away from the pitch he's a terrific fella. He's always willing to help others. A few years ago, a local rugby union player broke his neck. When his mates rallied round to help, Moz was there to lend his hand. That's the kind of bloke he is.

PROLOGUE

Cowering in a ditch, covered in mud, my eyes were stinging from the CS gas which had been sprayed in my face minutes earlier.

I closed them as tight as I could. Anything to ease the burning. My heart was thumping the inside of my rib cage like a bass drum.

Breathe, Moz. Breathe.

I shuffled forward on my knees, poking my head over the grass verge. I forced my eyes open to scan the landscape. I knew they were still out there, looking for me.

Think, Moz. Think.

Suddenly, something caught my eye. A movement. No, a reflection bouncing off a window. Blue flashing lights.

I ducked down and pushed myself further down the verge, hugging the ground.

I can't be caught.

Angry, depressed, half-blind, half-pissed and with adrenaline pumping through me, I tried to make sense of what had just happened. Why I was lying on a muddy slope, in the middle of the night, in the middle of Yorkshire, hiding from the police.

Two months ago I was playing in a Grand Final in Australia. Being talked about as one of the best players in rugby league.

Now, I was a piece of pub-quiz trivia, a laughing stock. The prop who'd been sent off after 12 seconds in a Test match. The player who'd cost Great Britain an Ashes win. The bloke who'd let down his team-mates and his country.

And now the police wanted me for drink-driving. And there was no way they could catch me, because the Ashes series was sponsored by the 'Think! Don't Drink And Drive' campaign.

'The press'll have a field day with this,' I thought. 'And what would I tell the RFL?'

Hi, remember me? I'm the bloke who cost you an Ashes series. Well, I've got some more bad news. I've cost you your sponsorship too.

No.

I'll stay here. The police can't stay out here all night. And it's not as if I've murdered anyone – they must stop people for drink-driving all the time.

Hang tight, Moz.

I rubbed my eyes, then blinked rapidly and forcefully, trying to push the CS residue out.

Suddenly, a noise. Footsteps. The policemen were coming into the factory grounds where I was hiding.

'I'll still be okay,' I thought. It was a big site, and I was in a good spot, down near the perimeter fence. Their muffled voices faded, until I couldn't hear anything. I debated risking a glance over the ledge, but thought better of it.

Have they gone already?

I listened intently, trying to pick up any noises, any clues that they were still out there. Then I heard the unmistakable sound which told me I'd been rumbled.

The barking of dogs.

A few weeks earlier, I'd flown back to England from Australia full of hope and excitement. It's a cliché that players love to play against the best, but it's true. In rugby league, the best are Australia, and I hadn't played them in nearly three years – a lifetime in rugby league terms. During that time, I'd been playing Down Under in the NRL, and I'd like to think I'd proved that English players can be as good as the Aussies.

Going into the series, I knew our biggest obstacle wasn't on the pitch, but in our own heads. I knew some of our players held the Kangaroos up on a pedestal, like Green-and-Gold superheroes. They'd lost 64-10 in Sydney in their last meeting a year earlier, when I was injured, and I knew that painful memory would still be playing on the lads' minds. But I'd been bashing them regularly in club matches Down Under. 'I'll show the boys that the Aussies are human,' I thought. Put them on their backsides. Prove that they can be beaten. The Kangaroos had been hit with a raft of injuries and withdrawals. Their squad contained players who weren't Test quality by their own lofty standards. By contrast, we were as close to full strength as we could have hoped to have been. If ever we were going to end our losing run, stretching back three decades to before I was born, this was it.

Before the opening Test, I'd never been so psyched up for a match. Out on the pitch at the JJB Stadium in Wigan, stretching my quads, minutes before kick-off, I was over-emotional. Shaking with nerves and excitement and energy.

Blaring out of the stadium sound system, an all-male choir sound-tracked our warm-up with *Jerusalem*. Then *Abide With Me*.

Get a grip. Concentrate.

Then the opening bars of *One Moment in Time* echoed around the stadium.

I began welling up. The enormity of the occasion – the chance to make history – had got to me. I tried shaking myself out of my trance. But when we walked, proudly, out of the tunnel minutes later, I was still zoned out. I tried to block out *God Save The Queen*, and drag myself back to the game. But I couldn't. The emotions and the music had whipped my mind into a frenzied state of energy and anticipation. I was clenching my teeth hard. I was pumped up. Like a provoked animal, I just wanted to get it on.

I decided, there and then, as we lined-up, that I was going to steam-train the first bloke. I wanted to make a statement. I wanted to show my team-mates that these blokes could be knocked down, beaten up. *Beaten.*

We kicked off and I missiled down the pitch ahead of my line. Robbie Kearns took a pass, and carried the ball back. Usually, players slow down to make impact. I didn't. I wanted to smash my shoulder into him like a wrecking ball, send him and his confidence three-feet back. But just before I hit him, Robbie jinked. He stepped. I was going at such pace, I couldn't change direction. Instinctively, I stuck my arm out and whacked him. Maybe across his chest, maybe his jaw. I wasn't sure. I circled around him and ran back into the defensive line. That's when I saw Robbie, flat out on the floor.

Job done, I thought.

Steve Ganson, the referee, called time off. Just 12 seconds on the clock. As I stood there, in my mind I went through what would happen next. He'll call me over, tell me to keep them down, I'll apologise and carry on. I was pretty sure he hadn't even seen the incident. But Ganson had his hand to his ear, taking instruction from the video referee. I walked over because I knew I was going to get a warning. Instead, he turned to me and said eight words which will haunt me forever.

'Adrian, it's a real bad one. You're off.'

He reached into his back pocket, pulled out a red card and thrust it into the air. I couldn't believe it. I was stunned. In a surreal haze. It seemed too crazy to be true. No one gets sent off in Test matches, do they? And especially not in the first minute.

But I didn't even stop to dispute it. I just wanted to disappear. I turned and ran towards the sideline.

Terry Newton grabbed my arm.

'What you doin'?' he said. 'He can't send you off for that.'

But I carried on running, not stopping, not speaking to anyone, until I reached our dressing room. Then I sat down, alone, on the bench. And began to cry. The severity of what had just happened floored me.

What the fuck have I just done? I've let my team-mates down. I've let my country down.

I was angry, and I directed it all at myself. It was the first minute of the game. I was still balling my eyes out when Kevin Sinfield walked into the room.

'Mate, get out the way, the camera's up there,' he said, nodding his head towards the Sky Sports camera fixed to the corner of the room. I appreciated that. Kev knew there was no way of cheering me up, but he also cared enough not to let the world see my misery. I shifted seats to the bench under the camera. Then I dragged myself up, showered and changed.

What do I do now?

I walked out of the dressing room and sat on the bench to watch the rest of the game. Every substitute patted my back, in a keep-your-chin-up way. The Sky cameraman kept trying to get a good shot of me, but every time he'd manoeuvre Dr Chris Brookes would shift into the way, shielding me from the lens. That meant a lot to me. The boys on the sidelines were looking after me.

And the boys on the pitch were doing great without me. We were only 8-4 down at half-time. Maybe they can still win, I thought. My mind raced back to Shaun Edwards being sent off at Wembley in 1994, and Great Britain won that game.

Come on.

Keith Senior scored early in the second half to put us 10-8 ahead. Then a penalty made it 12-8. A few frantic minutes later and we were 18-14 ahead.

I looked at the clock. Seven minutes to go.

Keep them out. Please.

Australia had the ball. Britain were holding them out. They were fantastic, the lot of them. They were winning without me, thank God.

Suddenly, a collective gasp from the 25,000 crowd. Craig Wing, my Sydney Roosters team-mate, had cut through. He had Kris Radlinski to beat.

Please Radders. Nail him.

But he never got the chance. Wing passed the ball to Darren

Lockyer, and he crossed the line to win the game. My head collapsed forward into my hands. We'd lost the Test. And it was all my fault.

I wanted people to think I'd recovered quickly from my red card. I even went out on the drink with the victorious Kangaroos players – I had a few of my Roosters mates in the touring squad – after they'd wrapped the series up 3-0. Laughing, joking. All good fun.

'*Moz, stick your arm out . . . Robbie, run at Moz . . .*'

All the while, drunken Australian players would snap pictures of Kearns colliding with my forearm, in slow motion, and collapsing on the floor. And I'd laugh with them.

But inside, it was killing me. I tortured myself over what I'd done. I'd always been a person who enjoyed life, who never worried about anything. Now, all I could think about was how I'd let my country down. Mates tried to comfort me, tried to tell me that it was one of those things, but nothing could shake me out of my mood. In my mind, I'd cost us the Ashes series. We had a chance to make history and blew it, and it was all my fault.

After a night out around Manchester with my brother Chris, I went home. Alone. It was two in the morning, and my girl-friend, Clare, was at a house party in Pontefract, in Yorkshire. I was desperate to see her.

Feeling down, feeling drunk, I made one of the worst decisions of my life. I got into the car Terry Newton had leant me, and set off on the hour-long trip to Yorkshire. I wasn't going to tell Clare. In my mind I pictured her turning around and seeing me, running up to me and hugging me, and it made me smile.

Trouble was, I didn't know where her friend lived. So I called Clare, playing it cool, trying to find out the address without giving away my game plan.

'Are you having a good night?' I said. 'I've just been chatting to a lad from Pontefract . . . what street does your mate live on?'

She rumbled me immediately.

'Adrian,' she said. No one else calls me that, only Clare. And Steve Ganson.

'If you're coming over, you'd better be in a taxi.'

'Yeah, of course. I'm not stupid . . .'

I turned off at the right junction, and called back for directions.

'Go down the lane. Second right. D'you see a petrol station?'

A drunken voice interrupted Clare, trying to give clearer instructions. But failing, miserably. I was getting nowhere.

'Text me the address,' I said. 'I'll ask someone.'

And that's when my rear-view mirror exploded into life. Flashing blue lights. It took all of two seconds for me to realise I was in the shit.

I indicated, and pulled over to the side of the road. I wound the window down. The policeman walked over.

'Do you realise why I pulled you over?' he said. 'You were talking on your phone while you were driving.'

'Oh sorry about that.'

'Have you been drinking?'

He could tell from my speech, or my eyes, or my smell, that I had.

'I had two beers earlier on, but it was a few hours ago,' I lied.

I looked for any signs that he recognised me. I'd played for Leeds Rhinos for seven seasons, so it wasn't uncommon for me to be stopped for autographs anywhere in Yorkshire. I had a bag in the boot containing some signed Kangaroos shirts. A flash of recognition, I decided, and I'd offer them to him as a bribe. But he showed no sign that he knew me.

'I'm arresting you for drink driving,' he said.

'What?!' I said. 'You've not even breathalysed me.'

I caught him off guard. He paused for a minute, wondering what to do next.

'Stay here. Don't move.'

He walked back to his police car, speaking on his radio. Either he had a breathalyser kit in the car, or he was radioing for one. Either way I was in trouble.

If they find out who I am, I am fucked.

So I did what anyone else would have done with those thoughts running through their drunken, confused, miserable mind. I ran.

I shot out of the car, and sprinted straight down the road in front of me.

'HEY! STOP!'

The policeman began to give chase. I had 30 yards on him, easily. But I had no idea where I was going and, with the street lighting, there was no way I was going to lose him. So I turned, without losing pace, into the driveway of a house. I shuffled past the parked cars in the drive, straight into the garden.

I leapt the fence into the garden next door.

I'll hide here until he's gone.

But a light went on – one of those motion-sensing security lights.

Bollocks.

I sprinted across the width of the garden and vaulted the fence into the next garden. And the same thing happened. Lights.

I leapt into the next garden and, incredibly, the same thing happened.

Will you security lights just FUCK OFF!

I jumped the next fence, and my prayer was answered. No lights. I turned 90 degrees, and ran to the back of the mid-sized garden, diving head-first into a hedgerow.

No way will he see me here.

I got my breath back, listening for the copper, looking for a torch beam. But there was nothing. I hatched an escape plan.

'Right,' I thought, running through the sequence in my mind, convincing myself it'd all be fine. Like Hannibal Smith from *The A Team*, it would all come together perfectly.

'Here's what I'll do,' I said to myself. 'First, I'll phone Tez and tell him to report his car stolen. Second . . .'

Bollocks! My phone's in the car!

I knew then that I was screwed. I tried to think my way out of trouble, but there was nothing I could do. I was stuck in a bush, in a garden, in Yorkshire, without a phone.

Reluctantly, I decided to hand myself in. I climbed out of my hiding place, walked down the side of the house to the street. I came out about 100 yards down the road from where I'd pulled over. By that point, a couple more police cars had arrived. I walked down the middle of the road, straight towards the group of policemen.

Head dipped.

Defeated.

Deflated.

As I got close to them, one of them ran towards me. Without saying a word, he raised his arm – and sprayed CS gas right into my face! My eyes caught fire. It was the most unbearable pain imaginable. I couldn't see. I screamed in agony. I was hysterical.

'You wanker,' I thought. 'There's no way you're getting me now.'

So I twisted around and shot off down the road again. I was running full speed down the middle of a street. Only, this time, I couldn't see.

I was frantically rubbing my eyes. I heard the commotion behind me. The multiple footsteps, slapping the ground as they chased after me.

I opened my eyes momentarily and saw the car I'd rushed past a few minutes earlier. Again I turned and ran down the driveway, into the garden. I could just about see through my right eye, in a blurred, under-water kind of way. I turned and began leaping the fences again. Just like before, the gardens lit up as I raced across them.

Then there was darkness, which I figured was the garden where I'd been hiding minutes earlier. But now I knew there was an army of coppers out there – well, half a dozen – there was no way I was stopping this time. Especially when they were all armed to the teeth with CS bastard gas.

All the fences were waist height – they were easy to vault. But the next one was a full-sized panel, five or six feet high. I knew I'd need a big leap to clear it. I pushed my foot down to leap, but with only one eye – and a blurry eye at that – I mistimed it. I smashed straight into the panel.

My head went clean through, followed by my shoulders. From the other side, I must have looked like a trophy reindeer head on a country club wall. As I wriggled the rest of my body through, the upstairs light went on and the home-owner drew the curtains. I looked up, apologetically.

'Sorry', I mouthed, to the silhouette in the window. I had no choice but to kick the rest of the panel in, to get my legs through.

Two gardens later, I reached the end of the row. I was out in the open. There was a junction in the road, so I sprinted right, and straight through an open gate, into the cloak of darkness. I rushed to the right, where the ground sloped down to a peri-meter fence, and threw myself at the floor. I turned around, looking for the police. No one.

My eyes followed the fence, but I couldn't see any other exit and, with the ditch, climbing over the fence was impossible. I hung tight, until I heard the Alsatians. I knew it was only a matter of time before I was found. And I knew that, if one of those dogs got a grip of my hamstring, I really could be in trouble.

For the second time in 20 minutes, I surrendered.

'Put the dogs away,' I yelled. 'I'm coming out.'

I climbed to my feet and walked out slowly, hands up, making sure they had no excuse to CS me again. But that didn't stop two of them pouncing on me, forcing me to the ground while they handcuffed me. I felt like a terrorist.

At the police station, I again clocked the officers to see if anyone recognised me. I was still pissed off, partly because I'd been caught, but mainly because I'd had CS sprayed in my face.

'What's your name?'

'Lee Butler,' I said. Lee's my best friend. And one of the only blokes my age who's date of birth I knew off by heart.

'Date of birth?'

Yep, right on cue.

'24 November, 1976,' I replied.

The policeman stopped scribbling and looked up from his desk at me.

'Listen. You've got a chance to change it now. You don't want to get yourself into more trouble.'

Did I not say the date of birth convincingly enough? Or did he know who I was?

Either way, I had no intention of making things easy for them.

'I don't know what you're talking about,' I said. 'It's Lee Butler.'

If the officer had any worries that he might have made a mistake, that maybe he'd booked someone who just happened to look a bit like the rugby player who'd been sent off in the first minute of a Test match weeks earlier, then that doubt was rubbed from his mind as I was being marched into a cell.

Clare burst through the door at the station. She and her friends had seen the whole drama unfold from the window of the party. It turned out that her friend's house was one of those with a security light.

'You have my boyfriend and I want to speak to him,' I heard her demand.

'What's his name?'

'Adrian Morley.'

'Thanks for that.'

CHAPTER ONE
KID FROM CORONATION STREET

'D'you want a shy-tash?'

I'd never heard of one of those before. I was six, maybe seven, but more wise to the world than most kids my age, simply because I had two older brothers. Stephen is seven years older, Chris nearly four.

'I don't mind giving it you,' Chris continued, doing his best salesman pitch. 'You can have it for free.'

'But what is a shy-tash?'

'It's hard to say . . . I'll show you if you want.'

I considered his offer. It wasn't in Chris's nature to be kind, at least not to me; he only showed generosity when Mum, Dad or Ste told him to, never without prompting, and never with such enthusiasm. My childlike intrigue couldn't handle the suspense.

'Yeah, okay then.'

And with that, Chris put his hand behind his back, and then brought it back out. His first finger was covered in goo, poo, deep brown. I sat frozen still, unable to compute what he'd just done. His finger inched closer to my face, allowing me to get a better look. I'd seen enough, but I couldn't keep my eyes off his hand. I thought this was as bad as it could get. I thought wrong, as he wiped his finger across the top of my lip.

'There you go,' he said, wiping his finger down the side of

the hand-me-down Manchester United top I was wearing. I know, because at that age I never wore anything else.

'You've got a shite 'tash.'

I was stunned. I didn't know whether to cry, or argue, or wipe my mouth, or try and least get one punch in before he'd retaliate with many more. So I did what most boys my age would have done in that horrible position. I screamed.

'MUM! MUMMM!'

By this point, one of two things should have happened. Chris should have clamped his hand around my mouth to shut me up, or run downstairs to get his version of events in first. Instead, he just sat there smiling at me. *What the hell was he doing?*

My mum walked in. I quickly told her where Chris had stuck his finger and where he'd wiped it. The brown goo was still on top of my lip and was beginning to itch my nose.

'Mum, he's lying,' Chris said, leaning behind his back to bring a jar out. 'It was Nutella. I was being kind and sharing it. He's just trying to get me in trouble. As usual.'

And that was my home life in my early years. Steve was good as gold, though there was too big an age gap for us to be really close when we were kids. We only really bonded later on. Chris was nearly four years older and we shared a lot of the same friends and played the same games, but that didn't stop him being horrible to me growing up. He tormented me. He educated me the hard way about wedgies and wrestling, and when he wasn't being out-n-out torturous, he'd get me in trouble other ways.

Like bed time. We shared a room for a spell, and if we were making too much noise, my dad would stomp up the stairs to tell us to shut up.

'There'll be trouble if there's one more peep out of here,' he'd warn us.

The door wouldn't be closed for a second when Chris would whisper into my ear, 'peep', which always had me rolling around in hysterics, and always got me in trouble.

I grew up on Coronation Street.

Remember the old opening credits to the long-running TV soap? The cobbled street, the seemingly endless row of terraced houses and backyards? It was my claim to fame when I was younger – and even now, occasionally – that the scene was filmed on our street, Cedric Street, in Salford. Mr Tandy lived at No.22 and, if you looked closely, you could see his car in the scene. The street was cobbled, quiet with traffic, with a fence at the end, on the other side of which was a reservoir. The locked gates made perfect goalposts.

I never met any other Adrians growing up. The only one I saw on TV was the woman in *Rocky*, which wasn't the best thing to brag about to my mates. I can't tell you how many times I heard people yell 'Yo A-driaaannnn' in Sylvester Stallone's punch-drunk accent. My dad – Leo – is a strong Catholic, hence my older brothers are called Stephen and Christopher. When my mum, Mary, was pregnant with me, she wanted to avoid any obvious Biblical names – James, Luke, Matthew – and having met a couple on holiday with a boy named Adrian, asked my dad about it. To her surprise, he loved it. Adrian, Dad informed her, was the name of the only English pope, so they were both happy!

At school, the teachers called me Adrian, but to my parents I was always Aje, to my mates I was always Moz, and to my brothers I was always 'Chink' (they claimed, long before the word became socially forbidden, my narrow eyes made me look Chinese. I never saw it, though.).

I remember a lot of my early childhood, even if I can't remember which memory was my first. I remember crying on my first day at All Souls Primary School, but I soon learned to love it. It was only a five-minute walk away from our house, and my mum was a lollipop lady and a dinner lady too, which served to make me both popular and well-behaved at the same time. We only had eight in our class, three girls and five lads; incredibly, three of us went on to play international rugby league.

Nathan McAvoy and I represented England, and Carlo Napolitano played for Italy. As I write this, Carlo is the current Italian team coach and preparing for their first World Cup appearance.

Carlo and I became good friends quickly. He's had alopecia since he was little and, being the only bald Italian kid living in Salford, he developed a thick skin, a silver tongue and – when that failed – an ability to look after himself.

I was always the tallest of my age group and sports came naturally to me. I won a mini-marathon when I was in the Cubs, giving me my first sports medal, and I was always the quickest, the strongest and the fittest without having to train. Nathan was a real athlete too, and sports day was always about the duel between him and I (for the record, I never lost . . . though he did trip up over his own shoelaces one year).

I did pretty well at school. I kept on the right side of the teachers and my half-decent right peg at football made me a popular team-mate. I was never red-hot at football, but I could hold my own in the games we played at school and at home, and I did alright for a local Saturday morning team, Seedley, as well. I even won a five-a-side tournament with the Cubs, which convinced me I could go on to make it professionally.

Unlike most of the other kids, I preferred defending more than scoring, but whatever position I played I was always Bryan Robson. He was my hero growing up. My bedroom looked like a giant Man United badge had spewed up everywhere; it was on my walls, bed sheets, pyjamas, you name it. My mum's a huge United fan and so it was inevitable that we'd grow up supporting them, too. Every Saturday afternoon, I'd rush in from playing football outside, on the street, to catch the scores on the BBC. I'd wait for United's result, check how their closest rivals had got on, and then hang around long enough to find out how Morley rugby union club had done, just because we shared a name. United's FA Cup Final win against Everton in '85 was one of my earliest memories of being excited at a sporting event on TV. From then on, every time I played football, I had to be Bryan Robson. One time, at school, we were told there would be a special guest from Man United coming to visit us the following day.

I prayed before I went to bed that it was the England captain, and again when I woke up. I convinced myself that it would be him. And so when our teacher welcomed Brian Kidd to the assembly, everyone smiled and cheered and clapped, apart from the rangy, tall lad at the back who fought back the tears. Poor Brian must have wondered what he'd done to offend me!

I got my first job working security when I was eight years old.

Cedric Street is only a few hundred yards away from The Willows and, while rugby league didn't play much of a role in my early years, we'd often hang out outside Salford's old ground. There always seemed to be something going on. A game, a training session, a hen party in the bar. One evening, I was hanging around outside the ground when an old man in a suit walked across the car park in my direction. I thought he was going to tell me to clear off and go home.

'Lad, mind my car and I'll give you 50p,' he said. 'Some bugger put my window through last week.' That was nothing new to me. A few months earlier, I'd been to Maine Road to watch a Manchester City game (I'd won tickets in a competition at school in which we had to draw an anti-smoking poster; 'Think Twice or Pay the Price' was the slogan I came up with, which I'm still quite proud of) and a group of black lads had offered to watch my dad's car for him when we parked up in Moss Side. Wisely, he paid them.

And so I gravitated around his car, taking my role seriously at first, as if people were just waiting in the shadows for me to nod off so they could smash up his nice motor. He came out of the building two hours later, thanked me and paid me. The next week he was there again. It didn't take me long to realise his regular pattern, nor for me to work out that I could go home for a couple of hours, and as long as I returned five minutes before he came out he was none the wiser. I'd just got my first girlfriend, long before I knew what having a girlfriend actually meant – Sarah, a cute blonde-haired girl my age who lived across the street – and so the money came in handy for buying her sweets from the corner shop. I'm romantic, me.

That carried on for a while, until one day when I returned, five minutes before the fella was due to come out, I spotted his car in its usual spot . . . with a side window smashed in. I legged it before he got out, and gave The Willows a wide berth for a few months.

My mum and dad were great parents. They left us to play and find our own way in life, but they were firm with us. Dad wasn't old-fashioned, but he was big on tradition and routines. We all went to church together on Sundays, and we'd all sit down together at the table at meal times each night. We'd even have a set meal for each day of the week. Saturday was steak, Sunday full English breakfast followed by roast dinner, Monday gammon, Tuesday Shepherd's Pie, Wednesday bacon and egg, Thursday spaghetti bolognese and Friday – of course – was chippy tea. It was at the dinner table one evening that Mum asked the question which would go on to change our family forever.

'How would you like a sister?'

I was only nine or 10, but I already knew enough about biology to know parents their age didn't usually have more children. My dad was 36 when he had me, my mum about the same.

'We're thinking of adopting a little girl,' my mum said. 'So . . . d'you fancy it?'

A few Sundays earlier, a nice lady from the Catholic Children's Rescue Society had spoken at our church about the kids who don't get a chance in life. It struck a chord with my mum. She loved raising kids and I knew she'd always wanted a girl. So after running the idea past us three boys, Mum and Dad went through the process of seeing if they were eligible, which entailed endless visits from social workers, who even quizzed me about whether I'd be upset if a little girl took my bedroom. But I wasn't bothered one bit. I wanted a sister, I looked forward to not being the youngest, plus I was always a bit jealous that Chris and Ste shared a bedroom and I missed out, so it was win, win, win for me.

I even made a nice book for the social worker to pass on to my new sister, to welcome her to the family. I'd never been into colouring pictures before, or making cards with glitter and glue. It was a new experience for me, and I liked it. My mates were excited too. Carlo didn't have a sister, and every day he'd call at the door and ask, 'Is she here yet?' After what seemed like an eternity since my mum first put the idea in our heads, Victoria arrived.

I took to her straight away. She was hard work at first, but she was so funny and sweet. Seven years younger than me, I spoiled her rotten – we all did – and she settled in straight away. People have asked me whether it feels different because she's adopted; not one bit. If anyone asks me, I have two brothers and a sister. There's no distinction at all. When I took my son Leo to visit Vicky in Australia, where she now lives, after the 2008 Rugby League World Cup people commented that he looked like her. She just smiled and said, 'Yeah, he's got my genes.'

CHAPTER TWO
PLAYING WITH FIRE

Sharing a room with two older brothers, I grew up quickly. I watched 18-rated films long before I should have and I knew about beautiful women before puberty, thanks to Chris's posters next to his bed. He convinced my mum that they were art, but they were really just pictures of fit girls with their tits out.

Until I was about 12, I was happy where I was knocking about on or around Cedric Street. As long as I had a ball and a couple of mates to play with, I was content. As I got older, I started venturing further afield. Me and some mates would go into Manchester every Saturday, looking around, having a laugh, convincing ourselves that we would chat up girls. We rarely did, though. The one time I thought I was making progress with a brunette my age, she left me in the queue at McDonald's to go to a Take That record signing at HMV. I wasn't the jealous type, but on that occasion I couldn't help myself; I used my milkshake straw as a makeshift pea-shooter and fired pieces of chewed up paper at Robbie Williams!

It wasn't long before we started drinking. My mum and dad had a spirit cabinet, which they monitored keenly. But Chris convinced me that, if we each had a swig of every bottle – and there were about 12 of them – they'd be none the wiser. And his plan would have worked, had I not thrown up every-where in bed that night. I woke up nursing the mother of all hangovers and as a 13-year-old vowed never to touch the stuff again.

My promise didn't last long, though. After Chris signed for St Helens on his 17th birthday, he'd regularly receive free crates of McEwan's lager, their principle sponsor. Chris kept some cans for himself, and sold the rest to me. When I was 14, the police caught me and my good mate Neil Farrow drinking and marched us home. We called at Faz's first, where I saw his dad flip his lid at him, which made me fear the worse for when I got home. But my dad was more embarrassed than angry. He sat me down and said, 'If you want a beer, come and see me and have it in the house.'

His logic was that he didn't want me and my friends drinking on the streets. And he was true to his word. The following weekend, he came up with a bottle of really cheap lager – Saracen, 3% proof – and my mates and I sat and drank it from beakers. We probably couldn't even get drunk on the stuff, but we were made up. We stayed in playing cards, not bothering anyone and feeling like real men. His idea probably helped rein me in a little bit, because I was at an impressionable age and had started getting into mischief.

Growing up in Salford, I saw a lot of lads become plastic gangsters, sometimes overnight. They were good lads, who liked a laugh one day, but the next they started carrying knives and pretending to be hard. The change in them was amazing. I saw some great lads who just woke up one morning and decided to become knobs.

They started stealing, from shops, houses and cars. They'd hang out around Salford Precinct, which is a rough area, but a lot of what they came out with was hot air – they created reputations for themselves without ever doing anything. Plastic gangsters. Dickheads, basically. The kind you see on Jeremy Kyle these days – the type you almost sympathise with, rather than fear.

I came from a good family, so I was shielded from that kind of behaviour a little; all my focus was on playing sport. The worst thing we ever did was light fires in the park. Once, we came across an air vent which led into a warehouse unit. Inside were three new motorbikes, with the keys still in the ignition. We could only drive them three or four metres but, kids being kids, we thought it would be fun to fool around with them. Then we found a canister which said 'Explosive' on it.

'I'll have that,' I thought. It only just fitted through the air vent we'd gone through. Back in the park, we gathered some wood and started a fire. Then I threw the canister on. We all stood back a few yards, not knowing what would happen.

BOOM!

Suddenly, everything went white. I came around a few seconds later, still disillusioned, and my first thought was one of devastation – my tracksuit pants were singed. But then I stopped worrying about my pants as the burning sensation on my face got hotter and hotter. My mate, Faz, poured cider on me, but that didn't help. The heat got worse. The side of my face felt like it was on fire. My tracksuit pants actually were still on fire. It was horrendous. Like giving birth through my cheek. I'd never experienced pain like it and nothing I've been through since has been as painful. I've broken my arm, my jaw, my cheekbone, one rib, two thumbs, my nose, ruptured a bicep, and had surgery on a wrist. I've had my eye taken out of its socket, had surgery on my spine, dislocated fingers and had countless stitches. And nothing has ever been as agonising as that night in a Salford park. If I could have ripped the side of my face off, I would have. But I couldn't, so I got on my bike, and pedalled as fast as I could to my friend's house. The pain was getting worse and worse. I ran into his house, filled the sink full of water and ducked my head under.

A flash of extra agony, then relief.

My mate's mum phoned for an ambulance, which I was happy about. Then she phoned my mum, which I definitely wasn't happy about. I knew she'd be disappointed. I was taken to Hope

Hospital and then my mum had to bathe saline onto my face, until I was transferred to a burns unit.

I was 14. I was vain. All I could think was, 'I'm going to be scarred for life'. I pictured the war veterans I'd seen on TV, with their disfigured faces, and feared I'd look the same. I feel guilty admitting that now, but I was just a kid. The doctors put a mask on half of my face, and I missed a couple of weeks of school until it recovered. Thankfully, the scarring is minimal – I notice it, but no one else has. And I've never played with fire since.

Chris jokes now, saying he made me the man I am, and maybe he's right. I learned early on to cope with the rough stuff and stand my corner. But that wasn't his noble intention. Strangely, while he was more than willing to torment me relentlessly, he protected me fiercely. On my way back from primary school one day, a high school lad whacked me. No reason, no warning, he just came up to me and clocked me across the side of my face. I went home in tears, and after I'd sobbed to Chris about what had happened he stormed out of the house to look for the lad, but to no avail. About two years later, I saw that same guy outside the shops in the precinct. My heart started racing. I tugged on Chris's top and said, 'That's the lad who hit me'.

'Watch this Chink,' he said. 'I'll steam him.'

From nowhere, I got a rush of adrenaline.

'No it's alright,' I said. 'I'll do it.'

Trouble was, Mum was with us, so we made our excuses and held back until she was out of sight. We walked past this kid, really casual, as if I didn't remember who he was. Then, I shot my right hand out from my side, launching my fist at his face and catching him sweet across the jaw. I didn't drop him, but he was stung, and didn't even attempt to fight back. It was the first time I'd hit anyone for real, and I could tell Chris was proud of me.

Without intending to, Chris had made me tough, simply because I had to tolerate him at home. But he also showed me when to fight and, before long, he ultimately shaped the way my life panned out.

I've heard about musicians and artists having thunderbolt moments early in their lives, which mapped out their destinies. One minute they were just regular kids doing regular things, and then they'd hear The Beatles for the first time or see Robert De Niro for the first time and know – just know – that they had to do the same thing. I was the same. Many rugby league players grow up with the sport, watching it with their dads and playing it at school. It's part of their lives from an early age. But not me.

I had little interest in rugby league until the summer between leaving primary school and joining high school, when I went along to see my brother play for the first time. That was my thunderbolt moment. Until then, I'd been Man United mad, worshipping Bryan Robson and trying my best to emulate him. Watching Chris and his Langworthy team take on Eccles, as an 11-year-old, changed all that. I pictured myself out there, taking the ball in, hard and fast. The 'smack' of the collision. And then there was the tackling. How I'd love to tackle! To launch myself into an opponent, hoping to hear that satisfying, deflating 'grunt' from the boy I'd just floored. Finally there was a sport that didn't stifle and punish my aggression. It was my calling.

Chris was playing in the back-row and he looked so hard and cool, covered in mud. But as good as Chris was, there was another kid who caught my eye.

He played stand-off and he was rapid, with a great chip over. No one could catch him. Every time he'd get the ball, the mums and dads would shout 'Come on Wilson' and when he didn't have the ball, they'd shout 'Give it to Wilson'. I heard one of the grown-ups say that St Helens were already looking at this wiry-framed kid with the mop of curly hair. He never went on to make it professionally in rugby league, though. But don't feel too sorry for him.

Instead, he changed his surname, changed his sport, and Ryan Giggs went on to have a pretty decent career in football.

CHAPTER THREE
COCK OF THE YEAR

I made rugby league history in one of my first games for Eccles and earned a record that I'm convinced has not been beaten since.

It was my first full year in the sport, I was 12 years old, and we were playing a side from Oldham (including a fresh-faced Paul Sculthorpe, playing a year ahead of his age group). Early in the first half, I was sent off for a high tackle. It was a fair call – I'd caught the lad across his chin and dropped him. But at half-time, as our lads huddled on the touchline, the opposing coach walked over and said he was going to have a word with the referee. 'I don't like seeing lads missing out, not at this age,' he gracefully explained. I watched as he strolled over to the ref, the pair looked at me, and then I saw the official nod his head. I was elated. I went back on, determined to make an impact. I wanted to make amends to my team-mates, and give them a lift. A couple minutes into the second half, one of their forwards drove the ball in, I clothes-lined him, and before I had time to say, 'Honest, Sir, it was an accident,' the referee had his red card back out of his pocket. Sent off twice in the same match!

The opposing coach approached me after the game and said, 'Son, you're going to have to cut the high-tackles out'. And I did, for a while.

Having developed a fascination for rugby league in the summer before I started at high school, I put my name down for both school teams – football and rugby league – as soon as term started. But after one game of playing league, I knew it was for me. I ditched the round-ball game, quit my local football side and put my hand-me-down replica United shirt at the back of my wardrobe.

Nathan McAvoy and I had become really close, and he shared my enthusiasm for league. He only lived around the corner, and so we'd walk to school together, and at weekends I'd sleep over at his house. Nathan's one of 13 children, so my mum used to go mad.

'Freda doesn't need another mouth to feed,' she'd say.

But I didn't eat much back then, and I wasn't any bother.

Rugby league started to take over our spare time. We started paying more attention to games at The Willows, sneaking in when they opened the gates mid-way through the second half, until we decided to splash out and become Junior Red Devils season-ticket holders. That entitled us to watch the A team – the reserves – play on Thursday nights. To this day, Terry O'Connor still says he remembers me going up to him and asking for his tie-ups – the laces that held up players' socks – after a game one night. But I say to him, 'Not me Tez. I only asked the first-team players.'

I loved playing for my school team so much that I joined a club side, Eccles, which was a half-hour bus ride from my house. John Barlot, the coach, really encouraged me. He made me captain for my first game, on the basis that my brothers had been good, so I must be.

Paul Watson, father of the future Welsh international, Ian, was great with the Salford lads. He lived a few miles away in Eccles but he used to drive out of his way to pick us up and take us to training sessions and matches. If it wasn't for him, I and the other Salford lads would have had to get the bus. If I missed the bus or it was raining, would I have bothered? I'm not too sure. That's why I'll always be grateful to Paul.

Nothing frustrated me more about playing football than seeing a little whippet dashing past me and being powerless to stop him. But in rugby league, I could whack anyone who dared come my way, and not get sent off for it (well, most of the time). I loved tackling more than anything. As captain, if I won the coin toss, I always opted to kick off so I could get stuck in straight away. Despite my occasional red cards, I had a great technique, bulleting at players' legs, a bit like one of my early heroes, Shane Hansen – dad of Wigan forward Harrison – was doing at Salford. Getting hurt never bothered me so long as I hurt them more; that's all I cared about. I made it personal. Regardless of the result, I cared about whether an opponent had got the better of me or not. I was probably a marked man, even back then, for the simple reason that I had the unofficial tag of being the school 'cock' – the hardest lad in the year. It was a reputation I had earned for not doing a great deal; Chris was a tough lad, and being 'Moz's brother' carried more weight than anything I ever did. Truth is, as hard as people thought I was, and as well as I did at rugby league, only once when I was at high school was my resolve really tested. And I failed, miserably.

My dad was a mechanical engineer for Royal Ordnance Factory, making munitions for the military. It sounded like a cool job, and it was. If I'd been a bit sharper back then, I'd have used it to try and impress my mates. Every year Dad's company would take us to a pantomime and we'd meet Father Christmas and we'd have a party with the other dads and lads. We loved it. But all of those privileges went when he was laid off.

My dad was out of work for the best part of a year before he landed a job as a maintenance man at a nearby hospital. Dad is a very proud man – even now, he says, 'We always took you on holiday every year', and they did. They even managed to scrimp and save enough for a camping trip to France while he searched for work. And it must have been tough, having so many mouths to feed with such little income.

During that time, I was entitled to free school dinners because of the family's low income. But I'd seen the kids with the meal vouchers at school; they'd go first at dinnertime, to cruel sniggers from the rest of us. I pleaded with my parents not to make me go on free dinners, and so each day my mum would give me £1.50 so I could continue buying my own dinner.

I still feel bad for doing that. It's one of my early regrets.

I've said sorry to my parents since, because that money could have been used far better. They said they didn't think anything of it, but I remember it, because I regret not being brave enough not to worry about what others would think of me. And this from the lad who was apparently the hardest in his year.

Throughout high school I made the lower representative sides, like Salford's town team, without scaling the heights of the regional or national levels. I played rugby because I enjoyed it; the laugh with my mates, the training, the games. When Salford took on St Helens' town team – a representative side comprised of all the best juniors from the town – at their place, my uncle John came to watch me. I played alright, and afterwards he said, 'There might be a career in this for you.'

Chris had signed for Saints and I wanted to do the same, but I wasn't as good as he was. Chris was dominant in every team he played for, a big, strong, angry human being who tore into defences. Widnes and Salford had also been in for him before he signed for Saints. No one had ever really taken much notice of me, or even given me an inkling I might be good enough to make it professionally, until my uncle John planted the seed in my mind that, maybe, I could make it too. Lads were being signed up at 12 and 13. There were some brilliant players at schoolboy level who never kicked on, whereas I was the opposite, the average toiler who developed late on. I knew I wasn't the most skilful player, I wasn't particularly strong, I didn't have a step and I was just about functional with the ball in hand. But I prided myself on my tackling. I'd pressure myself to put some big shots on. Our Salford town team couldn't compete with the likes of St Helens and Wigan. We'd go into games knowing we would lose, so to make it interesting I'd challenge myself to make sure I wiped players out. It was nothing I practiced or worked on. People talk about God-given talent, and if there was one thing I was given, it was the ability to floor opponents, so I decided that that was the part of my game I should really focus on and become known for. I loved the lift it gave my team-mates, and their congratulations only fed my desire to hit even harder next time. I started off tackling around the legs. But by the age of 15, I'd mastered the art of smashing players with my shoulder around the ball area, to try and force an error, and I earned a bit of a name for myself as a big hitter.

I did quite well at school. My brother Steve's quite academic. Chris, not so much. With an A in PE, four Bs and two Cs, I'm firmly in the middle.

I earned a bit of extra cash during the summer after I left school, a fresh-faced 16-year-old, manning a car park for a Test cricket series at Old Trafford; the £120 a week paid for a holiday to Kos for Faz and I. Foolishly, we blew most of our spending money on hiring mopeds. I say foolishly, because I nearly killed myself one afternoon when I took a corner too fast descending a mountain and came off, sliding across the road. Three feet further and I swear I'd have gone over the edge, and that would have been the end of me!

My grades were easily good enough to get me into college and continue studying, but my brothers were working, and I envied their lifestyles and incomes. They had money for the pub, and for new clothes, and for going out. And so, while I harboured a dream to follow Chris into rugby league, I started down the same path as Steve, training as an electrician.

NG Bailey's was a Manchester firm, but I alternated between spending six weeks on site in Liverpool, and six weeks at college in Leeds. It was tough going. I woke at six, then had a half-hour walk to Eccles, where a sparky picked me up. We'd drive the hour to Liverpool, work two four-hour shifts sandwiching a half-hour break, and then make the same journey back to Salford.

I'd walk in 12 hours after leaving home, and all for £1.52 an hour. Our job was fitting out the Liverpool Women's Hospital, which was just a shell when I started. In the winter it was unbearably cold, working in a building with no walls, which offered us no protection from the icy winds.

Between work, and training for Eccles Under-18s on Tuesday and Thursday evenings, and games on Sundays, I didn't have too much time for anything else. But there was a sense of satisfaction about what I was doing with my life. I worked there for two years, and I thought that was me for life. The hours were long and the travel was hard, but it wasn't the worst job in the world. It felt good to be doing what my brothers did. Work hard in the week, head to the pub on Fridays, play on Sundays – I enjoyed it. I was only earning a pittance, but it was a pittance more than my mates who went to college, and it was enough to pay for everything I needed, namely a new pair of boots every few months and a few pints every Friday night.

The lads I worked with were a great bunch. Before I'd started, I'd heard rumours of new-starters being greased up or having compound rubbed on their balls, but I was alright because I was bigger than most of the fellas, and I wasn't a gob-shite either.

CHAPTER FOUR
SIGNING

I've often wondered whether I'd have ever made it as a professional if it hadn't been for Nathan McAvoy.

He was the gun player in our Eccles side. The one all the girls fancied, the one destined for the top. By the time we were 16, playing in the Under-18s league, most of the stand-outs we'd grown up playing against – Paul Sculthorpe, Keiron Cunningham, Sean Long – had already signed contracts, and Nat had plenty of clubs chasing him, too. But he carried on playing for Eccles, biding his time while he decided what to do. The scouts continued to come down and watch him play, and eventually they started taking notice of me as well.

I went along to train with my brother Chris at St Helens a couple of times, hoping to catch their eye, but the only offer that came my way wasn't from Saints but from Swinton, who offered me and Ian Watson £1,500 a year each. They said it was the most they'd offered juniors, which sounded appealing. 'Swinton's highest-ever paid junior' . . . it had a ring to it. As I mulled over that offer, Halifax invited me and Nathan for talks – they were interested in signing us both. They picked us up outside my house and drove us the 30-odd miles across the Pennines to their ground.

Unlike Swinton, Halifax were in the top flight, and the thought of playing for them was even more attractive because the Great

32

Britain coach, Mal Reilly, was in charge. He was already a legend; my dad had told me what a great player he'd been.

Mal showed us around the ground, asked us about our aspirations – 'Just to make it,' I remember mumbling – and shook our hands as Nat and I split up to meet with the Halifax officials. A middle-aged man in a suit said they could offer me £4,000-a-year, for two years. The same as Nathan McAvoy, he said. Suddenly, Swinton's record-breaking offer wasn't quite as tempting!

My mind was made up. I instantly set my heart on Halifax, but I'd promised my dad that I wouldn't sign anything until I'd spoken to him first, so I reluctantly asked for a couple of days to think about it.

Nat and I rode back in the same car.

'What do you think?' he asked.

'Are you kidding? Mal Reilly's the coach and I get four grand a year.'

'Four?' he said. 'They offered me eight.'

'Eight a year?'

'Yeah.'

Nat was the better player and it didn't bother me that he'd been offered more. But the fact that they'd lied to me left a bitter taste in my mouth. I was so pissed off at the way they'd tried to trick me – they must have thought Nat and I wouldn't discuss figures – that I instantly went off the idea of playing for them. I didn't tell them 'no', but I kept them waiting. I didn't want to make a decision I'd regret, so I waited to see if my anger would recede. As well as that, I was still hoping Salford would come in for me. They were my home-town club, the only club I'd ever supported.

At around the same time, Eccles made it through to the Lancashire Cup Final against Blackbrook and, in a quirk of fate, it was at The Willows. 'Right,' I thought. 'If they don't notice me when I'm playing on their own ground, they never will.'

I saw it as my last chance to impress them. I gave it my all, throwing myself into tackles with even more enthusiasm than normal, volunteering to take the ball in whenever I could, barking instructions at my team-mates. I've always been a big critic of my own performances, but at the full-time whistle (we won) I knew I'd given my all, and played pretty well.

It was the first major trophy I'd won with Eccles, so it was a great feeling. As we cracked open the beers in the dressing room, my dad popped his head through the door.

'Aje', he said. 'There's a scout out here who wants a word with you.'

Finally, my moment had come. Nathan and Ian Watson had already been offered contracts with Salford. Now it was my turn.

I came out of the dressing room, and spotted my dad talking to a fella, who I instantly presumed was the scout.

'Aje,' my dad said, 'this is Bob Pickles. He's a scout for Leeds.'

With the look I gave, Bob must have thought I was hard of hearing, or a bit slow, or both.

'Leeds?' I asked.

He nodded.

'Yes, Leeds,' he repeated slowly, as if talking to a child. 'I've been very impressed with your performances lately and was wondering if we could talk about a contract.'

'Definitely,' I said, soon warming to the idea of signing for them. I'd had it in my mind that the Lancashire Cup Final was my last chance to impress a club. If Salford didn't want me, sod them. Their loss.

Leeds' interest made the win even more enjoyable. I went out celebrating with my team-mates and, when I got back, my dad was waiting up for me.

'Doug Laughton has already been on the phone,' he said. 'He's coming round tomorrow.'

My mum spent the following day cleaning and tidying, as if Doug was royalty. He was rugby league royalty, at least, having had a great career as a player and made a name for himself in coaching at Widnes, and then at Leeds.

When he arrived, my dad let him in and walked him through into our front room.

'Would you like a cigarette,' my dad asked. My mum shot him a piercing I-can't-believe-you've-just-asked-him-that look, presuming he wouldn't smoke.

But Dougie surprised my mum, and myself.

'I will have one thanks . . . and I'll have one for later,' he said, taking two cigarettes, lighting one up and putting the other in his shirt pocket.

'Right, Adrian,' he said, getting straight down to business. 'We want to sign you. How much do you want?'

I'd already gone through this in my head before he'd arrived. The offers from Swinton (£1,500) and Halifax (£4,000) were still on the table. But Leeds were a much bigger club, and looking like the only side really capable of keeping up with Wigan. They also seemed to give young lads a chance in the team, which was appealing. But the overriding swaying factor was that I was already spending every other six weeks in Leeds with my work commitments, meaning training would be on my doorstep for half the year; it wouldn't disrupt my apprenticeship.

I was still only 16. I was earning £1.52 an hour. I had no bills to pay. In my mind, I'd settled on £2,000 a year, just so it was at least more than what Swinton had tabled.

I shrugged.

'I'm not sure,' I said to Doug.

'Right, well how about we say £6,000 up front – tax free – and £3,000 a year,' he said.

If my eyes could have popped out of my head cartoon-style, they'd have knocked Doug clean out. I couldn't believe it. But before I could control my delight enough to say anything, he cut in.

'Oh sorry, sorry, my mistake,' he said.

I knew it was too good to be true.

'It's not six grand tax free. It's eight and a half. And there'll be match fees and bonuses as well, on top.'

In the space of him remembering the upper-limit for tax-free payments to amateurs, I'd earned an extra £2,500!

'Sounds good,' I said. I could tell my dad was happy, too, even if he was trying his best to look like he negotiated contracts all the time. Doug stood up, and shook both of our hands.

'Would you like a brew?' my dad asked. He accepted, sat down, and began telling us about his plans for me and the team, and talking about the game in general. He's engaging company, Doug. He must have talked for an hour, cracking jokes, making comments, asking questions.

My dad offered him another drink.

'No, I'd better not,' he said. 'The wife and kids are in the car.'

CHAPTER FIVE
CARE IN THE COMMUNITY

I was never worried, until the day my own lawyer told me I might go to prison.

I was only 17, and the thought of being the fresh piece of meat in jail was enough to make the pit of my stomach churn. I was nearly sick, right there in the office.

'If you're found guilty there's a chance of a custodial sentence.'

That clumsy, two-word phrase was racing through my mind on auto-repeat.

'Custodial sentence. Custodial sentence.'

Until then, I'd taken my first brush with the law in my stride. Wasn't concerned, certainly wasn't losing any sleep over it. Maybe it was my youth, or maybe it was the naive notion that because, in my own eyes, I'd done nothing wrong, everything would work itself out.

A few weeks earlier, I'd tagged along with my brother, Chris, and his mates to Blackpool. All of my mates were broke, but because I'd recently signed with Leeds, I had a bit of extra cash so I spent more and more time hanging out with Chris and his pals. Chris had made a bit of a name for himself at St Helens but – like me – he kept the same friends he grew up with, and they were a good bunch too.

We had a great day session on the beers, nothing too rowdy or daft; just a few lads having a laugh and enjoying the day out. As the afternoon rolled into the evening, we walked over to Brannigan's night club.

'Not tonight lads,' one of the doormen said, blocking our path. 'You're not coming in here.'

Maybe we looked more drunk than we felt. Or maybe the doorman was just on a power trip. I turned and walked away with the rest of the lads. In the corner of my eye, I saw another bouncer jog over to a pair of Specials – the equivalent of the Community Support Police Officers now. They listened to him, looked our way, and paced over in our direction, one of them talking into his radio the whole time.

They stopped at our Chris. Suddenly, one of them grabbed his arm. Chris shrugged it off. Then, from nowhere, two or three other coppers raced over and grabbed him.

I ran over to them.

'What are you doing?'

One of them grabbed my arm. I smacked it off. 'What are you doing?'

I was grabbed again, this time more forcefully. A police van screeched to a halt near us, and Chris was frog-marched towards the back of the van.

'Don't worry Chris,' I yelled to him, hoping to reassure him. 'I'll get you out.'

But then I was pushed towards the van as well. I resisted. I'd done nothing wrong. Two of our mates were grabbed too.

Inside the van, and on the way to the station, I asked Chris what the hell was going on.

'That fuckin' bouncer,' he said. 'He dobbed us in because I chinned him.'

Smooth move, Chris! I hadn't seen him hit anyone after we'd been refused entry. We were booked at the station, and all put in a cell together. Then, 10 minutes later, an officer walked in.

'You,' he said, pointing my way. 'You're too young to be in here. Come with me.'

My raised hopes of an immediate release were crushed seconds later; they just put me on my own in the cell next door.

They interviewed us a couple of hours later. I was still pissed.

I expected a ticking off, the proverbial slap on the wrist. But what they said cut through my drunken cloud.

'You hit a policeman. We could prosecute you with assaulting an officer.'

Then, just like in the films, they tried the 'Good Cop, Bad Cop' routine, seesawing between pointed threats and niceties as they asked whether I'd seen my brother hit a policeman.

It was awful. My entire legal knowledge until that point had been learned from watching *The Bill* and there I was, 17 years old, in a police station, being interviewed half-pissed, with no solicitor with me. They carried out their threat, charging me with assaulting a policeman; my brother got an extra one on top for assaulting the bouncer. I couldn't believe a skirmish – at most – had turned so serious and nasty, so I got a solicitor for help. Thankfully, I was entitled to legal aid, though the £15 a week I had to contribute took a fair chunk out of my wages. I was determined to fight it all the way, though. I told everyone that I was not guilty, and that I'd take it to the Crown Court if I needed to. In truth, I didn't know what was happening. The mechanisms of the legal system were baffling, and grinded so slowly, that eventually it wore me down. Before it got to trial, I went for a meeting with my solicitor. And that's when he first uttered the two words which still – half a lifetime later – drag up that same fear I experienced back then.

Custodial sentence.

He said courts looked favourably on guilty pleas, usually resulting in lesser sentences. Reluctantly, I agreed to admit to the charge. I didn't want to. I knew my pride would take a denting after I'd told everyone I'd not done nothing wrong and, besides, assaulting an officer was one of the most frowned-upon charges around, and rightly so. But I couldn't take the risk of going to prison.

Our parish priest, Father Quigley, came to court and gave a testimonial, saying what good lads the Morley brothers were. I'll always be grateful to him for that. We avoided jail but the magistrates still hammered us – I was sentenced to carry out 90 hours of community service, Chris 120.

I was gutted. I'd never been in serious trouble in my life. I knew a lot of lads who had, and I was known as one of the straight ones. Sure, I'd done plenty of daft things, but assaulting an officer? No way. The whole saga made me wary of the police, and the legal system. Still am, to be honest. I resisted arrest, nothing more. It was a wrestle, at the most. I was livid at the idea of having to carry out community service for something I hadn't done.

So I didn't.

A friend of ours, John 'Yuzzer' Hughes, worked in an old people's home owned by Frank Evans, the Salford Bullfighter. Frank went over to Spain and became the only Briton to get full matador status. He is a legend in Salford and certainly a legend in my eyes, after he agreed to help Chris and I out.

We had a meeting with our community service officer.

'Do you currently do any voluntary work?' he asked us.

'Yeah, tons,' Chris said, as if insulted at the question. 'We're always helping out at an old people's home.'

I nodded my head in agreement. Not surprisingly, the officer thought we were bullshitting, so he went to see Frank.

'Yeah, the Morley boys – they're here all the time, helping out,' he told him. Not even a community service officer dared question Frank's word, not in Salford, so he signed it off and allowed us to do the community service there. At the end of the week, late Friday afternoon, we went for an appointment with our probation officer and showed him our work dockets.

We'd each clocked 40 hours.

'How've you done that so quickly?' he asked me. Usually, I later discovered, it can be a struggle just to squeeze eight hours in during a week.

'We both took a week off work,' I said. 'Thought it was best to get a head start. We'll be there Monday, too.'

Truth was, I'd been to the home for the first time on the way to collect our falsely stamped work dockets.

'Is that so?' he said, refusing to be hooked in by my Oscar-winning performance. 'Well I might pop in and see you down there on Monday. See how you're getting on.'

Fearing we would be rumbled, three days later Chris and I both phoned in sick for work, and went into the old people's home for the first time. We spent the full day there, offering to help where we could but basically just feeling like we were in the way of the staff. We spoke to a lot of the old people and they were terrific. They were happy to have new faces to talk to, and for our part we were happy to make their day. One of the nurses came along and saw how well we were getting on.

'Take them out for a walk, if you like,' she said.

So Chris, me, and a group of the better-abled old people left the home, walked down the drive, down the road, and into the first pub we saw.

They loved it. It was obvious they'd not been out for a while, certainly not to the local boozer. I turned to our Chris and raised my pint glass.

'To community service,' I said.

'Community service.'

We clunked glasses, and neither of us could stop laughing at the fact that our first – and, as it turned out, only – day of community service had ended in the pub.

CHAPTER SIX
THREE-DAY WEEK

It was the loudest whisper I'd ever heard in my life.

'Hey mister. What's your name?'

I'd prepared myself for the noise of the crowd and thought a lot about the intensity of the match. I even considered how I'd celebrate if I managed to score a try. But nothing on my imaginary debut tip-sheet had prepared me for this.

'Hey mister,' the same voice repeated. A hushed yell which she knew I could hear, loud and clear. 'What's your name?'

I was stood on the dead-ball line at Headingley, waiting for Hull to kick-off to restart the game after a try, trying my best to ignore the young female fan positioned just a few yards behind me.

Months earlier, I'd been playing amateur level after leaving school. Hours earlier, I'd been on a construction site in Liverpool, spending the day before the biggest night of my life working as a trainee electrician. When I'd signed for Leeds at the start of the season, I'd set myself the modest ambition of making the first team before I was 20.

But fate couldn't wait that long, and I was now on my debut for Leeds at the age of 17, at Headingley, surrounded by legends who I'd cheered for as a fan. Everything was going to plan. Or at least, it was until the voice behind me turned up the volume and asked – for a third time – who I was.

I looked to the players closest to me. None of them were looking at me. So I half-turned towards the crowd behind me.

'Adrian Morley,' I whispered, hand at the side of my mouth to shield my voice from the playing field.

'Who?'

I took a cautionary look around again, and then repeated: 'Adrian Morley.'

'Oh . . . I've never heard of you.'

One of the first things I did when I joined Leeds in the summer of '94 was lie to them. I dipped into my signing-on fee to pay for a holiday to Tenerife with Chris and his mates but, just before we left, I checked Leeds' pre-season training schedule to see if it clashed. It did.

I'd presumed that, because Chris was off from St Helens, I would be too. I called up the club and lied to them, telling them the holiday had been booked long before I signed the contract. Thankfully, they allowed me to go. They even gave me a pair of shorts before I went; I don't think I took them off in two weeks!

That holiday was carnage. I'd decided before I went that I wouldn't blow my signing-on fee in two weeks, so I set myself a budget and kept to it religiously. We found a bar that offered unlimited alcohol from 7pm til 8pm for the equivalent of £10, and I'd go with the sole intention of getting hammered, just so I didn't spend too much for the rest of the night. Chris's mates were all seasoned drinkers, but I held my own. I don't know if the place is still standing and, if it is, whether my record of 14 Malibu and Cokes in one hour is still scrawled on the wall behind the bar!

When I got back, I knew I had some serious catching up to do with my training. All the other lads had got a two-week head start on me. I'd only met the academy players once before, when months earlier I'd been invited to go to Wembley with them to watch the first team in the Challenge Cup Final. Not one of the bastards came over and spoke to me all the way there or back, so I reported for training at Headingley not knowing anyone, and a little worried about settling in. Thankfully, Kris Smith – who later lived with Dannii Minogue, with whom he has a son Ethan – had signed at the club, and his parents gave me plenty of lifts over to Yorkshire and back. I'll forever be grateful to Kris and his family for helping me out. If ever Ethan's auntie Kylie needs a lift anywhere, I've told him to give me a shout!

During the summer pre-season, we trained Tuesday and Thursday nights with the first team. I was never the type to be in awe of big-name players – maybe because I supported Salford as a kid. But there was one player who I was star-struck about. Ellery Hanley. He was 'Mr Rugby League', a phenomenal player and the Great Britain coach at the time. He had a presence about him which is difficult to describe – he would walk into a room and everyone would notice. When he turned up to training it was like a film star had arrived on set, he was the coolest man in the world. Or at least he was to me. For a 17-year-old trainee electrician, it was quite intimidating being in his company, but once I'd plucked up the courage to speak to him, he was very approachable and really helpful to all the young lads.

The culture seemed different back then. There seemed to be more respect for the senior players, for the blokes who had been before us. The academy lads trained with the first-team, but we didn't dare say anything to them. None of the young lads did. We had to earn their respect, earn the right to voice our opinion, and that was fine with me – I was just happy to be in their company. I just listened, watched and learned. My fitness worked in my favour, too. I've always been naturally fit. I'm blessed in that area – an ability to go out and play how I want, without worrying about fading or easing off to conserve energy. I'm lean, with not much body fat, and I've always loved the hard stuff. It's like sado-masochism – you know it'll hurt, but in a good way!

By the end of pre-season, I felt as fit as I ever had; I was ready to make a big impression. That enthusiasm got the better of me when I was sent off in my first academy game for a high tackle. But after that early hiccup I settled into the side, and after a few weeks I finally felt like I belonged at that level. I never excelled in matches, but I was never embarrassed either. In my own mind,

I was happy to tick over, tread water. Sure, I *wanted* to progress, but I wasn't overly driven. I was comfortable with my life. I was working during the week as an apprentice, playing on Saturday mornings, earning £30 win, lose or draw and instantly spending it on beer over the next two days. Life was good.

When I was at school, I'd watch my brothers get in from work on a Friday and the first thing they'd think about was going for a pint. At the time I didn't get the appeal. But once I started doing a week's graft, I understood – it felt like I deserved it, and those evenings brought me, Ste and Chris closer together. We'd go out Saturday nights together and then the following night. Then, on the Monday morning, they'd drag themselves out of bed to go to work, nursing monster hangovers, while I'd decide whether to phone in sick or not. With the three of us often taking advantage of the cheap drink on Thursday student nights – and phoning in sick the day later – my nickname was 'Three-day Week' for a while!

Not long after the season had started, I was picked for an academy match between Lancashire and Yorkshire. I was made up. Until I found out that I'd been picked for Yorkshire! The rules selected players based on what county a player's club was in, rather than where the player was from, so I had to line up against my own county – and mates like Keiron Cunningham and Sean Long.

About halfway through the season, the A team – the name for the reserves – were struggling with injuries, so I got a shout to play for them at Bradford. These days, the second string is almost exclusively an Under-20s side, but then there were a lot of men at that level, seasoned pros looking to get back into the first team, or trialling for a contract. I played centre that night, a position I wasn't used to playing in, scored a try, and after the match Bob Pickles – the scout who had seen me – told me that Doug Laughton had been impressed. I didn't even know he was watching. Hearing that gave me the kick up the backside I needed. I threw myself into the next two matches for the A team with reckless enthusiasm. I was a pinball, a dynamo; I was desperate to impress. Suddenly, I caught the scent that I may not need to wait three years for my first-team shot after all.

The following Tuesday evening, I got a message that Doug wanted to see me in his office.

'Adrian,' he said. 'I want you to play against Hull on Friday.'

'For the first team?'

'Of course for the first team. You alright with that?'

'Yeah,' I said, trying to keep my cool. And that was it. No detailed brief, no long spiel, no clue as to what role I might play. He walked off, leaving me stood there, absorbing the news. I told my family when I got home and they were all really pleased for me. Ste, my eldest brother, never made it as a pro like Chris and I. He was a really good player who just wasn't blessed with the same size as us two, but he was never anything other than really proud of us both, and really supportive.

On the Friday morning, I asked my foreman if I could clock off work an hour early. I drove home, grabbed my boots, a quick bite to eat, and got back into my Volkswagen Polo (I'd passed my test weeks earlier. First time, thank you very much) for the hour-long drive over to Leeds. That's when the nerves began to niggle at me. By the time I'd arrived at Headingley, I was a full-on nervous wreck. I parked up and made my way to the first-team dressing room, spending the whole walk worrying that I would be the first to arrive and I'd accidentally sit in someone else's place and get yelled at. Fortunately, all the shirts were pegged up, so I knew where to go. All the senior players kept to themselves. There were no arms around my shoulder, no handshakes or words of encouragement. But Francis Cummins and Phil Hassan were great with me, and showed me the ropes. As a substitute back then, there were no guarantees you'd get on the pitch. And as it was only a two-man bench, there was no inkling about what position you might play if you did.

I quickly got dressed and sat down, waiting to find out what happened next. I looked around at the company I was in. Kevin Iro, Richie Eyres, Ellery Hanley. It felt wrong being in the same dressing room as them.

Ellery was captain, and as such it was his job to give the pre-match talk before the game. In the academy side, we'd huddle, jog on the spot, shout out instructions about 'getting our heads on'. It wasn't unusual for players to wrestle, just to warm their shoulders, so I expected the first team to be twice as intense – like an American Football film, with Ellery delivering a Churchillian speech to get us ready to run through walls.

But Ellery was quiet and composed. We walked out, I took my place on the Headingley bench, and for the first time I noticed just how much quicker the first-team game was than any game I'd played before. The hits seemed just as hard, but the pace was incredible. I was desperate to get on, but in a stupid way I was desperate not to; I was worried about looking out of place. After 20 minutes, Marcus Vassilakopoulos went down injured. The call came from the end of the bench.

'Moz, you're on.'

I took my place at second row, defending one in from Iro. A few minutes later, he got the ball out wide, and in space. I was hovering on the inside as he burst through Hull's line. A New Zealand international and one of the best centres in the game, everything he did was copybook. He drew the full-back, arcing away from me to peel the defender away from his inside support. I looked to my left, to my right. I was the nearest man to him and, even better, no Hull players were tracking back. The full-back moved in, Iro twisted his body and released the ball. It was the perfect pass . . . and I dropped it.

How could I be so stupid?

I couldn't believe it. I'd snatched at the ball – I'd scored the try in my mind when Iro threw the pass, and lost all concentration. The collective gasp of 10,000 fans only amplified my agony, my anger. I looked up at the try-line and thought, 'That would have been the perfect debut'. Franny Cummins came over and patted me on my shoulder.

'Don't worry about it,' he said. But I couldn't think of anything else. I was fuming.

Well done Moz. You had your chance. And you blew it.

A few minutes later, when we were defending, the Hull hooker Mike Dixon had the ball and beelined right for me. He must have thought I was shattered emotionally, a beanpole physically, and an easy target. He was right about the first two. I threw myself at him and caught him with a good shot, and he spilled the ball. The fans went wild.

'This is what it's about,' I thought. From that moment, my confidence grew, and I finished my first game (we won) proud of my performance. I knew that – aside from bombing a try – I'd played pretty well, and the newspaper match reports the next day were generous in their praise. Unfortunately, during the game Ellery went off injured a few minutes after I'd come off the bench. We never played in the same side again, but it's a claim to fame of mine that we were once in the same team – even if it was only for five minutes. I can always look back and say, 'I played alongside my hero'.

And he can always look back and think, 'I remember playing with Moz . . . he bombed a try!'

Afterwards my thoughts turned to my grandad. He had been a big supporter of mine throughout my amateur days. He died just before I signed with Leeds, but I knew he would have been so proud.

I got out of Headingley with no autograph requests and over the next few weeks started training more with the first team. Before the end of the season, I played in two more games; games which would have been instantly forgettable had it not been for two quirks.

I was on the bench against Wakefield when my future Great Britain coach, Brian Noble, was playing, still sporting his porn star 'tache. And I also played at Halifax, my first start, and scored my first top-level try, though I remember the game more for the fact that it featured the shortest, and funniest, pre-match talk I've ever heard.

We were all changed and ready to go out when Dougie walked in. We all hushed silent, waiting for our final instructions before kick-off. Instead, he took just a few seconds to deliver his pearls of wisdom.

'I know you'll win today lads,' he said. 'Because they're shite.'

TRIBUTE: BY ELLERY HANLEY (FORMER LEEDS TEAM-MATE)

I only ever played alongside Adrian for a few minutes – but I saw enough of him then to convince me he was destined to be a great player.

I have the absolute pleasure of being able to say I was one of the foot soldiers when he burst onto the scene at Leeds as a teenager. And from those few minutes I saw him play, and from the few sessions I trained alongside him, I knew he had the potential to go on to great things.

When I left Leeds at the end of the 1994/95 season, I gave a speech at the club's presentation evening. Adrian was only 17, and had just finished his first year at the club. But as I stood on that stage, I didn't hesitate to predict that Leeds would be in safe hands with Adrian Morley at the club. He, and Leeds, went on to make the inaugural Grand Final and win the Challenge Cup in 1999 – but they only scratched the surface of what Adrian has achieved in his fabulous career.

Far too often in rugby league, and other sports, journalists and broadcasters are quick to talk up the talents of players who, with all due respect, are average first-teamers. I've seen so many come and go over the years. If someone wants my respect, they have to do it consistently.

Adrian has my complete respect. The fact he has been at the very top of rugby league for nearly two decades is incredible, and a massive tribute to his dedication.

I hold him up there as one of the very best there is, and has ever been. I get goose pimples just talking about him. And when we meet face-to-face, at functions or major finals, we always hug each other – and I can feel the enormous amount of mutual respect we have for each other.

As a former player and coach, I still follow the game. And when I'm sat in my living room, watching Adrian Morley on TV, I get a thrill from watching him play. I play tennis, squash and racquetball to a good level, and when I go on court I'm inspired by his performances. He never hides from the hard work, never shirks a challenge.

The biggest test for any rugby league player, I believe, is going over to Australia to see if they can hold their own in the NRL. Adrian did more than that – he took it by storm.

Unfortunately, in Super League we have pundits like Stevo who tell fans – year after year – how much better the British game is getting. But he's probably better saying nothing.

The NRL is still the benchmark competition. The intensity is ferocious, week in, week out. I went over to the Australian competition in different circumstances – at the end of my season with Wigan – and nothing has changed in its intensity. It was another level up then and it is now. Adrian did well season after season. And he earned the complete respect of the players over there. He's a legend in England and a legend in Australia.

Journalists and broadcasters write and say nice things about Adrian, but if you really want to know how good he is, speak to the players. His team-mates, his opponents. They know how much work he gets through, how hard he hits, how dominant he is, how strong he is. The amount of respect they have for him is immeasurable. And that tells you everything.

It's impossible to compare players in different positions; you can't compare a back with a forward. Andrew Johns was brilliant. Brad Fittler was brilliant. But if I was picking my dream line-up, I know that Adrian would be one of the first names on my team sheet.

He is a real enforcer. He never goes sideways, never goes backwards. Opponents have to battle for everything against him. He is, in my eyes, a true champion.

I wish Adrian and his family good health and happiness forever.

CHAPTER SEVEN
THE PRO GAME

The first time I ever stepped foot on the Wembley pitch, I was nearly arrested.

It was 1996, Challenge Cup Final day, Bradford against St Helens. I'd been there the previous year with Leeds as a travelling reserve, and in '94 with the rest of the academy lads. But the fact that my team weren't in the final gave me a rare weekend off during the season, so a group of us headed down to Wembley to watch the game. For everyone else, it was just a chance to have a few scoops and enjoy the match. But my brother Chris was in the Saints squad and so I had more reasons than most to cheer for St Helens. And more reason to hit the beer early.

Chris had played for St Helens in all of the rounds leading up to the final. Fourth round, fifth round, quarter and semi-final. Played well, too. But for the game itself, the coach, Shaun McRae, dropped him from the team and put Simon Booth in instead. I was gutted for our Chris. I knew what it would mean to him to play at Wembley – he'd talked of little else for the previous two weeks – and the fact he'd been involved with the team in all of the previous rounds must have made it all the more painful for him.

I started early on the beers to drown my sorrows. I didn't think I was that drunk by the time the game started, but when I saw Booth take the ball in and started booing him I realised I must have had a few. It was a great game, which Saints just edged. The players were ecstatic, not only to win the cup but to win what everyone saw as Wigan's cup, given that they had monopolised the competition for the previous eight years. As the St Helens players celebrated, lapping the crowd and soaking up the atmosphere, the coaching staff, club officials and squad players – including our Chris – went onto the pitch to congratulate the lads. I saw Chris in his suit, walking among the players, shaking their hands, smiling. He was happy for them, but I knew that he must have been devastated inside. So I decided to do what any caring brother would do. I decided to go and give him a hug.

He wasn't even 50 yards away from me, but the only trouble was there was a fence between him, on the pitch, and me on the terraces. A pretty high fence, too.

I walked down to it to take a closer look.

'Moz, what are you doin'?' asked Marcus Vassilakopoulos, who was in our party. I didn't have time to tell him that I had to get on the pitch, that my brother needed me. Besides, I knew he'd try and stop me. So I quickly vaulted the fence – it wasn't hard to climb, it was a series of parallel washing lines pulled tight – and ran towards Chris. His back was to me, so I gave him a big bear-hug and lifted him off the floor.

'How you doin', kid?'

Shocked doesn't cover it.

'Aje, what you doin' here?'

'I just wanted to let you know pal, chin up, it's alright, you'll get here soon.' I'm pretty sure he was able to decode my drunken rant enough to appreciate the gesture. But I know for certain that before I or Chris could say anything else, two heavies in bright jackets had grabbed an arm of mine each and, flanking me, started dragging me towards the side of the pitch.

Fortunately, Mike Gregory – the St Helens assistant coach – saw what was going on and paced after us.

'Lads, he's alright – he's with us,' Greg said. They didn't believe him. The fact that I stunk like a brewery might not have helped.

'Look, he was just seeing his brother, he meant no harm.'

By this point, we'd reached the side of the pitch, where more stewards and two policemen were waiting to take me away. But thankfully, Greg's plea worked. They let me go.

I scanned the crowd in front of me for Vassy. I didn't see him. But I did see Lee Butler, one of my closest friends who had travelled down with the St Helens academy. He was stood on the steps, looking directly at me and laughing his head off – he'd seen the whole thing unfold. This was long before mobile phones and, after spending ages trying to find Vassy outside the ground, I decided to jump on the coach with Butler and head home.

I didn't see Vassy until training at Leeds two days later.

'Where the bloody hell did you go?' he asked. He looked relieved to see me. But not really *happy* to see me.

'D'you know how long I was looking for you? D'you know how many stewards I spoke to? D'you know many police stations I went to looking for you?'

I suddenly felt guilty for what I'd put him through.

'They let me go,' I said, in explanation.

'Let you go? Who was your lawyer, Perry frickin' Mason?'

'No,' I replied. 'Mike Gregory.'

I was still combining work as an apprentice sparkie with playing for Leeds. But Super League changed all of that. The launch of a full-time, summer competition whipped up a lot of hype and, being a young player, I was caught right in the middle of it all. It was exciting. We were being told there would be games all over the world. Promised the sport would have a profile to rival the Premier League. I had a mental image in my head of each match having a carnival atmosphere, and the razzamatazz of an American football game. I was excited at the thought of playing on firm pitches in the sun, rather than mud-baths in the rain.

Then there was the cash. Mates of mine were getting payments of 20 grand from the competition bosses, just to reaffirm they were going to play in Super League. We heard rumours of some of the Wigan players getting ridiculous money; money for nothing because they had no intention of going anywhere. And those that did – Gary Connolly, Jason Robinson and Lee Jackson – got even more for signing with the ARL, the rival competition in Australia. I wasn't established in the team, so I never got any bonus, but I never begrudged anyone for getting big paydays. Garry Schofield moaned about it, and I can see why; he was Great Britain's most capped player. But he was coming to the end of his career – he'd missed the boat. I never heard anybody else complain about it, though, and why would they? Everyone's contract was being upgraded. We were all, finally, getting the chance to do what Wigan had done for years – train and play as a full-time job. Young lads now can't believe it when I tell them my old routine in my Leeds days; work five days a week, 6am starts, train in the evening, games on weekends. But that was how it was always done, and before I'd heard of Super League it was the way I thought it was always going to be. I never thought I'd be able to play sport as my job – I'd resigned myself to always having to support my income with a 'real' job, too.

Maurice Lindsay, the driving force of Super League, wasn't universally popular. I remember watching the TV news and seeing an effigy of him being burned by Featherstone fans in protest at his plan to merge their club with Castleford and Wakefield to form a Calder side. Lindsay also wanted Salford and Oldham to merge to form one Manchester side and – being a Salford lad – I saw how much it rattled people. But I had no problem with it. I thought it was a tremendous idea. I can see why the old supporters dug their heels in, but in hindsight I can't help wonder whether they regret it now. I've since seen it work in Australia where once-fierce rivals – Western Suburbs and Balmain Tigers – have come together, and their fans have all come together as well.

To make way for Super League they crammed the '95 Centenary season into just six months, instead of the usual 10, which often meant two games a week. With work or college as well, it proved too much for me. Knowing Super League was a few months away, I told my dad that I wanted to pack in my apprenticeship. He had his reservations, because he wanted me to have a trade to fall back on, but my mind was made up. I went to see Dougie Laughton and asked whether I could go full-time with Leeds.

'What are you earning at the minute as a sparky?' he asked.

'£80 a week,' I replied.

'Is that all!?' he said, stunned. 'Yeah no problem. We'll match that.'

Good work Moz. I still don't know why I didn't tell him £300 a week!

That was probably one of Dougie's last pieces of business as Leeds coach. Dean Bell was supposed to come over from New Zealand to become his assistant, but Doug spat his dummy out and thought he was being squeezed out – and he may have been right – and so Deano and Hugh McGahan took over. Dean had only just finished playing with Auckland Warriors, and was completely new to coaching, so he had it pretty rough. But I liked his approach and, more importantly, he seemed to like mine. The game switched from two subs to four, and I began making some real money. We were paid £300 a game, and some weeks I'd come off the bench for 20 minutes on the Wednesday night, 20 minutes on the Sunday, and I'd earn £600 a week, on top of my £80 weekly 'salary' and my annual instalment. Everything was going beyond my wildest expectations. I was playing for Leeds, I was getting recognised, I was earning money. It was as if someone had floored the accelerator on the career plan I'd mapped out. Then Dean did what no coach had done before and what no coach has done since.

He dropped me.

And I always thought he was nicknamed 'Mean Dean' because it rhymed! In fairness, Dean was great with me and he explained his reasons. He never yelled at me. Actually, that's a lie. The first time I played against my brother Chris, our duel had dominated the build-up to the game, and we'd promised the local papers that we'd smash each other, but when it came to the game itself we never clashed. Not once. I'm not sure whether we operated on opposite sides – we were both second-rowers, who tend to operate on either the left or right flank – but we just didn't seem to come into contact. Truth was, once the game started I just saw him as an opponent. If that sounds a cliché, apologies. But it's true. He was just another face in another St Helens shirt. I wasn't going to go out of my way to run at him, just because he was my brother.

'Have you two made a promise not to hurt each other?' Dean sniped after the match. Apart from that, Dean was terrific with me. He had dropped me earlier in the season, and I was gutted. I was only 18, so I had no grounds to complain, but I took it really personally. He asked me to go back and have a run for the reserves, so I played my balls off, and he reinstated me the following week. That was as good a lesson as I could have had, because Dean took away my complacency by putting me on ice. I'd fallen into a comfort zone; not only did I not think I'd be dropped, but I didn't push for a starting spot either. From then on, I really kicked on, and I finished the season with a regular spot in the second-row and a new contract, too; a four-year deal starting on £20,000 a year . . . just a few months after accepting a basic wage of £80 a week.

Dean may have been new to coaching, but he had the benefit of his playing experiences with Wigan. They hadn't just beaten sides in the past few years, they'd trampled all over them all, winning an obscene amount of trophies, and Dean had been a big part of that team. Dean wanted to make us fitter and stronger for the start of the Super League season, so he brought over Edgar Curtis, a conditioner who'd worked in American Football. No one had ever done sessions as brutal as the ones we did with Curtis before. We carried out the pre-season with the academy lads, and one of them caught my eye immediately. He was shorter than me, stocky, with a wide neck. The players were split into groups for 400m runs – a horrible distance – and this chunky bulldog finished top of his race, was promoted to the next group up, and won again. He wasn't naturally quick or fit but he was packed with raw enthusiasm, determination and aggression. I knew immediately that Terry Newton and I would hit it off.

He'd been sidelined the previous season because of a contract wrangle with Warrington, and he was an animal. Players at a rugby league club are usually mates with everyone else, but within the group inevitably close friendships are forged, usually along the lines of age or where the players are from. I was only 18 months older than Tez and because we had similar back-grounds, and came from Lancashire, we spent more and more time together. He was the king of the one-line putdowns, but he'd take no crap. He'd say something smart and cutting and funny, but then spit his dummy if someone replied with their own witty remark. He was a bit like Joe Pesci's character in the Goodfellas film, only tougher. He was an animal on a night out, he feared no beer, but in training he was a legend, and we used to motivate each other to get bigger and stronger.

I'd hardly done any weights before then, but with Edgar willing us on we hit the gym hard. I naturally have a good engine, and that had got me through games until then. But Edgar brought in the techniques from gridiron – the Olympic clean and jerks, the squats – and in four weeks, he'd put muscle on to my scrawny frame. I felt strong and fit. I was slender and cut, if a bit dispro-portioned because I had a big backside – more like Serena Williams than Sylvester Stallone – but I knew it was what I needed to progress my career. It was the start of an exciting era for everyone. It was the first season of this headline-grabbing, money-swelling phenom-enon that was Super League, and I was ready to make a big impression. What I wasn't ready for was a battle against relegation.

"Bloody hell Moz, you could have knocked," came the alarmed and sleepy voice from the bed. "Did you have to kick the door in?"

It was my 19th birthday, and I was in Paris. I'd just scored two tries and won the Sky Sports Man of the Match in a great win against Super League's most glamorous new outfit, Paris Saint-Germain. If I could have mapped out the perfect birthday for a teenage rugby league nut, it would have gone something like this. We stopped overnight in Paris and took the win and my birthday as the perfect excuse for a few beers. It was paradise. Or at least, my version of paradise. I was living a life I thought had slipped by me just months earlier; I'd thought I was the bloke destined to combine Eccles amateur side with long shifts as a sparky, and not a very good one at that. And so the French beers flowed easily, too easily, which was why, when I got back from the bar to be told George Mann had gone to bed early, it didn't go down too well with me. In fairness, I did try knocking when I went to his room to convince him to stay up. But he didn't answer. So I gave the door a small barge with my shoulder – literally, one step back and 'thud' – and it smacked open against the wall.

I assessed the damage – two twisted hinges. Not too bad. But a week later, Leeds received a repair bill from the hotel for £300!

'Are we all chipping in here?' I asked the rest of the lads. 'It's only £20 each?'

But the tight sods all shook their heads and told me where to go, leaving me to pay the over-inflated invoice.

Those early days with Leeds remain some of the fondest of my career, even though the team struggled. Really struggled. We started Super League at home with a defeat to Warrington, and the losses just kept on coming. After all the hype, all the expectation, we were stunned. We had trained hard and prepared well, and we honestly expected to be challenging at the top of the ladder. Instead, we spent most of the season dancing around the bottom spots, with the threat of relegation hanging over us like a rolling, black cloud.

Our win in Paris on my birthday was one of only six in 22 games all season. Another of those was the return fixture against Paris at home, when Dean Bell came out of retirement and selected himself to play in the centres. Paris were one of the few teams worse than us. Strangely, Dean didn't select himself the following week to play against Wigan! But it was nice to say I had played with a legend of the game, however briefly.

Dean was a good coach and we respected him. The defeats hurt him, but he handled it well. He never tore strips off us, no matter how angry and upset he was. The older players had mortgages to pay, families to feed, and just months after giving up their full-time jobs to turn professional at rugby they faced being made redundant if we were relegated. That fear-factor festered a nervous and miserable working environment. Everyone tried to have fun in training, but it was hard. And it didn't help that Leeds' directors felt entitled – almost obliged – to come into the dressing room on match days to tell us what to do. They would either try and motivate us during their brief visits – 'Come on lads, we can do this. Wear the shirt with pride,' – or, worse, try and coach us. That really pissed the lads off. We knew how to play, but when confidence is low balls get spilled and tackles get missed. We respected Dean and, when he told us what to do, we listened to him. Not nameless, faceless old men in suits. We also heard the rumours that the club was in trouble financially. For years they'd spent money trying to compete with Wigan. But Wigan continued to win all the prizes, and all the prize money, and Leeds found themselves trying to operate successfully against an impossible business model. By '96, the last of the superstars (Hanley, Schofield) had gone, the crowds were down and it was a glum place to be.

And – incredibly – I was loving every minute of it.

Being 19, and not living in Leeds, I didn't really feel the pressure that Dean and the other players felt. I was still so new to the idea of being a full-time professional sportsman. I wasn't walking around pinching myself, but I had a definite appreciation that life could be a hell of a lot worse. It was only a few months earlier that I'd been combining rugby with early starts and eight-hour shifts on building sites. Now, I was earning decent money, training with my mates, playing pretty well and getting more and more attention. Even the drives over to Leeds were great. Except the one time when my brother Ste gave me a lift over. We stopped at Birch Services on the M62 for some sandwiches, and when we got back to his car, it wouldn't start. So while he got towed back to Salford, I had to walk around the service station and beg for a lift to Leeds. Finally, I found a girl heading that way, and after I called the club and explained my situation she agreed to take me the 40-odd miles to Headingley!

CHAPTER EIGHT
TAKING IT ON THE CHIN

It's a pretty well-known fact in rugby league circles that, when the police were given the power to use CS gas, the first man they sprayed was my Leeds team-mate Barrie McDermott. It's less known that, later that same year – 1996 – I was with him when we were both subdued by the spray. And when I say subdued, what I really mean is enraged! It was a Thursday night and, with the Friday off ahead of a Sunday match, we had arranged a night out in St Helens with George Mann, Phil Hassan and my mate, Lee Butler. Barrie's infamous incident, outside a club in Oldham, had made national headlines and, in turn, made him a marked man for every bouncer who wanted to score points and brag to their mates. I could picture them, bragging to their mates that they'd chinned Barrie Mac. And that was the case in St Helens. At the end of a great night out, he left the club in front of me and a doorman kicked-off with him for no reason. Within a flash, bodies rushed in, arms were windmilling around and chaos erupted. I rushed in to grab Barrie and pull him out – we'd both been in trouble with the law and neither of us needed the aggravation. And that's when it happened.

One moment, I had hold of him, trying to pull him away. The next, my eyes were on fire. Instructions were barked at me but, in the confusion, I couldn't register anything. All I was concerned about was stopping the burning in my eyes. I kept my hands over my eyes, trying anything to ease the pain. It was excruciating. Then the police gassed me again! Maybe they were trigger-happy – CS gas was a relatively new addition to their arsenal. Or maybe they just thought it'd be fun to see me in tears. Either way, I went wild, telling them to fuck off, and so they gassed me yet again. I just wanted them to stop, but I lost all rational thought. The more they gave it to me, the more I fought back – I was caught in a vicious circle, until I was pushed or tripped, and ended up lying on the floor. A body leapt on me and my wrists were cuffed together. Slowly, my eyes began to recover from the trauma they'd just been put through. I started to make out shapes – and there was no mistaking the white, square blur in front of me. It was the back of a police van. They threw me inside, next to Barrie. I sat there, blinking to try and force the CS gas from my eyes, trying to comprehend what was going on and what had just happened.

Suddenly, the door swung opened. It was my mate Butler. There was no policeman next to him, just Lee, in the opening. 'Brilliant,' I thought. 'He's rescuing us.'

Even for Butler, that was a ballsy move. But instead of ushering us out, he climbed into the van and sat down next to me.

'What the fuck you doin'?' I asked him.

'I'm coming with you,' he replied. 'I don't know my way around St Helens, and I can't find George.'

He rode with us to the police station, and the copper got a real shock when he opened the door and saw three of us! Lee was released immediately, while Barrie played it smart, apologised, and they released him too. But my attitude was, 'You wankers, I've done nothing wrong', so they locked me up for the night.

The next morning, sober, they interviewed me.

'We know you play rugby,' one of the coppers said.

I went into deny mode.

'I don't play rugby. I don't know what you're talking about.'

'We could charge you with assault.'

'I didn't assault anyone. I don't know what you're talking about.'

The verbal sparring went on for a while, before I was charged with being drunk and disorderly. I hired a solicitor and, just like after the Blackpool incident, he advised me to accept the charge, so I took the £500 fine on the chin.

Barrie felt bad, like it was all his fault. And it was. But I didn't hold a grudge and, thankfully, neither did he when I crashed into his car a few days later while parking mine! His repair bill came to nearly £500, so we were evens.

As for my eyes, they were back to normal within a day or two, but the CS gas left rashes on my face. On the Saturday morning, two days after our night out, Dean Bell pulled me to one side.

'What have you been up to?' he asked. I could tell from his pointed question that he knew something had gone on. I later discovered that the police had phoned the club.

'Nothing,' I said.

'Why have you got rashes on your face?'

'Oh that,' I said, trying to conjure a believable excuse. 'It's from . . . the . . . soap. In the shower.'

Barrie, who was eavesdropping nearby, heard me. And like a true team-mate, he tried to validate my ridiculous claim.

'I got a rash off that soap as well,' he said, in mock-outrage. 'I'm going to tell the kit-man. It's bang out of order.'

And off he stormed!

But Dean didn't buy any of it, which was hardly surprising. De Niro and Pacino we weren't.

I came clean and, the following day, we got hammered by London Broncos. Dean didn't hold back afterwards.

'No wonder we're getting beat when some of you are out on the piss on a Thursday night,' he shouted during our dressing down after the game.

He was right, of course. He didn't mind us having a few beers, but going out on the lash was out of order – especially when it was landing us in trouble with the police. Being out with Barrie in St Helens that night showed me how rugby league players can be targeted when they go out. Maybe other lads see it as a chance to score points, to brag to their mates that they'd hit a player . . . I don't know. I've only ever been a player, so I can't see it from their perspective. All I do know is that the episode should have taught me to develop a thicker skin, and not to react when provoked.

But it didn't.

And two years later, in 1998, that ignorance came back to bite. It was a nothing incident, really. A silly fallout in a pub. But when I saw a picture of me, sporting a black eye, on the front page of the *Yorkshire Evening Post* with the headline 'Morley Wanted For Assault Quiz', or something like that, I knew it had gone too far.

I was in the Chained Bull pub, in Leeds, having a beer and minding my own business, when a lad came over to talk to me. And when I say talk, what I mean is verbally spew drunken abuse at me. He was being a real prick.

'Listen pal, get out of my face,' I said, but he ignored my warning. So I did what anyone else would have done in that position. I uppercutted him.

I know my own strength – if I wanted to drop him, I could have done. Easily. But I thought a clip would teach him a lesson, and it did. He ran off without saying another word.

I thought nothing of it, until the guy behind the bar shouted my name a few minutes later.

'Phone call for you,' he said.

I walked over to the bar, leaned over and grabbed the receiver.

'Hello, Adrian speaking,' I said. I had no idea who would be calling for me in the pub.

'Morley. My dad's a copper, and I'm going to get you arrested.'

'Look, you were being a prick, you deserved it,' I said. 'Just leave it.'

But he didn't leave it. The police went to the training ground two days later, when I wasn't there, and when I was shown a copy of the local newspaper – and my mug was on the front page – I drove to the police station and tried to explain what had happened.

I was hoping for leniency, but I had no chance. I told them he was being an idiot and he deserved it, but they didn't listen. Apparently, you're not even allowed to give smartarses a good slap.

Gary Hetherington, CEO of Leeds, and Graham Murray, head coach at the club, came to court to give me their support, which I appreciated. Waiting outside the courtroom, Gary leaned towards me.

'Maybe after this you'll not go drinking,' he said.

As he was saying that, I could see a familiar face walking towards us. It was a lad who I knew from the academy ranks, a real character who was obviously in court for a similar reason as myself.

'Mozza, how are you doing?!' he said, walking on after brief handshakes.

Gary shook his head.

'And maybe you'd better look at who your mates are, too,' he said.

I had to pay the 'victim' £800 compensation and carry out 80 hours of community service. And this time, there was no Salford Matador to rescue me. I did 10 full days of the most mind-numbing, tedious labouring imaginable. I had to put together wooden camel figures which, I was told, were to be given to old people for them to put in the garden. The first one was kind of fun to do. The second, not so much. By the time I'd polished off 50 by the end of the first day, I knew it would be a long, hard slog.

A year or two later, I was in a different Leeds pub, when a lad came over to me.

'Adrian, do you want a drink?' he said.

'No thanks.'

'D'you remember me?' he asked. I studied his face, but couldn't place it. 'I'm the lad you chinned in the Chained Bull.'

All his mates started laughing nearby and, right there and then, I nearly launched my fist through his face. But I didn't. I bit my tongue and walked away. For a moment, I considered ringing a mate and asking him to come and do it, but then I thought the better of it. I didn't want one of my friends to have to go through what I had – the police interrogation, the court case, the costs, the community service. My rational thinking took over and he genuinely wasn't worth it.

It took me a while, but I learned my lesson in the end.

CHAPTER NINE
INTERNATIONAL
DISASTER

I sat in the dressing room, alone, my head in my hands. All I could hear was the muffled sound of stadium chatter and chants. Spikes of encouragement silenced immediately after.

Just nine more minutes.

Suddenly, there was an explosion of noise above my head. I knew New Zealand had scored a try and, two minutes later, that same roar from the home supporters told me the conversion had been successful.

I tallied up the score in my head. We were still 12-10 in front. There must only be a few minutes left.

Please God. Don't do this to me.

It was bad enough that my first game for Great Britain, my lifetime's dream, had been cut short by a referee's yellow card just five minutes after coming on as a substitute. Now, I had to sit and wait to see if my team-mates could cling on to the win they had worked so hard to achieve.

Seven minutes left.

I walked over to the TV, pinned to the wall in the corner. It wasn't working. I searched the wall for a nearby plug socket, but couldn't find it, so I went and sat back down.

Six minutes.

The silence was painful, but I assured myself it was a good

sign. If we were doing well, then the home fans at Ericsson Stadium in Auckland wouldn't have anything to cheer about.

Then my self-encouragement was interrupted by a ripple of noise. The Kiwis must have the ball. I waited for the collective sound of disappointment from the fans, but instead the noise was amped up. Louder and louder until it exploded on top of the ceiling above me.

The Kiwis had scored and taken the lead.

Come on fellas, there's still time. Please.

Until then, time had dragged painstakingly slowly. But now it was in a rush, racing, it seemed, towards the referee's whistle. Suddenly, a cheer. But not the euphoric cheer of a dedicated bunch of English fans, nor the sound of the home fans' spontaneous applause at the sight of another try. I correctly deduced that the Kiwis had kicked a drop-goal, cushioning their lead and eating up the clock. Then the applause. The game was over.

Well done, Moz.

How could I have been so stupid?

But then I thought back to the sin-binning, and replayed the incident in my mind. Sean Hoppe had been tackled, and was trying to get to his feet. We'd worked all week on slowing down the Kiwis' play-the-ball, on interrupting their attack. Some players are good at holding players down on the ground, but wrestling was never my game. I was more about collision. Knock them on their backs, rather than twist them onto their backs. But who was I to argue? I was 19 and I'd done nothing in the sport – if they wanted slow play-the-balls, they'd get them. I held Hoppe down.

The trill of Bill Harrigan's whistle told me I shouldn't have. I cursed myself for giving away a penalty. I looked at Harrigan, as he pulled a yellow card from his back pocket, pointed to me and then to the touchline. I was stunned. I jogged off the pitch and into the changing rooms on autopilot.

The first signs of activity seeped through the door, snapping me out of my flashback, and then I heard that all-too-familiar percussive sound of studs on cement. The door opened, the players filed into the room, their heads bowed.

Phil Larder, our coach, was the first to speak.

'You can't win a Test with 12 men,' he said, addressing the room.

He was right. And if we'd held them out, we'd have been in a great position. History shows that whoever wins the first Test usually goes on to win the series.

I was heartbroken. It took all my strength to stop myself from crying. If I'd been anywhere else in the world, surrounded by any other people but rugby players, I'd have broken down on the spot.

Terry O'Connor was the first to come over and put his arm around my shoulder, telling me it wasn't my fault.

'We fucked up – it had nothing to do with being out-numbered,' he said.

Andy Farrell came over next. He leaned into me, whispering-distance away.

'Moz, listen to me – it wasn't your fault,' he said to me. 'We should have done better with 12.'

Faz was only 21, but he carried the captaincy so naturally. He had an aura and authority about him which just commanded respect, and it was nice of him to say what he did.

But it didn't make me feel any better. My first really important game, my first Test, and I screwed it up.

Even now I'm amazed at how rapid my rise to the Great Britain side was. Sure, I aspired to get to the top, but not many thought that would be achievable when I was an amateur. I certainly didn't. My plan when I'd joined Leeds was to make one first-team appearance within three years, which didn't scream ambition, but in my mind that was the realistic limit of my talents. Occasional bench player, first-team battler. One of those players who didn't quite fit in, but no one wanted to criticise because 'he tried hard'. But as I progressed, I felt comfortable at every level I played at.

It just seemed normal, like it was meant to be. I took it as a huge compliment that Dean didn't want me to play for Great Britain academy side for their mid-season internationals in '96. He said I was too important to Leeds and, with the side struggling in the league, eventually they compromised and agreed that I could play in the second Test, in France.

I played loose forward that day, we won the match and I scored a hat-trick – the only one of my career. But I remember it so fondly because our game was the curtain-raiser to Wales's game against France, in which my brother was playing.

Chris had broken into the Welsh squad that year. Mike Gregory, the assistant coach at St Helens, was also the Wales assistant. One day, when he was leaving training at Saints, he just so happened to mention he was heading to train the Wales team.

'I'm Welsh,' Chris told him. 'Well, my gran is . . . I'm not sure if that counts or not.'

It counted. He travelled down with Greg to the training base, where he was asked more about his Welsh ancestry. And so Chris told them that she lived in a little village, just outside of Swansea which – even after all these years – he still couldn't pronounce. Aber-something-or-other. Our gran hardly spoke a word of English, he told them, and she loved Wales more than anything.

None of which was true, of course. My gran didn't really speak fluent Welsh, but fortunately for Chris he spoke fluent bullshit. His little white lie proved his passport into the Wales team and, to make it even sweeter, it activated a clause in his St Helens contract which gave him a payment of a few grand for playing international rugby!

I remember him phoning me up.

'Aje, if anyone asks you, our gran is Welsh,' he said.

'I thought she was from St Helens.'

'Not any more.'

Wales had a strong squad back then, and for Chris it was a chance to play at the top level. As time went on it soon stopped being a family joke – he became really affiliated with Wales. He starting cheering for them in the rugby union and football, too, and even learned their national anthem. I know he had no Welsh link, but I saw how proud he was to play for Wales. Years later, I was actually offered the chance to play for them as well, and I was tempted. Really tempted. The main team was Great Britain at the time, so fixtures for England – or Wales – were few and far between. I saw how much Chris enjoyed it and what it meant to him, and the chance to play alongside him really appealed, but in the end I stuck with England. I thought, being English, it was the right thing to do. A couple years after that, my own big mouth nearly got me into the Irish team, too! Terry O'Connor and Gary Connolly were in the side, and I made a flippant remark how I wish I hadn't injured my ankle because I'd love to play for Ireland. If I remember rightly, there were only four people there when I said it – Gary, Tez, myself, and another fella I didn't know. And he just so happened to be a journalist.

'Morley Pledges His Allegiance To Ireland,' read the headline, above a story including my quotes. Good work, Moz. Get yourself out of that one. Fortunately, the story was soon forgotten.

My hat-trick for GB academy must have impressed Phil Lowe, our team manager. He was a solid bloke Phil, who I recognised as the freakishly tall guy who used to lead Great Britain out when I saw them on TV as a kid. He must have had a word with Phil Larder, the England (and Great Britain) coach, because a couple of days after getting back from France, a woman phoned our house.

'Adrian I'm calling from the RFL to inform you that you've been selected for England.'

I went into camp with the England squad to prepare for their Test against France. It was great to train with players like Andy Farrell, Martin Offiah, Shaun Edwards and Jason Robinson. They were all good lads, too.

The match was up in Gateshead, way out of rugby league's

heartland. We walked out of the tunnel into a near-deserted stadium. The roar of the crowd, I had to convince myself, was deafening. At least the national anthem got me going. I'd always loved it, from watching the Olympics or football or rugby on TV as a kid. I'd learned it in Cubs and when it was played over the loud speaker at Gateshead that evening, I'd never felt so proud. It's a cliché that a shiver runs down your spine as you stand, shoulder to shoulder, with your team-mates when *God Save The Queen* is played, but it's true. I belted out every word, knowing that a couple of hundred miles away my mum would be watching on the small screen in our front room to make sure I did.

The match itself was a no-contest. We won 73-6, I came off the bench for the last 10 minutes, managed to put a decent shot on one of the Frenchies, and the rest I don't remember. Maybe because I was so young, or maybe because I was working so hard trying to play well for Leeds, but I never really gave international rugby much thought after that. I was 19. I knew I had time on my side. But late in the year we played Wigan and, though we got well beaten, a couple of the lads – Faz and Terry O'Connor – said I might be in with a chance of making the Great Britain tour to the Southern Hemisphere. Sure enough, a few weeks later, a letter dropped through the door informing me I'd been selected.

I was elated. It was like being picked for England, only amped up and a whole lot better. Even just meeting the lads to get measured up for a Great Britain suit, and collecting a big bag of swag – all emblazoned with the Great Britain logo – was amazing.

I'd heard all the stories about cannibals before we set off for Papua New Guinea. After an exhausting flight involving a mid-journey training session in Hong Kong, one connection and a bumpy bus ride down a rickety road, we arrived at our hotel.

As we huddled in reception, waiting for our room keys, team manager Phil Lowe walked over to address us all.

'We've been advised not to go outside of the hotel complex,' he said.

'Why's that?' someone asked. 'In case the cannibals eat us?'

'No. Someone's just been shot dead nearby.'

Phil's expression told me he wasn't joking. Older players had tried to warn me what to expect in PNG. Alan Tait, my old Leeds team-mate, told me how he once threw one of his boots into the crowd after a Test match. The lucky recipient spent hours walking the several miles to the team hotel to ask him for the other one!

Despite the advice, we did venture out. While our hotel was a modern complex, it had been parked smack bang in the middle of an under-privileged country. It fitted in as uncomfortably as a director's Rolls-Royce in The Willows car park. The locals treated us well, and everywhere we went we'd be greeted by their smiling faces. Which would have been nice, had their teeth and mouths not been stained blood red by the Betel nut they seem to chew on incessantly. Rugby league isn't just PNG's main sport, it's like a religion. They are devoted – devoted – to the sport and its athletes. We were unknown to them, but treated like rock stars. Those players who I had thought would be treated like rock stars, were treated like gods. There were posters every-where of Adrian Lam, the PNG half-back who had captained Queensland the year before. He was worshipped. Their fans are more passionate about the game than anywhere else in the world. When Lammy flew in for the Test match, I was told the airport was busier than when The Beatles hit America. No such clamour or glamour for us boys in the mid-week side. We had to get on a small, rickety, single-propeller plane to take us to our match. It was the first time I realised just how huge and vast Papua New Guinea is. In every direction, all I could see were the tops of trees. Eventually we spotted a scar in the sea of lush, dark green, a clearing which didn't look wider than a regular house but somehow proved big enough for us to land in.

From plane to mini-bus to rugby ground, we were on the

pitch within an hour. I love the way the PNG boys play. To a man they were short, stocky and built like granite. Imagine facing 13 Stanley Genes. They were powerful and physical, they hit so low and so hard and when they had the ball they tried to put on a show for the hundreds of fans who were packed around the ground to see. If they couldn't see, they climbed trees to get better vantage points.

We won quite comfortably and, when the final whistle went, the supporters rushed onto the pitch. It wasn't scary as much as it was surreal. Why would a fan want to touch me, 19-year-old Adrian Morley from Cedric Street, Salford?

The touring squad was effectively split into two – the Test team and the mid-week team. It was a fluid system, but in truth few players were promoted. Those of us in the mid-week side had hopes but few expectations of cracking into the Test side.

After our win, we had a few days to relax. I went sea fishing with Jimmy Lowes and caught enough tuna on one glorious afternoon to fill an entire aisle at Tesco. I also took up an open invite to listen to a fella called Jack Gibson deliver a coaching clinic. When I asked Jimmy who he was, he pulled me aside.

'He's just about the greatest coach rugby league has ever produced,' he said.

'Oh *that* Jack Gibson,' I said. 'I know who you mean now.'

I still didn't have a clue who he was. Years later, at the Roosters, I got quite friendly with Jack. A great mind and a great man, I was sad when he passed away in 2008.

When it came to the day of the Test, the mid-week boys went along to watch the game with the fans. 'If there's any trouble in the crowd,' our tour guide told us, 'they may set off some tear gas which might sting your eyes a little bit.'

But it wasn't scary. I never felt threatened or in danger. The people couldn't have been more welcoming, and the fans couldn't have been more passionate in their support of their Test team as they gave our lads a real scare. Some of our boys needed oxygen on the sidelines – the heat and humidity proved a real leveller – but we got the win in the end.

I thought PNG was scenic and naturally beautiful, but it had nothing on Fiji. The country wasn't as developed, but the beaches were picture-postcard. Palm trees, white sand, turquoise ocean. It was there that I was introduced to Kava, which the Kiwis drink over here. Apparently, there's a drug in it which acts like an anaesthetic, but it's all natural and legal. You drink it from a coconut shell, clap three times and down the hatch it goes, but I needed to drink 20 glasses – or rather, coconut shells – of the stuff before I felt it taking any effect and relaxing me.

We won our mid-week match with ease, and the Test itself would have been a completely forgettable affair had Bobbie Goulding not made it unforgettable. He was a real wind-up merchant. The game flared up, punches were thrown but – as so often happens – it was all calmed down pretty quickly. Until one of their props decided to try and remove Bobbie's head. He charged straight at him, and the crowd – and we were sat among them – were screaming for blood. The match itself was one-way traffic; this was their only real hope of any real drama. Bobbie kept his cool, and waited until the last possible second to step out the way and unleash a right hook, which sparked another brawl.

Bobbie was a prickly player, who thrived on irritating opponents. He'd niggle at them and taunt them, and he didn't mind throwing punches when he felt he needed to. But his combative style only annoyed people who were playing against him. As a team-mate, he's great company.

I was the only Leeds player on the tour, and with many of the lads strangers to me I was worried that they might not like me. My style of play was all about aggression. Hit now, think later. But as I got to know them, I could feel the other players warming to me. They didn't say it, but I could tell from reading their facial expressions and the way they began relaxing in my company. By the time we landed in New Zealand, I felt they'd accepted me, and I'd convinced them that the fist-throwing hot-head on the field was actually an okay fella off it.

It was Denis Betts and Andy Farrell who helped launch my Test career.

For the first two games – in Papua New Guinea and Fiji – I didn't even make the starting line-up for the mid-week side. But Denis and Faz approached Phil Larder and asked him to give me a crack.

Denis had taken me under his wing. He was playing for Auckland Warriors, and he showed me around, took me to his home and really looked after me. He knew I was from Salford, like him, and growing up he was one of my heroes.

I really rated him as a forward and, when I toured with him, I realised that his success on the pitch wasn't a fluke. He and Faz were forever staying for extra fitness sessions or spending time working on specific drills. Faz was only a couple of years older than me, but I looked up to him like he was 10 years my senior. He's got a physical presence because of his size, and he also had a real aura of authority about him. He'd told me he'd been championing my cause, and after playing well against a Red Lions select side Larder gave me the nod. There was no fanfare or fuss to getting my first cap, nor was anything said when I was dropped from the team after the yellow card in the first Test. I was rooming with Terry O'Connor and he was terrific. He took care of me, he cracked open the bottle of Jim Beam he'd bought in Duty Free, he took me out on the drink, he took the piss out of anyone around us. Anything to try and raise a smile out of me.

But all I really wanted was my mum. I phoned home. Tez was sat on the bed, so the last thing I wanted to do was cry in front of him.

'Hello.'

That was it. As soon as I heard her voice, I couldn't hold the tears back any longer. My mum tried to tell me it was alright, but I knew it wasn't. I just wanted to get back home. Five minutes must be the shortest Test career in history, I told myself. Tez told me I had my whole career ahead of me, but I was so down I couldn't see that. I only saw doom and gloom. I kept my head down and my mouth shut. I wish I'd had the courage to stand up and apologise to the rest of the lads, but I didn't.

I'd just about picked myself up when I was floored again – Great Britain lost the second Test 18-15. The series was lost. I craved home even more.

By a fortunate twist of fate, the RFL decided to recall a dozen players home as a cost-cutting measure. Some of the lads were furious. We'd gone out there together as a team, and it wasn't exactly costing a lot – we were only earning £200 a week. I fully expected to be sent home, but when they read out the names of the departing players, I wasn't on the list.

'Either someone's tormenting me or I'm in with a chance for the third Test,' I thought. It was the latter.

I was made up to get another go. Injuries had bitten into the squad and we were well beaten in the last game, but I scored a try just after half-time, which helped me get over the disappointment of my debut. It was my first try for my country, and I'll never forget it. My Great Britain career was up and running.

CHAPTER TEN
LAND DOWN UNDER

If someone had said early in my career that rugby league doesn't offer enough travel opportunities, I'd have laughed at them.

I'd played in Ireland, France, Papua New Guinea, Fiji and New Zealand during my first 18 months in the first team, and 1997 started with another country chalked off – Australia. Each Super League club provided one player for the Great Britain squad which would compete in a 9s tournament in Townsville. It was my first trip to Australia and, when I landed in an uncomfortably hot, unbearably humid north Queensland, I didn't think I could ever settle there. In my naivety, I presumed all of Australia must have been the same.

I was still a relative newcomer to the scene but our team had plenty of big names, players like Andy Farrell, Denis Betts and Tommy Martyn. No one, though, was as recognised as much as our coach, Andy Gregory. Everywhere we went, the Aussies would welcome him like an old friend and buy him beers – which annoyingly came in tiny glasses called schooners, rather than pints.

And we had plenty of beers, too. Greg realised that, with the squad consisting of a player from each club, he had to work fast to build team spirit, and nothing builds it better than two days on the drink.

By the third day, we tried a game of touch rugby but after 15 minutes we couldn't cope in the heat. Everyone was dripping with sweat.

We were due to train the next day, but instead Greg took us scuba diving. Our manager – John Wilkinson, the Salford chairman – voiced his concerns that we weren't doing enough training.

'They're underwater,' Greg apparently told him. 'All the swimming they will be doing will be great exercise.'

Samoa knocked us out at the semi-finals stage, but we took some comfort from the fact that we'd beaten the eventual winners, New Zealand, in a group match. We finished with a day on the drink around Townsville, which qualified me to be the unofficial tour guide when Leeds went there later that year in the World Club Challenge to play the Cowboys and Adelaide Rams. It was a great concept, involving all the Super League-aligned teams Down Under and the English competition. The only reason it was a failure was down to us, the players. Across the board, none of our clubs performed, and some of the scorelines were just embarrassing.

Leeds had a decent squad that year – Gary Hetherington had led a consortium buy-out, and brought in some good players from Australia as well as his old club, Sheffield – and we'd started the year well, beating the reigning champions, St Helens.

I'd played in the Townsville humidity during the tour Down Under earlier in the year and I knew we'd messed up during the warm-up for our opening game against the Cowboys. There was no shortage of enthusiasm; if anything, there was too much. We went through our drills at 100mph and exhausted ourselves too quickly. It was like playing in an oven; we just had no energy when it came to the match.

Many clubs spent three weeks Down Under but we only had the two, which everyone in the Leeds squad was gutted about. Everyone but Terry Newton. He hated Australia and Australians; and couldn't wait to get back home.

Adelaide was a lot more comfortable, a lot more English. The Rams beat us easily, but a few weeks later we got revenge at Headingley. When most of our teams were getting smacked, we pulled one out of the hat, thanks in part to an amazing try from Paul Sterling – one of the best I've ever seen (the full-back he skinned to reach the line was a certain Michael Maguire, the future Wigan coach). The World Club Challenge was a massive wake-up call, and one we needed. I realised that – just because we were now full-time professionals – we weren't as good as we probably all thought we were. What started out as a great concept ended farcically, with my brother's team St Helens making the quarter-finals even though they hadn't won a group match, and two Aussie sides contesting the final. Thankfully, our domestic form fared better. We stayed in the top half of the table all season and reached the semi-finals of the Challenge Cup, where we lost to Bradford.

Our season was simmering along quite well. But I broke my jaw in a game at Wigan – Anthony Farrell and I went in to make a tackle, and his big nut swung around the player's body and whacked me square in the face in the very first minute. I immediately knew something was wrong. I tried biting, but my teeth weren't aligned. I stayed on for the rest of the half, and then in the dressing room at half-time I told the doctor it felt wrong. He examined me, and said, 'You're fine.'

I knew I wasn't, but I never needed a green light to continue playing. It was only the next day, when my face had swollen up like a hamster, that I was sent for a scan and the full damage was revealed.

They offered to plate the jaw, but that would have finished my season and I was desperate to play for Great Britain. There was a five-week window before the first Super League Test against Australia at Wembley.

'Well, it's a risk,' the doc said. 'But you might get away with it.'

So I turned down the operation and, once the pain of my injury had dulled, the swelling had faded so I didn't look too much like a hamster and I got to a point where I could eat most solids, I went on holiday to Ibiza with Tez Newton, Phil Hassan, Phil Cantillon and Leroy Rivett.

We'd all become pretty close. Tez and I were home-birds and split our time between the north west and Leeds, where Tez stayed with the two Phils, while I slept at Neil Harmon's pad. Quite a few of the apprentices crashed at Harmon's place as well. It was called The Palace, and if those walls could talk they'd tell some good stories. Not quite Motley Crue stories; but the unofficial rule was that if any of the lads pulled, they could take the girls back to The Palace. Neil only charged me £40 a week, which wasn't a bad price, considering Dean Bell had persuaded the club to give me £2,000 as a relocation package.

In Ibiza, we were young enough to hit the beer pretty hard each night and still get up in the mornings. As close as you become to your team-mates, you still learn a lot more about them when you live with them for a week.

Take Leroy, for example.

There were quite a lot of stray cats around the hotel site, scavengers with no owners. I was sat down one day, eating a sandwich, when one of the cheeky little moggies kept trying to take a bite out of it every time I put it down.

'Right,' I thought. 'I'll teach the little fucker a lesson.'

So the next time it came to take a nibble, I scooped it up, and without looking, just launched it – American Football-style – into the pool. Except, the pool was further away than I thought it was. And the cat was heavier than I thought it was.

Bollocks, it's not going to make it.

Tez was pissing himself laughing.

For a split-second, I pictured the hungry little fur-ball crashing into the terracing. But as it fell from the air, I heard the reassuring 'splash' as it just made the pool.

I breathed a sigh of relief and grinned to the lads, as if I was always confident it would make the pool. Terry was bent double laughing. Phil Hassan was, too. But I looked at Leroy, and he was glaring at me in disgust. He couldn't believe what I'd just done.

It was then that I discovered that Leroy has a soft spot for cats. Well, all pets really. In fact, I'd go as far as saying he was a part-time animal rights activist.

'You wanker,' he shouted at me. He looked distraught. He ran over to the pool to check the cat was fine (it was) and then stormed off. He didn't speak to me for the rest of the night! I apologised to him later on, though, and we were fine.

When I got back to England, I started training with other Great Britain boys whose sides weren't involved in the Premiership. I made the Rothman's Team of the Year and got a lot of accolades, but I still felt I had a lot to prove. Sure, I'd played for Great Britain, but I wasn't an established player. I knew a big series against the Aussies could change all that.

CHAPTER ELEVEN
SEND HER VICTORIOUS

I was waiting for *God Save the Queen*. Arms linked, chest out. I scanned the faces of the Australian players, until my eyes fell on the player I most rated and respected – and he was staring straight at me. His face was angry, twisted, enraged. The type of expression which screamed out, 'I want to kill you'.

We'd been stuffed at Wembley 38-14, thanks largely to a terrific performance from Laurie Daley, who scored a hat-trick, but I'd felt I'd done okay coming off the bench and Great Britain coach Andy Goodway promoted me to the starting side for the second Test at Old Trafford. For me, that was as big as playing at Wembley. I'd grown up marvelling at the Theatre of Dreams and envying the players who ran out there, admittedly with a different shaped ball. To have the chance to do the same, just a few miles from my house, was as big as it could get.

I was only 20, about to take on the best players in the world again. I'd played them the previous week, but now I had a starting spot and I knew it was my big chance. I scanned their line-up.

There's Laurie Daley, there's Wendell Sailor. There's that kid Darren Lockyer, I bet he has a decent career. And there's Gorden Tallis, the best forward in the world. Why is he eyeballing me?

I turned to my left and right, to check whether I'd been mistaken. No. He was looking straight at me, and not a casual glance in my direction, but a piercing stare which was burning a hole in my head. He didn't mouth anything to me, and he didn't need to. His expression could only be translated one way: 'I am going to rip your Pommie-bastard head off'.

When I'd seen him play for Brisbane, I thought he was a nut case. When he brawled with Tez O'Connor earlier in the year, Tez said his wife hit harder, but I wasn't convinced. Rugby league players don't show fear or admit if they're intimidated, but we're all humans and some get more scared than others. I noticed that a lot when I played alongside Terry Newton. It wasn't always about what he brought to our team, but the way he would unsettle theirs. Blokes were scared of playing him, and Tallis was the same. It wasn't just that *he* brought his talents to the party, it was the way he scared his opponents into forgetting theirs. He was trying to unsettle me by staring at me both barrels. Shoot me down before a ball had been kicked. But it had the reverse effect. I didn't try and stare him out, I just smiled to myself, content in the knowledge that Gorden Tallis, the best forward in the game, must think I'm alright if he's targeting me. Nothing could have fired me up more. It gave me a buzz, a 'fuck you' mentality.

We spent the entire match smashing into each other. I never gave the Aussies an inch. I took in every carry as hard as I could, I ripped into the tackling, and I never felt dominated by the opposing forwards. In those scenarios, it's easy to fall into the trap of B-lining for one player, creating space in your defensive line that could be exploited. I didn't do that. I didn't lose my head, I just wanted to make an impression for Great Britain, against the Aussies, against Tallis. He even cleaned out my second-row partner, Chris Joynt, with a high shot, as Andy Farrell went over for a try.

It was my fourth game for Great Britain and the first in which I'd felt I'd made a real difference. We won 20-12, and my mum still has a picture on her wall of me, fist clenched, minutes after we'd beaten the Aussies. The feeling of beating them was amazing. Paul Sculthorpe, a school year younger than me, was loose forward and he'd played a stormer. He'd been a stand-out player in Super League that season, but that game put him on the map, and a lot was said afterwards about us two young forwards who were going to be there for the long haul. My focus was on the short-term, though. The series was level 1-1 and you couldn't pick up a paper without being reminded of the fact it had been 27 years since our last Ashes win.

The deciding game was at Elland Road and we went into it confident, but that melted away within the first few minutes when the Aussies rattled up the early points. The final scoreline of 37-20 flattered us. The Aussies had a crash hot side which was drawn from only half their pool of players, due to the Super League war Down Under which saw two rival competitions run simultaneously. I still find it incredible that we can count those matches on our Test records but the likes of Lockyer for the 'Super League Australia' side can't; those matches were real Test games, and far more ferocious than the games the 'real' Kangaroos were facing during that time, against Fiji and a Rest of the World side.

That was my first taste of losing to the Aussies, and as much as I wanted to, I couldn't bring myself to hate them. Before I became friends with any of them, before I lived in their company, on their soil, I wanted to despise them. But the trouble was, even after they'd won a series, they were great blokes. They were modest and gracious, offering nothing but praise and kind words to us. Maybe if they'd acted like wankers it would have been easy to hate them, but they didn't. To a man they were terrific, and when I asked Tallis whether he'd swap his jersey with me at the end of that third match, he didn't hesitate.

'I remember watching you play against North Queensland earlier this year,' he said to me. 'I said then you were going to be a good one.'

Not everyone thought the same about the Aussies. 'Diesel' Dean Sampson, the brickwall former Castleford prop, had taken offence to something the Australian full-back Brett Mullins had said to his missus that evening when we all went out after the game. To this day I'm still not sure what it was, all I know is that one minute we were all drinking in the same Leeds pub, and the next Diesel had stormed off to the Aussies' hotel. No one followed him because no one thought he was serious but, credit to him, later that night, word got back to us that he'd stormed straight into their place, found Mullins and given him a beating!

The party was still going strong the next day, only I'd moved 70 miles from Leeds to Wigan with the rest of the North West-based players. I got on well with Kris Radlinski, and he told me a few of the Wigan lads were heading to Tenerife the following morning, if I fancied it. I couldn't turn it down. He phoned the travel agent and added me to their group which included Craig Murdoch, Andy Johnson and Gary Connolly. I didn't know Gary too well by that point, but everyone knew of two legends about him: his drinking ability and his freakish gift for arm-wrestling. Both were true. I actually managed to beat him with my left arm, but his right arm was his gun, and I didn't stand a chance. I gave a good account of myself on the drinking though, and had a great time making some new mates. Only trouble was, I was supposed to have been back at Leeds the Monday after the Ashes series finished. Players usually get five or six weeks' holiday after their final game, but I'd taken my break before the Tests began. This was long before mobile phones, and each time I called my mum from Tenerife she said, 'Leeds have been on again, wondering where you are.' On the final day, Kris Rads suggested we extend our stay for another couple of days, but I couldn't put off the bollocking that awaited me any longer. When I got back, Dean Bell tore into me, telling me I was out of line. I pleaded my case, saying I had needed a break after the Test series, and he could see my reasoning – he'd only just finished his own playing career. But he said I should have approached him and asked beforehand, and he was right. The club fined me, but suspended it, in part due to my good form that year and in part because I think they understood where I was coming from.

CHAPTER TWELVE
PLAYING CHICKEN

I'd never been so happy in my life.

It was a perfect autumn Sunday morning during the 1997 Test series, crisp but sunny, and I was heading down a deserted dual-carriageway towards Salford. I was 20, I'd made my Great Britain home debut the day before, played my first game against the Aussies, and my first at Wembley.

I'd been on cloud nine for the past few hours and, just when I thought life couldn't get any better, Barry White came on the radio! I love Barry White.

'. . . and the answer, to all of my dreams,
You're my sun, my moon . . .'

I had the driver-side window on my Vauxhall Carlton wound down and my hand on the roof, tapping along. I was heading towards church to surprise my mum and dad. I hadn't seen them for a few days, and I knew, just knew, how proud they would be see me there – dressed in my smart Great Britain suit – alongside them at mass.

I couldn't wait to see them.

'. . . my guiding star,
My kind of wonderful,
That's what you are . . .'

A quick glance at the clock. Twenty past 10. Five minutes away. Perfect timing, Moz.

'I know, there's only, only one like you . . .'

I approached Eccles roundabout, one car in front, turned the volume up.

'There's no way, they could have made two . . .'

The car in front moved off, he'd spotted a gap, he was away. And here came my favourite bit. I turned the volume up again.

'You're all I'm living for . . .'

I put my foot on the accelerator, knowing I could squeeze into the same gap as the driver in front.

'Your love I'll keep for evermore.

You're the first, you're . . .' – SMASH!

I jolted forward in my seat. All around me went chaotic. I was deafened by the shattering of glass and the ear-piercing screech of metal being twisted. From start to finish, it must have only lasted two seconds, and it took at least the same amount of time again for me to register what had just happened.

The car in front, the one which had spotted the gap, had – I now realised – not pulled off. The driver had stopped. I hadn't.

The back of his car was caved in; I edged by bum up from my seat to assess the damage to the front of my car; my treasured Carlton was a full foot shorter than it should have been.

I turned the radio off. Not today, Barry. I'd just totalled a car and, worse, I had no insurance (with the cheapest quote £2,400 – more than half the value of the car – I thought I'd take my chances). All I could think was how much trouble I was in. The driver in front got out of the car and stormed over towards me. He was blazing. He was only small, five-feet nothing, with steam coming out of his ears, his arms waving around wildly and a pace in his step which said, 'I'm going to deck someone'. As I stepped out of the car, towering above him, he instantly changed tact.

'Are you alright mate?' he asked. I was dying to laugh at the way he'd become so caring all of a sudden. Had I been smaller, he'd probably have taken a swing at me!

His missus got out of their car and she was shook up. I apologised sincerely for what I'd done. It was my mistake, and I felt awful for them. I ran around to Carlo Napolitano's house – it was only around the corner – and woke him and his mates up from their drunken slumber. They followed me back to the roundabout to assess the wreckage. The police were already there; I went over and told them it was my fault, that I thought the car in front had set off when it hadn't.

The officer scribbled down my rambling apology and took my name and address.

'Now if you'd just follow me sir, we just need to breathalyse you.'

Now I knew I was in trouble. I'd spent the previous night out on the drink with Paul Sculthorpe, having an endless supply of beers bought for us by rugby league fans in the chain of pubs we called in around Wigan. A couple more back at his future in-laws' place in Orrell, and I knew the booze was still in my system, even though I didn't feel in any way drunk.

'Blow as hard as you can sir.'

I stuck my lips together and puffed my cheeks, making it appear like I was blowing hard when really I wasn't. It didn't matter. I was in the borderline category, just over the legal limit but flirting with the safety line. So they put me in the back of the police car and took me to the station. There, they breathalysed me again; again I was borderline. The policeman actually felt a bit sorry for me.

'You're just over,' he said. 'But what you can do now is ask for a blood test. It might take the doctor a couple of hours to get here, by which time you might be alright.'

I didn't need any convincing. I asked for a blood test, and then they took me to a cell to wait until the doctor arrived. Being locked up, alone, in a stone-cold room plays with your mind. I began panicking. *What will my parents say? What will Leeds say? Leeds! How the bloody hell will I get to Leeds if I'm banned?*

Think Moz, think.

Suddenly, a plan came into my head. I could sweat the booze out. So I dropped to the floor and knocked out 30 press-ups. Then I stood up and started jogging on the spot, thrusting my knees up high to get my heart racing. Then star-jumps, then sit-ups, then back to jogging. I was halfway through my second improvised circuit, when I heard the clank of metal outside. The door opened.

A policeman stood in the doorway, a puzzled look on his face as I stood, my breathing laboured, my nice Great Britain shirt and trousers soaking in sweat.

'Come with me,' he said. 'The doctor's here to take your blood.'

What happened to a couple of hours? It had taken him 20 minutes, at best. The doc took my test and apologised. I was still just over the legal limit.

I was banned for a year, fined, and gave my car to my brother Chris on the understanding that he could have it if he paid the two grand it would cost to fix it. The repair bill for the car I hit was more than seven grand, but the kind people at the Bureau of Uninsured Drivers offered to pay it for me, on the basis that I paid them back later.

I never did. I've always been told that if you ignore a problem it won't go away, but in this case it did. Every time a letter arrived demanding payment, I ignored it. I've always been pretty good at taking a blinkered approach to problems. If I know I'm going to get a bollocking in three days' time, I won't spend those three days stewing and worrying; I file it away and out of my mind until the time comes. I know not everyone is like that. Take my brother Steve, for example. He's more sensible, more of a worrier. I was living with him at the time – my mum and dad had moved out of Cedric Street. I didn't tell him I was binning the letters over the unpaid insurance bill, because I knew he'd spend his time panicking about it.

And I did a pretty good job of keeping it from him until we got an unexpected visitor.

'Aje, you wanker,' he said, as soon as I picked up the phone. It was my first mobile, the size of a brick. 'The bailiffs have just been round. BAILIFFS!'

'What did you say? Did they take anything?'

'No, I told 'em you weren't in.'

'Don't worry, I'll sort it,' I said.

They called again a week later, when I was in, but hiding like a coward behind the couch in the front room, thanking the heavens that Ste wasn't in.

After that, they never called again, but it wasn't quite the end of it. Years later, when Ste got married and went to buy a house, he had a bad credit rating because of his previous address, forcing him to put their first mortgage under his wife's name. I felt bad about that . . . even if it did save me seven grand.

Steve helped me out while I was banned from driving, without knowing it. Getting from Salford to Leeds every day proved pretty tricky without a car. At times, I stayed over in Leeds at Neil Harmon's place. Other times, Terry Newton would come over from Wigan and collect me. And other times, I just drove anyway.

I'm not proud of it. The first time I did it was an emergency, or at least, an emergency in my life at the time: I had to get to training and I had no way of getting there. I spent the entire way there and back worrying about being pulled over by the police. I knew I'd really be in trouble if I was. But I was driving Steve's car, we lived in the same house and with his date of birth at the forefront of my mind – I practiced saying '10 September, 1970' until it rolled off my tongue effortlessly – I reckoned I could pull off impersonating him if I needed to be.

Ste Morley. 10 September, 1970. Ste Morley. 10 September, 1970.

I never did get pulled over, so I drove again. And again.

Then, a few weeks before my driving ban was due to expire, I bought myself a new car in readiness for getting my licence back. I've never been a petrol-head, but I'd missed having my own wheels and I couldn't wait to take it out for a spin.

So I didn't wait.

When Leeds had a game at Warrington, I decided to take my new car and drive myself there. I'd taken Ste's car out four or five times without incident and I'd grown complacent, knowing the chances of being pulled over were remote.

On the way to Warrington's old Wilderspool stadium is a big roundabout. I had stopped at the junction, waiting for a gap in the traffic and just off to the left were three lads – all about 17 or 18 – harassing a kid who must have been at least two years younger than them. He was a nerdy little thing, but I felt sorry for him; he was getting picked on and it was obvious that he was getting upset, even though he was trying to pretend like he was in on the joke. It was like George McFly being bullied by Biff in *Back to the Future*, played out right there on a Warrington street.

As I pulled out onto the roundabout and drove past the group, I wound the passenger-seat window down.

'Hey,' I yelled. 'Leave him alone.'

The three lads looked up.

'Piss off you wanker.'

They all started giggling. Even the kid who was being bullied, in a nervous, trying-to-be-in-with-the-gang kind of way.

I'd driven past them at this point, but could see the tallest lad – and the obvious gang leader – giving me the fingers through my rear view mirror. It was a typical case of him acting hard as nails because he knew he could get away with it.

I'll show you.

Instead of going straight on towards Wilderspool, I drove around the roundabout to do a full loop. I didn't know exactly what I was going to do. Get out. Shout abuse. I wasn't sure.

I sped up and deliberately revved my engine so the pricks would hear it. It was only a 1-litre engine – a glorified lawn-mower, really – but I convinced myself it roared as I rounded the corner and they came back into view.

By this point they were crossing the road heading towards Wilderspool – the turnoff I wanted. Two of the three lads skipped across, but the one who had given me the fingers stayed in the middle of the road.

Goading me.

Provoking me.

I drove straight at him.

I had no intentions of hitting him – I just wanted to get close enough to scare the crap out of him. My left foot was hovering over the clutch, ready to slam on the brakes just in time. He stayed where he was, put his two hands out and motioned his fingers towards him – the universal sign language for 'come here'.

I got closer. Thirty feet. Twenty feet. My eyes locked on his, all the time. Then I saw it. In less than a second, his face turned from the arrogant, cocky, bullet-proof brat to the petrified, worried, scared bully that he was. He was frozen still.

I'd got him, good style. Mission accomplished.

I switched my foot from the accelerator and slammed on the brakes, all the time staring at him with a knowing, satisfied smile of a job well done. The car screeched in front of him.

Five feet. Three feet. But it was too late.

Biff got hit.

'ARRGHHH!'

I clipped him with my bumper. He didn't go down. I could tell he wasn't even badly hurt. He just started hopping around, clutching his thigh, shocked that someone had stood up to him. While driving a car, admittedly.

'That'll teach you to be such a cocky git, won't it?' I yelled at him through the window. I didn't feel sorry for him. I hadn't intended to clip him – I planned to just give him a fright – but I wasn't going to shed a tear for him, either.

He kept shouting abuse, calling me every name under the sun. His bravado was rushing back. I pulled away, carrying on towards Wilderspool, a proud grin on my face. But as I sped away and his voice tailed off, I just made out the final words he yelled after me.

'I'm calling the police'.

As those words slowly sunk in, I was overcome by a nauseous feeling; one that started in the pit of my stomach but quickly spread through me. By the time I'd pulled up on the deserted Wilderspool car park, I was a bag of nerves, clutching the steering wheel just to stop my arms from shaking.

It was a perk for the lads from Lancashire that they were allowed to make their own way to games in the north west – Wigan, St Helens, Warrington, Salford – rather than travelling with the rest of the team. Terry Newton, always the early bird, was already at the ground. Luckily, the team coach hadn't arrived, and wasn't due to for another half an hour or so, so I parked my car next to Terry's, got out and explained what had happened a couple minutes earlier.

'You've nothing to worry about,' he said. 'He was in the road and you slammed on your brakes. That's all you have to tell 'em.'

But it wasn't clipping the lad with my bumper that I was worried about.

'I can't,' I told Tez. 'I'm still banned. And I've no insurance.'

He'd presumed my ban had expired when I'd bought myself a new car. He stopped talking. It was obvious he was thinking of a solution to the new problem I'd presented him. Then it hit me. A way out.

Without saying a word to Tez, I ran over to the side of the car park, where a once-planted area was now covered by litter and rubble. It didn't take me a few seconds to find what I needed – half a brick. I ran back towards my car, cradling my new possession under my arm and then – after a cursory glance around to check no one was watching – I launched it through the driver's side window.

Tez looked stunned.

'What you doin' you dickhead?' he asked incredulously. I leaned my head through the window, picked up the brick, and started hammering it against the ignition point. By the third strike, it had smashed open.

'Moz,' Tez asked again, as I put down the brick and started yanking the ignition wires free, like I'd seen them do in *The Terminator* film.

'WHAT THE HELL ARE YOU DOING?'

I brought my head from out of the car and looked at him.

'Simple,' I said. 'If the police come calling, I'll just say the car was stolen.'

Tez was not a straight-A student, but he was one of the most streetwise people I have ever met. No one pulled the wool over his eyes. So, not surprisingly, he noticed the gaping flaw in my masterplan immediately.

'So you'll tell the police your new car was robbed,' he said, running through my chain of events. 'It was parked at your house, somebody nicked it, drove it here, hit the kid . . . that way you can't get done for it?'

'Yep.'

'But Moz – you play for Leeds. Why would a car thief bring it to the stadium that you're playing at?'

Bollocks. When I'd thought of the idea, when I'd found a brick, when I'd run back and launched it through my window, not once had that thought crossed my mind.

Thankfully, my attempts to make the car appear to have been robbed had not disabled it. I put the key into the ignition and the engine turned over. So the pair of us got in and drove it a couple of miles away and – when we were convinced no one was watching us – pulled over by the pavement.

I got out and realised I'd parked it flush to the curb. Car thieves wouldn't do that, I thought. So I got back in and angled it, trying to make it look like it had been abandoned, and then we double-timed it back to the stadium.

I spent the rest of the afternoon feeling petrified, regularly calling home to check if the police had been around.

They didn't call that day, or the following day. I spent two days as a nervous wreck at home, lounging on the couch, waiting for an unfamiliar knock on the front door. When, eventually, the police did call, it was on the telephone – not to my door – to inform me that my car had been spotted by a patrol, it had been impounded, and if I wanted it back I had to pay £500 for its release.

CHAPTER THIRTEEN
CHEAP SHOT

'What happens on the pitch, stays on the pitch,' has become as big a rugby league cliché as big hits, dumb football and 'the best season ever'. But that doesn't make it any less true.

And I can't think of a better example than during a Super League match at Wigan in 1998, when Mick Cassidy tried to remove my head with his elbow.

'That is an awful one from Cassidy,' Stevo said on the Sky Sports commentary. 'It's one of the worst I've ever seen in the game of rugby league.'

Earlier in the match – in fact, straight from the kick-off – I'd cleaned out the Wigan hooker, Robbie McCormack. He was only a little fella, and as soon as he collected the ball I monstered him. It was a tactic Iestyn Harris and I had practiced time and again, until we had it down to a fine art. He would kick the ball high so it would drop just at the right place, and time, that I was charging, and on that instance, as soon as McCormack had the ball in his hands I completely smothered him . . . and in doing so painted a big bright red target across my face.

'You cheap shot bastard,' Andy Farrell screamed, pointing his finger at me.

The atmosphere was electric. Leeds and Wigan had been the two best sides in Super League all year. We had a one-point lead nearing the half-hour mark and had forced a drop-out on their line. Back then, second-rowers stood where props stand now. I collected the ball and drove it forward. There was a three-strong welcoming committee waiting for me, but I didn't slow down.

The next thing I remember I was waking up on the floor.

'Where's the ball. FUCK! I've lost the ball.'

I had no idea what had happened.

The crowd was a dull roar. I was a bit worse for wear, so the physio picked me up and took me off. I was still in the dressing room, having a wound near my eye stitched up, when the lads came in at half-time.

'That Cassidy's a dirty bastard,' one said.

'He's a wanker isn't he?' said another.

Many other lads said similar things, but I still didn't know what had happened.

I told Graham Murray I was good to go back on for the second half. My eye had swelled up, but my head felt fine. I ended up providing the pass for the final try, which was sweet because we won the match, 15-8.

I saw Mick in the players' bar afterwards. I stared at him, still not knowing what he'd done.

'What's up with you?' he said.

'You know what's up with me.'

'I didn't mean it . . . it's just one of those things.'

It wasn't until I got home that I saw the incident. I've done some things on the field I'm not particularly proud of, but his was done with malice and intent. He clearly raised the elbow to my face-level at the last minute, for me to charge onto. It was a low act. But as pissed off as I was, Cass was right – it was just one of those things. That's the nature of the game, and when emotions are high, the stakes are high and players do stupid things. They have brain explosions. If I see Mick now, I'll say 'hello' – there's no grudge there.

In fact, the only time I saw two players fighting off the field, it was between two of my own team-mates – Terry Newton and Barrie McDermott!

Graham Murray took us away to Blackpool on a team bonding weekend. We were in one pub and Jamie Mathiou put a condom on Barrie Mac's shoulder. Which would have been okay as a prank, but Barrie didn't like Jamie. He didn't like smart-arses, he wasn't too fond about Aussies and he certainly didn't like Aussies who played in his position. Jamie was all three, so there was always a lot of tension between the two. Full of lager, it wasn't long before they were squaring off – just handbags, really – but Terry, Leroy Rivett and I decided to calm it down, so we took Baz to another pub.

Baz was fuming. Like a bear with a very bad head.

'Jamie's a wanker. He's a prick. Don't you think he's a dick-head?'

A short while later, Tez, being as compassionate as ever, was taking a leak next to Baz and thought it'd be funny to piss on his leg.

To say it was probably the wrong time and the wrong place would be an understatement. Barry shoved Terry back forcefully, and the two of them ended up throwing punches. I jumped on Barry's back, Leroy grabbed Tez and we split them up.

Baz had come off worse, so I walked back with him to the place where we were staying, trying to calm him down. 'He's a team-mate Baz – you'll end up in the shit,' I told him.

And Baz agreed with me. 'Yeah, I know. It was a stupid thing to do,' he said.

But as soon as we got back, he steamed the door open and they were at it again!

Earlier in the year we'd played Bradford at their place and smacked them. Bradford had earned the right to two titles at the time – they were Super League champions, and they had the most annoying player in Super League in their side.

Graham Bradley. Even his own team-mates thought he was a prick. I spoke to him after he'd retired and he said, 'If I was still playing, I wouldn't speak to you.'

He was a knob like that. Some players like to frustrate opponents by doing niggly tactics, like putting the knees on a player in a tackle, or standing on their hands or feet. Some others try to frustrate players, swearing at them and criticising their form, their looks, their mum. A select few get involved in both; Bradley was one of them. He was a grub. So when we smacked them at Odsal it was a great feeling, and made even better by the sight of Bradley, his hands on his nose, and blood dripping through his fingers after our prop, Darren Fleary, smashed him with a great shot.

In the video review, our coach, Graham Murray said, 'I wouldn't normally condone that sort of behaviour . . . but as it was Bradley, well done Daz.'

Muzza had come in at the start of the year. Dean Bell had done a decent job, but he'd been thrust into the role before he'd expected to be, and I think he was happy to take a step back.

Muzza brought so much experience and he made us a lot better with little simple things. He could have a laugh, he worked hard and he didn't tolerate dick-heads – I took to him straight away. Most lads did. When coaches have that personality where players want to play for them, then half the battle's won. They've cracked it. And that's what we had with Murray. I had faith in him and believed in him, and he seemed to like me. I got sent off for a mis-placed shoulder charge against Sheffield, but Muzz said he had no problem with my tackling style. I was only 20, but Muzza made me feel like a senior player.

We got knocked out of the Challenge Cup by Castleford at the start of the year, but from that point on it was us and Wigan leading the way all season, and it was fitting that we both made it through to the inaugural Grand Final. I know a few were against the concept, and they had a point – the first-past-the-post system is the fairest way of deciding who's been the best side during a season. But I was excited about the Grand Final and play-offs, and Muzza told us it was how things were done in

Australia and that even the cynics would learn to love it. I think he got that one pretty much right.

The atmosphere at Old Trafford was incredible. I didn't know what to expect, but as we lined up to go out I could feel the energy pouring through the mouth of the tunnel. There was a buzz, an excitement. I walked out, behind Iestyn Harris – that was the only quirky superstition I had pre-match – and I sensed it was going to be a great game.

It was. Only sadly, it went Wigan's way, with Jason Robinson scoring a great solo try and Andy Farrell's boot doing the rest. Our forwards were far better than Wigan's, and Iestyn had been on fire all year – so much so that he walked away with the Man of Steel – but Wigan just managed to nick it. It's never nice to lose a game so big, and it's made only slightly easier when it's to a piece of wizardry from one of the world's greatest wingers.

CHAPTER FOURTEEN
ONE CRAZY YEAR

E vander Holyfield is standing on an empty dancefloor. In a cowboy hat. Shadow boxing.

Maybe I shouldn't have been surprised. This, after all, was 1999. A year when I'd won a Challenge Cup Final at Wembley, been arrested for swimming naked in Queensland, sent off within a minute of one Super League game and been approached by a club 12,000 miles away in Australia. It wasn't supposed to get any weirder. Until one night in London, well, I ran into the champ . . .

Back then, the season started with the early Challenge Cup rounds before the Super League campaign began. Everyone knew that the '99 final would be the last at the old Wembley. It's a romantic idea that the historical significance somehow fired Leeds up but, in truth, none of the players thought anything of that. At the time, we thought the new one would be up within a year or two – few predicted it would be so long before rugby league was back there – and besides, we had plenty of motivation ourselves. We all carried so much disappointment from the year before because we felt we had a team good enough to win trophies. I'd grown up watching Wigan win the cup every year and no one else had a chance. Winning at Wembley felt unachievable. Then, when their dominance ended in 1996, it was by a shit-hot St Helens side.

But in '98, when Sheffield beat Wigan at Wembley, winning the cup felt more attainable. No offence intended, but man for man we were much better than Sheffield. We'd beaten Wigan home and away in '98 and, though we lost to them in the Grand Final, we felt we were a better team than them.

At the start of the year, the Leeds CEO, Gary Hetherington, flew us all out to Lanzarote for a training camp (credit to Gary, he's tighter than a submarine door when it comes to contract negotiations, but he's really generous when it comes to looking after the lads).

At the end of the camp, we had a team meeting and set our goals for the year, and then Gary went through the bonus structure. Usually, a player may be on £500-a-man for progressing past the first round, then a grand for the next stage, and so on. But Gary laid it on the line. He offered us each £13,000 for winning the Challenge Cup, or nothing. It was a bold move. Leeds hadn't won the cup since the '70s.

We looked at each other and everyone nodded in agreement. There were no complaints. We knew we were good enough to win a trophy, and we backed ourselves.

We were still at the camp when the draw for our first Challenge Cup game was made. Wigan at home. There were still many lower-league sides in the bag but, honestly, I was made up. It was the perfect draw – the team who'd beaten us in our last game, the Grand Final.

It was a brutal, brutal game. I did my best to smash Wigan's forwards off their game; for their part, our fans were trying to put Mick Cassidy off by chanting, 'Morley's gonna get ya' every time he got the ball! They'd not forgotten his elbow on me the year before, and I hadn't either, but I didn't hold a grudge. I'd done dafter things and had brain-snaps, just like he'd had; I'd hate it if the players I'd hurt held a grudge. Only once have I seen a player carry a grudge off the pitch and into the players' bar afterwards. And it happened in that game.

Early on, Barrie McDermott was sent off for a high tackle on Simon Haughton, leaving us a man down for the best part of an hour. But we had so much energy and determination, and were good value for our 28-18 win.

Afterwards, in the bar, Barrie saw Haughton, and made a beeline for him. Simon would have known from Baz's expression that he wasn't walking over to apologise.

'What are you doing staying down?' he shouted. Baz was livid and gave it to him both barrels. He was convinced Simon had milked the incident – a definite no-no in rugby league. I once read a great quote: 'Footballers spend a game pretending to be injured when they're not, and rugby league players spend a game pretending not to be injured when they are.'

For me, that sums up our sport perfectly.

We beat St Helens and Widnes in the next two rounds, and then knocked Bradford off 23-10 in the semi-final to make it through to the final. It was a great feeling; a combination of relief and delight, pride and satisfaction. We'd beaten three of the top sides to reach Wembley – it had been a tough run. Our final opponents, London Broncos, had some very good players, but with all respect they weren't in the same class, and maybe Graham Murray sensed that complacency might be a tricky obstacle. So the night before the game, he gave every player a pencil and a sheet of paper, with the squad list on it. He instructed us to write down what we thought about each of our team-mates, and hand it in. It was all done anonymously. It was such a simple idea, but that was part of Murray's genius. Later that night, a sheet of paper was slipped under my door with all of my team-mates' comments about me copied on it.

It blew my mind.

'I wouldn't swap Moz for anyone', 'It gives me confidence when he's in our team', 'He's a real leader' . . . the praise made me feel bullet-proof. From that point on, I had little doubt in my mind that we would win, even when London took the lead when Martin Offiah – who bloody else? – opened the scoring. Even when they were 10-0 up a few moments later, and even when we only held a slender two-point lead at half-time. London had a decent side back then, thanks to the investment of their millionaire backer Richard Branson, who looked like an ageing rock star when he led the side out in jeans and an open buttoned shirt. But we never let our heads dip. Our pack was granite: Barrie McDermott, Tez Newton, Darrell Fleary, Anthony Farrell, Marc Glanville. All tough, tough players.

Early in the second half, I made a good break when Andy Hay put me through a hole. The noise from the crowd was incredible and I made a cardinal sin – I chased individual glory. I had Francis Cummins open on my inside as I closed in on their full-back, Tulsen Tollett. But instead of passing the ball, I took on Tulsen . . . and lost. I apologised to Franny after-wards, but he still reminds me of the incident every time we catch up!

London really gave it to us, but Barrie McDermott scored a great try for us, barging through three or four defenders to score, and they ran out of steam in the final quarter. I've been in that position before when the opposition has got on an unstoppable roll, and it's an awful position to be in. Leroy Rivett finished with four tries, and as we edged in on the half-century, when I knew the game was won, I began to enjoy the occasion. I soaked up the noise, the atmosphere, the grand scale of Wembley's structure. And when the full-time whistle was blown, I felt elation I'd never felt before.

It was the first trophy of my embryonic professional career, but seeing how much it meant to the Leeds fans, who hadn't won the cup in 21 years, made me realise just how special it was. After we'd collected our medals, posed for pictures and sung *Simply The Best*, I jogged over to the terracing where my family were sat. My brother, Chris, had told me before the game that, if we won, he was going to jump onto the pitch – like I had three years earlier.

I gave him a hug through the wire fencing, and then motioned him onto the pitch.

'I can't Aje,' he laughed. 'There's too many stewards'.

'Fair enough,' I said. 'Where's dad?'

Chris pointed up towards the back of the stands. I scanned the crowd and I couldn't see him. There were too many fans, too many flags and arms being waved. Then, just as I'd given up hope, I spotted him. He was stood on a chair, waving at me, a proud smile beaming from ear to ear. And at that moment, right there on the Wembley pitch, I cried my eyes out.

That evening felt so surreal. It was an emotion that's so hard to explain, but I'll try: take the feeling of being a child rushing downstairs on Christmas Day, amp it up a notch, add Red Bull, and you'd be somewhere close. It's that same not-a-care-in-the-world happiness. That same permanent-smile giddiness.

In the dressing room, cans of Tetley's were opened and sprayed and poured all over the place, and then in the evening we had a formal team dinner to celebrate. Partners were invited, but I was single at the time so I took Carlo along. I don't exactly remember why, but he and Terry ended up diving into the pool at the end of the night. Tez was gutted in the morning – his nice, Hugo Boss suit was ruined!

The coach trips home from Challenge Cup Finals were, I'd been told, ridiculously boozy affairs. Ours wasn't. We had a game against St Helens just two days later, on the Tuesday night, and so the ride home was dry – which took a bit of the shine off the celebrations. But when we arrived at Headingley that Sunday afternoon, the scene brought the giddiness out of us again. There were thousands of fans inside the ground, the place was packed, and they were so happy. For the kids and those in their 20s, they'd never known success at Leeds. For those over 30, they'd had to wait 21 long, painful, frustrating years for silverware, and it was obvious how much it meant to them. After we'd paraded the cup we filed back inside the ground. Muzza congratulated us but left us with a parting instruction:

'Fellas, no drinking today. We've got St Helens on Tuesday.' Iestyn Harris was our captain, and he was the most professional of us all. Iestyn's side step was God-given, but that didn't mean he relied on his natural talent. He trained hard, ate well, always did the extras and lived an impeccable lifestyle. He was the model pro'.

He huddled us together.

'Right lads,' he said. 'We're going out on the piss.'

I couldn't believe it, but I wasn't going to question him. We went up to Headingley and had more than a few scoops and, looking back, I think Muzza knew we were going to go out. He probably told us not to drink to keep us in check, to make sure we didn't go daft.

On Monday morning, many of us had stinking hangovers, and on Tuesday night Saints murdered us 62-18. But I wouldn't have changed what we did. Winning a trophy is always a special achievement and when you do it in extraordinary circumstances – in our case, ending a two-decade trophy run, beating the top sides on the way and winning the last game at Wembley – it creates a bond. You don't have to be best friends with the lads, but when you achieve something together it feels special. We had a 10-year reunion in 2009 and it was great to see them all again. I'm looking forward to similar events in the future.

After the mid-week mauling by St Helens, we only lost two of our next 17 Super League matches. And I got sent off in both.

The first was at St Helens. We'd gathered momentum during an unbeaten 13-match run, so it was no surprise that Saints tried to rattle us early on. In the first minute, I drove the ball in and as I was being held in the tackle, Paul Davidson, the bald-headed forward, swung a punch. I swung my left hook and caught him flush on the chin, and the big fella went down. Russell Smith, the referee, didn't hesitate – he pulled out the red card and said, 'Adrian, you're off'. I couldn't believe it, and I don't think most of the crowd could. Thankfully, the disciplinary panel saw sense and didn't suspend me.

Three weeks later, they weren't as compassionate. We played Halifax in August and it was a really niggly game. We just couldn't get into our rhythm and, in the heat of frustration, I head-butted Paul Rowley on the ground. A few of their players rushed in, and I got red-carded straight away. I had no complaints about the decision, or the three-game ban. It's one of the few incidents I regret. As aggressively as I've played the game, I've never got involved in shit-house tactics like hair-pulling or sledging or any of that nonsense.

I returned to the side for the end-of-season run but we ran out of steam, bowing out of the play-offs to Castleford. We were disappointed at the time because we wanted to get back to Old Trafford, but we still had the satisfaction of having won the Challenge Cup, and – as I write this now in early 2012 – I find it incredible that a club the size of Leeds has not won the trophy since.

I only moved to the NRL in 2001, but the seed was planted in my mind at the end of '99. Great Britain toured Down Under for a Tri-Series tournament against Australia and New Zealand. First, we had a warm-up game against a Queensland lower league side, the Burleigh Bears. We only just scraped through, though in fairness jetlag wasn't our only obstacle – in a sleepy country town, out of the media spotlight, the subs weren't policed very well. At one point, I counted 18 of their players on the pitch at the same time! That performance gave me no confidence that we were capable of mixing it with the Aussies and the Kiwis, but our squad did. The fact we lost both Tests – 42-6 to the Kangaroos in Brisbane, and then 26-4 to New Zealand a week later – was baffling given our team included so many top-quality players. I know it's a popular discussion among fans to ask how many British players would make their opponents' side, and that year I'd have put the likes of Kris Radlinski, Jason Robinson,

Gary Connolly, Keiron Cunningham, Denis Betts, Andy Farrell and Paul Sculthorpe right up there with the best.

Against the Aussies, we only trailed 10-6 at half-time but they ran away with it in the final half-hour, which was disappointing. In the players' bar afterwards, a big, friendly Aborigine fella who I didn't recognise approached me.

'Hi Adrian,' he said, shaking my hand. He had a firm grip. 'I'm Arthur Beetson.'

I'd heard his name before, I knew he was an Australian legend, but I'd never seen a picture of him so had no idea what he looked like. Artie, who was working for the Sydney Roosters, told me that he thought I'd played well, which meant a lot coming from a man of his stature. Then he introduced me to Nick Politis, the Roosters chairman, and we made small talk for a few minutes before going our separate ways.

I'd been really pumped before the game against the Aussies and I'd put a couple of good shots on. I got quite a bit of praise in the press afterwards, which I took little satisfaction from – I was there to win with my team-mates, that's all I cared about. But I felt I had held my own, and I went to New Zealand ready to mix it with them. But I never got the chance to mix it properly.

About 20 minutes into the game, I drove the ball in and managed to offload to Jason Robinson. Job done. Suddenly, my whole face caved in, like I'd been thumped by a granite wall. I had, only that granite wall's name was Stephen Kearney! He came over the side and boom! He smashed me. I left the pitch completely dazed, but managed to regain my senses enough to convince Andy Goodway I was fit enough to go back on. I tried to get Kearney back but he was always too smart, and I never got a chance to get near him.

Our confidence was really low after that series. We genuinely felt we'd made progress up until then, but the Aussies and Kiwis out-classed and battered us. We were really down in the dumps. We managed to pick ourselves up to play the New Zealand

Maori in a curtain-raiser to the final – but talk about a kick in the teeth.

After the series, three of us decided to stay on in Australia for a bit. That's when I really fell in love with the place.

Andy Hay was a close mate from Leeds and, although Sean Long played for St Helens, I always got on well with him. He's got a screw loose but I love that in people; he doesn't take life too seriously. Sydney was going to be our first stop, and when we discovered how big it is we decided we needed a car to get around. We considered renting one, but then I remembered Nick Politis mentioning he owned a car lot, so I dug out the business card he had given me and phoned the number.

A secretary answered.

'Oh hi there, this is Adrian Morley,' I said. 'I spoke to Nick up in Brisbane and he told me he'd arrange a car for me while I'm in Sydney. Well, I'm here now . . .'

If I expected the English accent to impress her, it didn't. An apprehensive voice promised to get back to me, leaving me unsure about how we were going to travel the thousands of miles we'd planned to, without any wheels.

Graham Murray, who had left Leeds by that point, had recently been appointed as coach of Sydney Roosters for the following year. That evening, he laid on a nice barbecue for us all, up in Newcastle, north of Sydney.

'You fancy coming to Sydney with me?' he asked me.

The question threw me. 'What, next year?'

'No, now,' he replied. 'Nick's just been on the phone. Said he didn't remember offering you a car, but he's sorted one for you.'

So I headed with Muzza to Sydney, then drove back to Newcastle to pick the boys up for the rest of our tour.

We looked at the map, and the next notable place above us was Brisbane, so we decided to head there. No matter how big you think Australia is, it's only when you drive between two places – half an inch apart on a map – that you truly appreciate its grand scale. We drove the 500 miles up the coast, stayed there a few days, and then headed back, stopping at popular back-packing haunts and even picking up a backpacker – Longy's mate, Richard Owen – on the way.

On the Gold Coast we went to a club called Shooters, and had a great night out. We rolled out of the club around 6am, just as the sun was coming up, and the beautiful beach across the road seduced us. We crossed over and, as Andy and Richard sat on the sand, Longy and I stripped off our clothes and ran in. Longy and I started messing around, wrestling naked in the sea. It was brilliant. Not wrestling with a naked Sean Long, you understand, but just being in the refreshing water when we were so tired and drunk.

'Look who's here,' Longy said.

I looked to the beach, as two policemen were walking over to Andy and Richard. We strolled out of the water, our hands covering our privates. A small crowd had gathered. The coppers asked us to get dressed, which we did, expecting a ticking off. The next thing I knew, they marched us to a police van and locked us in the back. They drove us to the station, with Longy kicking-off all the way about how ridiculous it was to be arrested for something so minor. They let us out of the station a couple of hours later and told us we were due in court at 11am.

'And if you don't turn up, you'll find it hard to leave the country,' a policeman warned us.

We went back to the hotel and sat on our beds. I looked at Longy and he looked at me, we both smiled, and then put our heads on the pillows and slept off our hangovers instead.

We headed back to Sydney, where I'd arranged to meet with Dave Barnhill to talk to him about what it's like playing for Leeds as he was moving to Headingley the following year. We went for a drink with Richie Barnett and Adrian Lam, and they couldn't speak highly enough about the Roosters. The seed in my mind was growing, fast. Their enthusiasm for the Roosters, the Roosters' apparent interest in me – I guessed Nick didn't lend cars to just anyone – and Muzza's appointment as coach all seemed to make the club the perfect fit. I'd always wanted to go over to Australia at some point, just for the challenge, but the '99 Test series had taught me how much better they were and that chance to test myself against the very best each week really appealed to me. On top of that, the lifestyle and weather weren't too bad either, even though I wasn't naive enough to think I'd be spending all my time on the drink if I played over there.

Those thoughts were playing on my mind as we flew out of Sydney to head home (or at least they did, once we cleared customs – Longy and I were bricking it in case we were stopped for our no-show at court. Thankfully, we weren't).

Before the year was out, I ticked another box on my career 'to do' list – I was invited to the BBC Sports Personality of the Year event. I'd never been one to get star-struck, but sat right behind Muhammad Ali, and with David Beckham in our row, it was hard not to feel a bit out of place. There were top athletes everywhere.

On the way out, Iestyn and I bumped into Martin Offiah and Shaun Edwards. They asked where we were going next. We had no plans.

'Have these if you want – we can't go,' Martin said. They were tickets to Lennox Lewis's after-event party.

So we got a taxi to his huge mansion – I'd never seen anything like it in my life. Lewis's family and friends had taken over the main room and there, in the centre of the dance-floor, was Evander Holyfield! He was wearing an all-black suit, shirt and cowboy hat and he was dancing on his own; if I'd tried to pull that off I'd look like a dick, but he was the coolest man in the world. Iestyn and I stuck out like sore thumbs, for the simple reason that we were the only white fellas there. But a couple of minutes later I felt a tap on my shoulder. It was Ryan Giggs. I'd known Giggs casually growing up; he grew up not too far away, I'd played alongside his brother Rhodri and, without becoming mates, we had always got on well. He was with Teddy Sheringham and a few of the United boys, so we stayed with them for a few beers. We were having a great time. It had been a brilliant year, winning the Challenge Cup at Wembley and travelling around Australia. And now, here I was in a millionaire's mansion in London, surrounded by sporting superstars and having a laugh and a drink. I was single at the time and I knew my chances of finding a girl there, surrounded by so many stars and so much money, were remote.

'Come on Iestyn, let's go to a club,' I said.

'Are you serious?' he asked, looking around at the surroundings and the company we were in.

Reluctantly, he followed me and we ended up in a club. I headed to the bar and got some beers, and we stood there having a laugh, recounting the surreal evening we'd had.

'Back in a sec',' Iestyn said, putting his beer down and heading to the toilet.

While he was gone, I did what every bloke would do in that position and had a casual glance around the room to see how many girls were in. None.

There were men at the bar, men sat at the tables, men on the dancefloor. Camp-looking men.

Good work, Moz.

Iestyn came back from the toilet, and I told him we were going.

'Why?' he asked. I looked around the room theatrically, and he followed suit. The penny dropped.

'Oh perfect,' he said. 'Who'd want to be at Lennox Lewis's party when you could be at the Blue Oyster Bar?'

TRIBUTE: BY JAMIE PEACOCK (FORMER ENGLAND TEAM-MATE)

Each week, fans get an 80-minute snapshot into what rugby league players are like. But the impression they probably get of Adrian Morley could not be further from the truth. Because that same, aggressive, confrontational forward who has inflicted so much pain on so many, for so many years, is quite possibly one of the nicest people you could ever wish to meet.

He never gives an inch on the field, but he was so kind off it. Moz loves his life and he cares about people. Genuinely cares. And when we met up with the England squad, he was the first to go out of his way to make sure the young lads are welcomed. He covers all bases – he's a hard trainer, a great player and the life and soul of the squad. He's an all-round nice fella and no one – no one – could reach that conclusion from the way he plays the game, because he plays with such an unforgiving style. In fact, he's such a nice fella, I even feel bad taking his money off him at poker!

I'm the same age as Moz, but he came through into the first-team scene much earlier than me. When I broke through into Bradford's side in 1999, he was – and had been for several years – the benchmark forward. More than a decade on, he remains the same.

They may or may not admit it, but every forward wants to be as good as him. I certainly did. I respected the way he played, the way he worked, and when he decided to move to Australia I respected him even more. Moz was at the peak of his success – to put it all on the line and move to the NRL was a risky move, but it paid off spectacularly. In many ways, Moz was a pioneer, because when the game switched to the Super League era no one of Moz's stature had been over there. Since then, the likes of Brian Carney, Gareth Ellis, Sam Burgess and James Graham have moved to Australia, but Moz was the trailblazer. And it speaks volumes of the success he had that if you speak to anyone Down Under, they hold him in the highest regard. Walk down the street with him in Sydney, and it's like being with Austin Powers. 'G'day Mozza', 'G'day Moz' . . . they all love him. All of them – not just the Sydney Roosters fans. But he's still the same grounded, caring, genuine person he's always been and, in many respects, he reminds me of the early British explorers. They were fearless men, but they were gentlemen too. That's Moz all over. He's a world-class player, and over the years he's changed his game so that he's not getting sent off as much, but he's still retained his aggression. That's a real credit to him. He's been playing since there were three-point tries, and he's still one of our best players. But as good as he is on the field, the qualities of his character are far more enduring and far more sought-after than his qualities as a player. Everyone likes Moz. Players can't speak highly enough of him, even the blokes he's whacked high – and he's whacked quite a few!

CHAPTER FIFTEEN
LEAVING HOME

My good friendship with Bryan Fletcher got off to a funny start. Funny, in that I smashed him in the face and broke his nose.

It was England's opening game of the 2000 World Cup, against the familiar foes, Australia, in the unfamiliar setting of Twickenham. By that point, my pending move to the Sydney Roosters had been widely reported and talked about. I wasn't stupid – I knew the Aussie eyes were on me during the tournament. The organisers weren't stupid, either, and they made me one of the two poster boys for our match. The other, Sean Long, was featured on a big billboard alongside the title of a classic song – 'We Could Be Heroes'. It looked pretty good. And then I saw mine and I could have died right there on the spot. My semi-naked torso was accompanied by the headline, 'Sex Bomb'. Not surprisingly, I copped some abuse for that one.

A week earlier, I'd been with the squad to a training base in Florida, which was a great experience – the facilities were fantastic and they even opened Disney World an hour early for us, allowing us to go on the rides without having to queue! Nathan McAvoy was in the squad, too, which was a little surreal. We'd spent countless nights having sleepovers as kids, talking about and watching rugby league, and all of a sudden we were in the England camp together. Sadly, he injured his knee in a friendly against the USA Tomahawks, so we never got to play for the national team together.

While we were there, Andy Farrell chose me as the England vice-captain. I was shocked. There were other more senior, older players in the squad, I wasn't the most professional back then – my training was spot on, but I was drinking a fair bit – and I wasn't the biggest talker on or off the field, either. Afterwards, I asked why he'd picked me.

'Because I respect you and what you do one the field,' he told me. 'All the lads love playing with you.'

That meant more to me than any plaudits I'd ever had. I learned a lot about being a good captain from Faz. He distanced himself from the lads to some extent, maybe that was the way he prepared, but he spoke sense, was universally-rated, and tried his balls off at everything he did. He was also fiercely loyal to his team-mates and never got involved in back-stabbing or little digs. They sound like simple qualities to have, but there haven't been too many who had them like Faz.

I was struggling with a chest injury at the time (which ended up meaning that I only played in one more game during the tournament – the quarter-final against Ireland, which we won 26-16), but I really wanted to show the Aussies what they were getting. It was the coldest, wettest, most miserable night imaginable, and my enthusiasm was boiling over, which is why, when Fletch – the Kangaroos back-rower – drove the ball in, I launched my out-stretched arm at his chest. Right above the ball. With any luck, I thought, I might force the error. Only my arm didn't hit his chest, or the ball, but caught him square on his hooter.

The Aussies ended up winning the game, 22-2; big Wendell Sailor scored two tries for them on an otherwise forgettable night. Afterwards, Brad Fittler, the Sydney Roosters captain, made a point of approaching me and shaking my hand. 'Mate it'll be good to have you on board next year,' he said. 'Everyone's looking forward to you arriving.'

I thought that was a really nice gesture, but I wasn't sure I believed him. Especially when I saw Fletch in the players' bar a few minutes later. He was stood next to Gorden Tallis, who looked at me, pointed to Fletch's nose and shook his head.

Fletch looked over. His nose had really swelled up, but not that big that I couldn't see his eyes. He was still pissed off, so I went over to clear the air.

'I'm sorry,' I said, offering him my hand. 'I didn't mean to do that.'

He took my hand.

'Just as long as you know, I'm going to throw you some fuckin' hospital passes next year'.

Then we both laughed and that was it. We became good mates, right there and then in the Twickenham bar.

My move to the NRL clouded my final season with Leeds. I'd like to think it didn't impact on my form – I felt I played well – but it was a distraction. Dean Lance had replaced Graham Murray and I got on well with him. Solid fella, good coach. Not that our start to the season backed that up.

We lost our first five Super League games, and in a game at Wigan I caught Simon Haughton high and got a three-game ban. It was a miserable time for me, and it wasn't helped by the uncertainty and speculation about my own future. A lot had been said about me moving to Australia, but it took a while before formal offers began coming in. Brian Smith phoned me. He wanted me to move to Parramatta, and it was nice to know other teams were interested. But Graham Murray's presence at the Roosters proved the swaying factor. They put together a formal offer, yet just when I thought my decision had been made, Gary Hetherington countered with a package to stay.

It was a tough call to make. I loved Leeds. My mates were there, I loved the city and we'd won the Challenge Cup the year before. With Gary offering to double my money, and guaranteeing me a testimonial, I would earn far more by staying. On the one hand, it was nice that I had two great options – it was a win-win in that respect. But that only made the decision even harder to make. I was desperate to go to Australia, but how desperate?

Desperate enough to take a big pay-cut?

I took a few days to think about it and came to the conclusion that if I didn't go then, I might never go. It was tempting to defer the move, but what if I had kids? What if I settled down? I told Gary and Dean my decision, and they understood. At the next training session, I stood up and addressed the squad and told them that, even though I was leaving at the end of the year, I would give my all to the team until then. I meant every word.

We'd made the Challenge Cup Final at Murrayfield, Edinburgh, earlier that year and only just lost out to Bradford. Our scratchy form had recovered enough for us to string together a 13-game winning run, but our season fizzled out. We lost our last three Super League matches and then, in a play-off game at Bradford, we went down 46-12. I shouldn't have played that day, though. Three weeks earlier, I'd injured myself in a Super League game against the Bulls. Henry Paul was killing it for them that year, so early on I tried to smash him. But in the tackle, his elbow lodged into my sternum. It was agonising. My chest was in agony. So, in the warm-up to the play-off game, inside the dressing room, I asked Iestyn Harris to push me to see how it held up. He nearly dropped me like a Bruce Lee one-inch punch.

That's one thing which many people don't fully understand about rugby league. Sometimes we play at 70 per cent, other times at 50 per cent. Proud men will patch up wounds, wrap pads around bruises and have painkillers injected into their joints just so they can take to the pitch. It's what we do.

Against Bradford, I knew I was nowhere near my best. But I couldn't stand the thought of not playing for Leeds again, so I made myself available. I was devastated when we lost. I sat alone in the dressing room with all sorts of thoughts rushing through my head. I couldn't believe it was all over. And as much as I reassured myself that everything would work itself out, the self-doubt was niggling at me. I kept asking myself the same question, over and over.

Have I made the right decision to go?

TRIBUTE: BY CLARE RICHARDS (PARTNER)

If someone had told me – on the day Adrian Morley strutted into my life in a Leeds pub – that we would live together and have two kids together, I'd have laughed my head off.

He was cock-sure, he was too forward. And worst of all, he was sweating on me (he'd played a game a few hours earlier)! Love at first sight? No way. I couldn't stand him. I think my first words to him were, 'Will you please go away, I don't want a drink, I don't like you.' But he didn't go away. He did buy me a drink and – eventually – I did start to like him. But it took a while.

Unbeknown to me, my friend had given him my number – she was convinced I'd like him – and Adrian kept phoning me. I had a boyfriend at the time, and I tried my best to ignore him. I wasn't interested. He was a pest, who wouldn't go away. And when I heard some of the girls at British Gas, where I worked, talk about him (and yes, they did know him that way) it put me off him even more.

But I'd see him out around Leeds, and when I started talking to him I couldn't help but warm to him. He was so genuine, and nice, and funny. I was upset when he left to go to Sydney, but he kept in touch through email and when he came back at the end of each year. In early 2003, we pretty much spent a week together when he was over in England for the World Club Challenge. We were getting more and more serious. One night, he said to me, 'I want you to be my girl.'

Deep down, I wanted to be his girl, too, so I flew over to Australia for three weeks that August. When I landed at Sydney Airport, I had to write down where I was staying during my stay. I filled in the form, and two officials quickly ushered me into an interview room.

'Is this the same Adrian Morley who plays for the Roosters?' one of them asked.

'Yes.'

They looked at me quizzically.

'He's a good friend of mine,' I said.

They didn't believe me. They must have thought I was a crazed fan who had come all the way from England to stalk him. I had to convince them he was in the arrivals lounge, waiting for me, and one of them disappeared to check. Minutes later, he walked back in to tell me I could go – and asked me to get Adrian's autograph for them!

I discovered right there and then how popular he had become. And over the next few days, I also discovered the best and worst of Adrian.

'I'm taking you for a romantic break,' he said to me. He'd been banned for three matches – he joked that he did it deliberately to show me around. 'I'm taking you to the Blue Mountains.'

I'd read about them on the flight over. Seen how picture-perfect they looked. I was so excited. I tolerated his crappy old music (he absolutely loves Bob Dylan!) all the way there, and when we pulled up at this beautiful hotel, I couldn't have been happier. It was around 7pm, the sun had dipped and the setting was perfect. We parked the car, walked inside and found a roaring log fire. It was the best of England and Australia, combined in one place.

Adrian went to reception to check-in, while I snooped around the lobby. He walked over a few minutes later.

'Bad news, they have no rooms available,' he said, apologetically.

'You didn't book?' I said.

'I didn't think we'd need to.'

So we drove to the nearby hotels. No luck. Eventually, both tired, we found a room at the dodgiest guest house ever. The man behind reception told us we had two TVs.

'The sound doesn't work on one of them,' he explained. 'But it's okay, because the picture doesn't work on the other. So if you change channels, you'll need to change them both.'

We didn't have our own bathroom either, so Adrian peed in the sink at the end of the bed! Hardly the romantic break I'd planned. But that's what it's like living with Adrian. Nothing goes to plan. Everything is a great laugh with him.

When I moved over to live there permanently in 2004, I arrived to find a home with garden furniture in the lounge, a kitchen with no utensils, a bed with no sheets, and a training towel for a quilt. There were bed bugs – beetle-sized ones – which took six visits from the fumigators to rid, even after we'd burned the mattress!

For someone so charitable and generous, Adrian can also be quite prudent. He always does the big shop because, apparently, I don't get enough bargains. When we moved back to England in 2006, I was heavily pregnant, and we had nothing. No pram, no cot, no car-seat. So we went shopping at Mamas and Papas, and when we got to the checkout Adrian began bartering the price down! His love for a bargain also usually means he returns from the big shop with bags of rubbish.

'I've got bacon frazzles.'

'You know I don't like them.'

'Yeah, but they were two for one . . .'

One time, he really splashed out and bought me a car for my birthday, which was the best present ever. Then he gave me my birthday card, and it had a picture of a wheelbarrow on the front with the words 'My Forever Friend', and on the back was the price – 29p!

But that's why I love him so much. Adrian and I are polar opposites in many respects. I'm tidy and I like everything in order. He's scruffy and laidback. I'm straight down the line. Adrian knows people who can chip Sky TV boxes. I'm a stress-head. A worrier. He's chilled out and placid. His favourite saying to me is, 'Don't you worry that little pretty head. Moz is sorting it out.' But that usually makes me worry more!

Possessions mean little to him. If I knocked my car, I would be fretting until it was fixed. It would be the worst disaster in the world. But when Adrian has banged his, he just shrugs his shoulders and says, 'It's only a car'.

All he really cares about is his family. When he's with his brothers, they never stop giggling – it's like they speak their own language. But I love the fact that he loves his family. He's very close to them all, and he's great with our two kids.

Having kids has really mellowed Adrian out. He's matured. Grown up. He doesn't go out as much, and he rarely drinks. These days, his one vice is poker – he absolutely loves it.

Adrian is very traditional in many ways. He makes sure the kids have good manners, we always eat dinner around the table together, the kids have rigid bed times. He baths them every night, he takes them swimming every week, he takes them to church on Sunday mornings. Leo's his shadow, he wants to go everywhere his dad goes, while Maya has got him wrapped around her little finger!

On the rare occasions I go away, I never worry about them because Adrian's so good with them. The only problem is he manages to dress them in horrendous outfits. He sends me picture messages and my first instinct is, 'Aw, the kids look happy' . . . and that's usually followed very quickly by, 'Please tell me you've not been out the house with them looking like that!'

I know I'm not the easiest person to live with, but we keep each other in line. I hope Adrian knows how much I love him. I am grateful for our beautiful family and extremely proud of him.

CHAPTER SIXTEEN
POMMIE BASTARD

A knot of photographers, reporters and TV crews were waiting for me when I walked through the arrivals gate at Sydney Airport. For a split-second I honestly thought there must have been a star on our flight.

Well done, Moz. Brad Pitt was sat alongside you and you didn't even notice.

Only when they trained their lenses and flash bulbs on me did I realise they were my welcoming committee. My arrival was news. I was news. So much for the low-key introduction to Australian life I'd secretly craved.

It was New Year's Eve, 2000. I posed for pictures and carried out interviews, which took longer than they should have done because the reporters kept asking me to repeat myself.

It seemed they struggled to understand my northern English accent. I could understand them fine, because I'd played with a few Aussies at Leeds and I'd watched *Neighbours* as a kid. But they couldn't understand me. After the interviews, the Roosters CEO, Bernie Gurr, took me over to Roosters second-row Luke Ricketson's. We'd met during the World Cup the previous year and we'd gone to watch the Super League Grand Final together. Ricko took me out for a bite to eat, showed me around, and then drove me to Harvey Howard's place in Cronulla. I knew Harvey from Leeds, and he was heading back to England with Wigan. I saw in the New Year with a few beers and then, a couple of days later, Ricko told me the Roosters boys were going out for a quiet one for Craig Wing's birthday.

It started with a few beers. A few introductions, a few greetings, and the boys all seemed like sensible blokes. But fast-forward a few hours, and we were at Bryan Fletcher's place and the lounge room was wild. People were partying, bodies were wriggling, blokes had arms around each other as they jumped up and down and hugged and sang. In the corner, a group of lads were downing shots, like teenagers who'd just discovered alcohol. And then Fletch stripped off all of his clothes and began dancing, wearing only flippers and goggles, his todger wobbling around to the beat.

I turned to Craig Fitzgibbon.

'I thought you said it would be a quiet one,' I said.

He looked around, assessing the carnage, and flashed me a smile. 'What are you talking about,' he said. 'This is a quiet one.'

I knew then that I would love the Roosters boys.

They were my kind of people. I knew they played hard, I guessed they trained hard, and once I found out they partied hard, too, it was as if everything had fallen into place for me.

A couple of days later, I reported for training with my new club. Ricko took me around the gym to introduce the lads, the ones I hadn't already met, and they were all terrific with me. I'd done my homework before flying out, looking at their squad for names I recognised, and I was made up that Quentin Pongia was there. He'd always been immense for New Zealand in the games I'd seen him play. And Brad 'Freddie' Fittler was undoubtedly one of the best players in the world. I'd watched him play for the Kangaroos in '95, and not only did he have a freakish step, but back-rowers like Steve Menzies had a lot of joy running off his inside shoulder. I was looking forward to that.

I'd heard about Freddie being a real wild fella on the drink. When I was told the story of a taxi driver dropping him off at a police station because he was so drunk, I thought we'd get on like a house on fire! But when I got there, he'd turned over a new leaf. He didn't drink too much, didn't party too much. But we had a beer together eventually and, as I got to know him, I realised what a good fella he really is.

I loved Australia from day one. I'd been there before, but I was wise enough to know working somewhere was different from holidaying there. Graham Murray invited me to live with his family while I got myself settled. I can't thank his wife, Amanda, and daughter, Cara, enough for the way they welcomed me in. Of course, I got the staple stick from the lads for that – 'coach's son', 'teacher's pet' – so I didn't stop long. I found out that Muzza had a place on the outskirts of Coogee. It's a suburb, by the beach, which is popular with English tourists and ex-pats. It was perfect for me, so I walked into the estate agents, signed a lease for the first place I visited, and bought Harvey's furniture and TV off him before he left.

I loved my new home. It was two minutes walk from the beach, and for the first couple of months I went every day. But then the novelty factor wore off, and I never went unless family or friends were over visiting.

The Roosters were terrific with me, even if I didn't make the best first impression, on or off the training pitch. Off it, it took me all of two days to scrape the side of the hire car they had arranged for me. And within a month I'd accrued $1,000 in speeding and parking fines. I learned the hard way that Australia has some peculiar driving rules, such as not being able to park facing oncoming traffic.

In training, I heard the usual Pommie jokes, as well as some unusual ones. For some reason, they think we don't shower, which I'd never heard before. But when they laughed at me, I'd laugh too. That's part of being able to settle in somewhere. Another part is copying what they do – again, I learned the hard way not to ignore the communal sun-cream tub before training. My shoulders were burned to a crisp after our first session!

Sydney's spring and autumn weather is perfect, like really, really nice English summer days. But their summer is really hot, just like Greece or Spain in July. And that's how it was when I started training with them in January. I wasn't used to standing outside in such heat, never mind training in it. To make it worse, most of the boys had been in since November, and I wasn't in the best shape when I arrived at the Roosters.

Leaving England was a big deal for me. I had a leaving party, but not everyone could make it, so two nights later, I had another one; then the lads said I should have a drink in the local before I went. And that's how it went for six weeks. Every other night, it seemed there was an excuse for me to go out on the smash. Then I topped it off with a big Christmas and New Year.

While the Roosters had spent six weeks training, I'd spent six weeks on the piss, and it took its toll. In our first conditioning session, I nearly passed out. We were doing running drills at the army barracks in Sydney, and I just about managed to drag myself through it, but the other boys were flying. It was a shock to the system. I was embarrassed, and couldn't help thinking they must all be looking at me and wondering who the club had signed.

Graham Murray was fine about it and he said I didn't look too bad, and I probably didn't. But I knew my body and I knew I was nowhere near where I should have been. At Leeds I used to do my sprints with the backs because, without sounding big-headed, I was the quickest forward, and one of the fittest. When I got to the Roosters, there were a few forwards in front of me – Luke Ricketson, Simon Bonetti, Craig Fitzgibbon. They were all machines, and all better than me.

A big part of their training was swimming. I had learned to swim at school, and could swim as well as the next man. Or at least, the next Brit. I got my bronze, silver and gold certificates, thank you very much, and knew how to collect a rubber brick from the deep end while wearing pyjama pants. But most of the Aussie boys swam like fish, and I couldn't keep up. It got to the point where I had to swim in a separate lane, with a float between my legs to correct my technique, while they propelled past me like an army of Ian Thorpe clones.

Over time, I got better, and within a month my fitness was where I wanted it to be. In the build-up to the new season, I carried out a lot of interviews. Although Harvey and Lee Jackson, both Great Britain internationals, had been over to Australia recently, they probably didn't have the same profile I had. Rugby league in and around Sydney is covered like Premier League football is in London. It takes up eight pages at the back of the newspapers, dominates the discussions on radio phone-ins and it's all over the TV. There are two weekly magazines dedicated to it. It's everywhere. And for a few days, I felt like I must have spoken to every single one of the papers, magazines and stations. I loved the profile and attention the game got. I even ticked off one of my life ambitions, when I was featured in *FHM* magazine's Bloke Test!

Predictably, as Graham Murray had warned, many of the journos zoned in on my disciplinary record. The *Daily Telegraph* even recited my suspensions from my academy days. A few also asked me about growing up in Salford. They were angling for the story that I grew up on the mean streets, that if it wasn't for rugby league I'd be a criminal. Salford is a bit rough, it isn't the most glamorous place, but it has its nice areas and, to me, it's home. I was proud of my background, and I defended it to everyone I spoke to. I defended Super League, too. I felt like I was an ambassador for the competition – but there was no denying the NRL was superior.

They were training to a higher standard, the ball skills were intense, the fitness sessions were a step up from what I'd been used to. A big difference I noticed straight away was the strength in depth at the Roosters. There were 25 full-time players, who could all hold down a place. And every team had a scattering of big-name players – in the UK, Leeds, Wigan, Bradford and Saints held the monopoly. In Oz, even those who weren't Box Office were still very good.

When people compare Super League and the NRL, they make the mistake of looking at who's in the top teams. The gap is marginal. It was then, and it is now. It's no surprise to me that Gareth Ellis and Sam Burgess went over and killed it, and I've no doubts at all that James Roby, Sam Tomkins, Sean O'Loughlin, Ben Westwood and many, many more would be stars in Australia. But if people look at the players who can't make the teams, then they'll spot the difference. Down Under, the talent doesn't slope off as much as it does in the Super League. Also, NRL teams do a much better job of keeping hold of their marquee players – in Super League, even the ones who break through at less-successful clubs tend to gravitate to the big clubs.

After the hype my arrival had generated, I expected plenty of abuse on the pitch. I'd heard the Aussies love that more than in England. They even have a word for it – sledging – and being the only Englishman in the NRL, I was braced for the 'Pommie bastard' comments in the tackles. I heard a couple early on, but they wilted quickly.

I made a modest debut. More than 50,000 fans rocked up at Stadium Australia to see us take on Wests. We won the game, and made a solid start to the season. But it was two months later, against Brisbane in Round 9, before I played a game and thought I'd actually played well. I got the Man of the Match and felt like everything had come together. During the match (we won 20-18), I clipped a player high and got a two-game ban, ruling me out of the games against Melbourne and New Zealand. I came back and tried to get back into my groove, but then I broke my arm at Canberra, which ruled me out for a few weeks. In my third game back against St George I got Man of the Match, but ended up re-breaking my arm. It was one of those seasons when I couldn't get going. I struggled to find my feet, and in such an intense competition there is little respite. Firing up every week was harder than I expected. In Super League, getting pumped up to face Wigan or St Helens was easy, but everyone at Leeds knew they could thump the easy-beats like Huddersfield without getting out of second gear. It wasn't like that in the NRL, though. In my first year, we got beaten by Penrith twice – and they finished bottom – while we beat Brisbane twice, and they finished above us. It was a lot more evenly contested.

Around July, I began craving a return home. I'd not tired of the Aussie lifestyle. But rugby league consumes players' lives, and if they're not happy with how they're playing, they can't be happy. I wasn't. I was low, and I missed my family.

I was always going to see the season out, but I had reservations about staying beyond the end of the year. I missed the comfort blanket of the mates I'd grown up with. I missed pint glasses. I missed Indian food. I missed Guinness. I missed home. But I didn't tell anyone. Who could I tell? I had no family and close friends around me. Sure, the Roosters boys were mates – but they couldn't understand what I was going through. I convinced myself that I'd be fine, that I was going through a phase. Part of my contract deal was that I could have return business class flights each year, or I could transfer them for economy flights for my family. My sister Vicky took advantage of that offer and came over to visit me. She loved the country – so much so that she's still living in Australia to this day.

We finished the season in sixth place. Parramatta were on fire that year and we only lost to them 27-26 in our final game of the season, so we went into the play-offs pretty confident. The top-eight system was stacked so the two lowest-placed sides would go out at week one. New Zealand and St George were below us. We travelled up to Newcastle for our finals game, and had a shocker. We just didn't turn up. Andrew Johns took the game by the scruff of the neck and really punished us. He was a freakish player. And he could hit a bloke, too. We targeted him to try and blunt his edge, but that didn't seem to stop him putting in the big hits.

We weren't too disappointed after the game. We knew we'd

had an off-day and we'd have a second chance to put it right, as long as St George – who'd finished seventh – didn't beat Canterbury. We listened to the game on the radio on the coach ride back to Sydney. It was the quietest coach ride ever, with our finals series hingeing on another result. St George were six points up with 10 minutes to go. We were all keeping our fingers crossed for a Canterbury resurgence, but then Willie Peters dropped a goal. It was over.

I was shattered, like the rest of the lads. They had made the Grand Final the year earlier and really fancied their chances of doing it again. We knew we could beat anyone on our day. But that's the key in the NRL – you always have to be on your game.

Well before the play-offs, I started hearing rumours that Graham Murray would be sacked. At first I dismissed them as crap because, without excelling, we'd gone pretty well, and he'd reached a Grand Final the season earlier. It was obvious he was a good coach.

But he'd pissed a few people off earlier in the year. After a game, anyone who was anyone would pile into the dressing room. There was always a box of Crown lagers on ice, and the directors, sponsors and other suits and hangers-on would help themselves and chat with the players.

After the match Muzza would have important things to say to the players, and he didn't want those other people in the sheds. I thought he was right, but the club's bosses didn't, and nothing changed. The friction between Muzza and the board probably started then.

When he was sacked, they told him they didn't want him to go to the presentation night, which I thought was a cheap shot. He'd been our coach all year. Yet Ricky Stuart, who was swiftly confirmed as the new coach, was at the presentation. Ricky got up and said a few words, but I think he felt awkward being there. A couple of days later, Muzza rung me up, and we went for a beer with Fletch and Luke Ricketson as well. He'd been the one who'd brought me over from England, and I wasn't sure where his sacking left me. I hadn't been terrible in my debut year, but I'd not been as good as I knew I could be. Gary Hetherington had already been on the phone, offering me the chance to go back to Leeds.

It was reassuring that I had a plan B, but I asked for a meeting with Ricky, and he assured me he wanted me to stay. That was all I wanted to hear.

I returned home desperately hoping to play in the Ashes series. Great Britain had a new coach, Australian David Waite. That was a time before Sven-Goran Eriksson, before Fabio Capello. Appointing a foreigner to coach England was not the done thing, and it caused a stir among some fans, but I wasn't bothered. He was knowledgeable and passionate. Maybe he was too technical for some players at first. His game-plans were so detailed – every other coach I'd had could fit their pre-game tip sheets on one-side of A4, but his were pamphlets.

He was a smart man, though, and a fan of mine, and he told me he'd give me every chance to play in the series if I recovered from my broken arm. I'd suffered the injury playing against the Dragons in the second-last game of the regular season. The Roosters had been happy for me to take on Newcastle with it heavily strapped the week later, but didn't want me playing for GB unless it was fully healed.

In the hope it'd be okay, I went with the rest of the squad to a warm-weather camp in Spain.

In the airport, the team doctor – Dr Chris Brookes – asked if anyone was nervous about flying. A few of the lads put their hands up, and he gave them tablets. I put my hand up, and took one too.

I don't know why I did it. I'm not scared of flying, but I've always found it hard to turn down freebies, which is probably why, when the air stewardess came around offering a complimentary little bottle of wine on the plane, I didn't think twice about accepting.

Two hours later, I had to be carried off the plane. The drug combined with the drink had knocked me senseless. We were only at the camp for three days, and I spent the first two days asleep!

Brooksy, I have to say, is one of the most knowledgeable professionals I have ever met. Unfortunately, the same couldn't be said for another member of the GB staff. Conditioner Mike Sutherland had everyone fooled with his stories about working with the best athletes in the world. It was only the following year when, while he was working with St Helens, they discovered he was really a firefighter! Paul Sculthorpe told me that when club officials phoned to confront him, he denied it . . . but then the fire bells went off in the background! Fair play to him, though, I admired his balls to go in and pretend to be something he wasn't.

Unfortunately, my arm didn't heal in time and I never got to play the Aussies after all. But I enjoyed being in the squad, and as we were based in Worsley – just a few miles from my home – I had a great chance to catch up with my family and friends. I even had a beer with one of my mum's heroes, too.

In the hotel bar one night, a fella was sat alone, drinking his beer, passing the time. I went over to say 'hello' and was surprised that he knew about Great Britain's series against the Aussies. He knew about rugby league, so I bought him a beer and we had a good chat before going our ways. He seemed like a top bloke. I was sad when I heard on the news, a few years later, that George Best had passed away.

CHAPTER SEVENTEEN
SIDELINED

'There's good news and bad news.'

I stared at the surgeon's face, trying to read what was coming next. He was my last hope of curing a back injury which had plagued me for weeks.

'The bad news is, there's a 10 per cent chance that the operation won't have any effect, and it'll feel exactly the same as it does now.'

'Okay.'

'But the good news,' he said, his voice chirpier, 'is there's an 89 per cent chance it'll sort it out for good.'

He was upbeat and positive, which was encouraging. And I liked the odds – 89 per cent is pretty certain.

'And what's the other one per cent?' I asked.

The surgeon frowned. Maybe he'd expected me not to work out that 89 plus 10 equals 99, not 100.

'Well, there's a one per cent chance you'll lose the use of your legs. But I'm confident everything will be okay.'

I gulped. No matter how slim the chances, I couldn't help contemplate the thought of being stuck in a wheelchair for the rest of my life. But the alternative was to not have the surgery at all, and that was out of the question. I'd put up with the sharp pain in the centre of my spine for long enough. It was ruining my life. I had to walk around when eating my meals; lie down during video review sessions. My sleeping pattern was out of whack. To make it worse, the injury came just as I'd begun to put a good run of form together.

I'd trained really well in the off-season. Instead of spending the Christmas period on the piss in Salford, I went boxing training at Oliver's Gym – the same place Jamie Moore trained at and Amir Khan later went to. I wanted to be flying by the time I landed in Sydney.

Our first game of the '02 season was against Souths, who had just been readmitted into the competition. The fans in and around Coogee had told me all about the rivalry between the two clubs in the weeks before the game. I'd noticed pictures of past encounters on the walls of the Roosters' leagues club – another Australian quirk I'd grown to like. In England, clubs hold their functions at their home grounds. The Aussies don't do that. They each have an affiliated leagues clubs located nearby, each filled with 'Pokies' (poker machines, an Aussie obsession I never quite understood) and decorated with old shirts, trophies and pictures. They were like old-style amateur clubhouses, on a grander scale. With some of the NRL clubs sharing stadiums, and sterile modern ones at that, the leagues clubs were often the heart and soul of a club. That's how it felt at the Roosters.

For our opener, 35,000 turned up; it was strange – it was only a regular season game, but it felt like a final in itself. The fact that Russell Crowe, the South Sydney Rabbitohs' owner, was there just added to the occasion. Ricky Stuart surprised me when he started me at prop. I'd played there a couple of times over my career, in emergencies, and I didn't mind it, the only thing I didn't like was the shorter game time, as I was substituted. A player only gets 80 minutes a week to do what he loves; cut that in half and it's half the fun. We blitzed Souths 40-6 that day, and I felt good.

Some players obsess over stats. But I've come off the pitch knowing I've done well and the stats have been average; other times they look crash hot but I know for a fact I haven't played well. After the Souths game, the coaches, and even the press, praised me for making 26 hit-ups, and the week later I was in their good books again after playing the full match against the Warriors at prop. All I thought was, 'Stu Fielden's doing this every week for Bradford', but it was a rarity in the NRL. I was cited and suspended for clocking a Kiwi player with a lazy high shot, forcing me to miss the game against Brisbane, but after two pretty good games I finally felt in a good position to build some momentum. So you can imagine how pissed off I was when – against Manly the week later – I got up from a tackle to feel a rib poking out of my side. It didn't cut the flesh, but it was sticking out like a thumb. I tried to push it back into place, but couldn't. It was being a stubborn little sod.

They took me off, needled me, pushed it back into place, and I went back out. But it was no good. The injury forced me to miss a few weeks and, to compound my frustration, we were really finding it tough coping with all the injuries in the squad. Freddie Fittler was out. Fitzy, Fletch and Ricko were out too. We were 12th in the ladder and the following week we lost our fourth straight game, at home to Newcastle.

Ricky had arranged for the entire squad to stay in a motel the night before the game – an inexpensive place, the Ezron, just up the road from my home in Coogee – to try and strengthen the team spirit.

It worked. We lost, but the young lads did really well against the reigning champions – the 28-12 scoreline flattered them. From then on, Ricky decided that we'd stay over the night before every home game. It was a great idea. We could go to the cinema, play cards, walk to the beach. The older blokes didn't have kids waking them up, and those who had wives, or girlfriends, or both, weren't distracted. Two weeks later I'd recovered enough to play, but just as I felt hopeful of stringing some good performances together again, my back failed me.

It started as a niggle, a dull pain that would flare up occasionally. But quite quickly, it got worse and worse, until it got to a stage when I had to stretch every few minutes, just to try and relieve the pain. I'd had bad backs before, and time had always made them better. But this was getting worse, and within days I was waking up at 4am every morning with pins and needles in my legs. I tried physio but it didn't work. Deep massages didn't work. The Roosters sent me to hospital to have a cortisone injection to settle it down and that didn't work either. The longer it dragged on, the worse it got and the worse I felt. I'd started the season so well and then it had all gone tits up – first I'd been suspended, then I'd popped a rib, and now I had a phantom back injury keeping me out. Eventually, I was sent for a scan, which revealed part of my spine had fragmented and was pushing on my spinal cord. As soon as they mentioned there was a problem with my spinal cord, I began to worry. All rugby league players become hardened to dealing with injuries and having operations. But when there's something wrong with their spine, eyes, brain or balls, they are just like normal people. Petrified.

I was 25; Phil Clarke was the same age, at the same club, when a spine injury finished his career. It's hard to think rationally when you're scared. I thought, 'This could be it'. And when the surgeon told me there was a chance, however slight, that I could be paralysed, it made me worse.

As soon as I came around after the op', though, I could tell by his reaction he was really pleased with how it had gone. He even handed me a clear, plastic tub with a bit of my spine rattling about inside. I figured he wouldn't have done that if I'd been paralysed. Within an hour he had me on my feet, telling me to walk up and down stairs to get my body moving, and within a week I was back in training.

I returned for the home game against the Sharks in round 21, which we lost 34-20. It was our third defeat on the bounce, and with the finals a month away, the last thing we needed was a dip in form.

'We're still a good team', Ricky told us afterwards. 'Come on – we're all going out on the drink.'

We caught the ferry from Circular Quay – near to the

Opera House – to Manly, and had a great night out. We forgot about football for a few hours, had a laugh, a bite to eat and a few beers. I was just so happy to be playing again. It got to midnight, and the last ferry back to Circular Quay was leaving. Miss that, and it's a long and expensive taxi ride back to the city.

We all drank up and rushed over to the terminal. I nipped in to the toilet for a pee, and then ran to catch them up. I could already see a few of the lads were already on board, so I ran down the ramp . . . just as the ferry was pulling away. Without thinking, I leapt over the gate and sprinted as fast as I could down the wharf.

I could see the boys on the back of the ferry, cheering me on. I was running out of land. Eight metres, five metres. Then nothing but the ink black sea. I reached the end and leapt – and just cleared the gap, crashing onto the floor of the ferry. I stood up to applause and pats on the back, smiling that my stunt had paid off. What I didn't tell my team-mates was my ankle was in agony. When we reached Circular Quay, I limped to the nearest pub.

'Two beers . . . and a bag of ice please,' I asked the barman. I found a seat and iced my ankle.

By the Monday morning, it still wasn't right. I told Ricky about it when I arrived at training.

'Bloody hell Moz,' he said. 'You've missed nine weeks with a back injury . . . how am I supposed to explain to the board you've injured your ankle leaping onto a ferry when you were on the drink?'

But Ricky had arranged the night out. It was in his interest, and my interest, to say I'd twisted it during training. Thankfully, I only missed one game – which was a huge relief to me, because so far my 18 months in Sydney had been constantly interrupted by suspensions or injuries.

When I played, I felt I'd done okay. But it was frustrating

playing well for a week, then missing two, then returning and then sitting out again. I desperately wanted a good run of matches. But I had no idea back then just how good that run would turn out.

CHAPTER EIGHTEEN
SWEET VICTORY

It started in the Roosters leagues club. Two hours after we'd won the Grand Final.

At first it was just a murmur at the back of the room.

What are they saying? 'Boring'? 'Mooring'?

Definitely 'More' something.

I was stood on stage with my team-mates, going through the formalities of our post-match presentation in front of the fans, lapping up the celebrations, the achievement, the excitement. Brad Fittler had said some nice words about me and handed me the microphone, and I wanted to say a few words, but the fans at the back of the room wouldn't shut up with this 'More-whatever' they were chanting. And it was getting louder and louder. Until suddenly, it clicked what they were singing.

Morley.

Only, they were taking four or five seconds to get my name out, pronouncing it in a slow, low-toned 'Morrrrrrrrr-lll-eyyyyyyyyyyyyy' over and over again. In that moment, I can't tell you how proud I felt. Being serenaded to the collective voice of a thousand Roosters fans, all singing my name, made me feel accepted. No, more than that. *Wanted.*

I was the only Englishman in the team – the only one in the entire competition in fact – and it's no secret that Aussies don't always like Poms, especially when it comes to sport. If you're tolerated, you've made it. Aussie fans don't cheer like the English and they certainly don't have songs about individual players. The fact that they were chanting my name after we'd won the Grand Final was the ultimate compliment. And it came at a time when I thought my day couldn't have got any better.

Teams can cruise when they want to, and they can turn it on. They can go through blips and hit purple patches. But no side consciously times a run of form at the right part of the season. No player thinks, 'Right, it's the business end of the season, we'd better peak'. Actually, that's a lie. *Every* player thinks that. Which makes winning games at the end of the season, when players have the sub-conscious extra motivation of play-off positions at stake, even more difficult. In 2002, we finished strongly with a nine-game winning run, culminating in the Grand Final triumph.

Our defence has widely been credited for our success that season, and rightly so. We trained hard, and our pack was so fit that we were able to get off our line quick, swarming the ball-carrier and limiting how many metres our opponents could make in each set. The more we did it, the more success we had, the more pride we took. In video review sessions Ricky Stuart would say, 'Look at our line speed'. The cogs started to turn. It became our goal to get better and better. In that sense, it was completely organic – we just took it upon ourselves to improve. Ricky didn't come in one day and say, 'Right lads, I want you to do this or that.'

In the final game of the regular season, against Cronulla, their prop Chris Beattie tackled me. As I got up to play-the-ball, he stood on my hand.

'Sorry mate,' he said.

'No worries,' I said. It was one of the few Aussie terms I picked up.

The week later, in the play-offs, we played Cronulla again. Beattie tackled me again and – sure enough – he stood on my hand again.

I thought, 'You cheeky bastard.'

I stood up, played the ball, and before he could move, I shinned Beattie across the legs, Thai-boxer style. Both his legs went, he fell down, and I ran off as if nothing had happened. The referee had missed it, but the press hadn't. They made a beeline for me in the dressing room afterwards.

'You appeared to kick Chris Beattie, can you explain what happened?'

Players need to be on their guard with the Aussie journos, but minutes after a game, when emotions are high, it can be tough to do that. I should have been smart. I wasn't.

'He stood on my hand,' I explained. 'So I kicked him'. The journos didn't know what to say. They hadn't expected a confession, and it cost me – I was banned for one game, ruling me out of our next match against Newcastle, though I returned for the semi-final against Brisbane.

Laughably, the Sydney Football Stadium was used as the 'neutral' venue for the semis, even though it was our home stadium, but we weren't going to kick up a fuss about it. Brisbane were the gun team, with blokes like Lockyer, Langer, Webcke and Tallis, but our momentum, confidence and togetherness were off the charts; we beat them, I got the Man of the Match, and we booked ourselves a place in the final. Many of the other players in the team had played in the 2000 Grand Final and knew what it was about, but for me it felt surreal to think that I would be playing in such a massive game.

We all went to the pub the next day to watch the other semi, between Warriors and Cronulla, and I was pleased the Kiwis got through. We'd flogged them 44-0 weeks earlier, and I knew that was a psychological advantage for us. We had the confidence of knowing we had it in our arsenal to blitz them. And they knew it, too.

That week, the whole place went nuts. The Grand Final was huge news. All over the radio, all over the newspapers, front and back pages. The Roosters' main support base comes from a pretty small geographical base – Coogee, Bronte, Bondi, Randwick. It's not a huge area (fans at other clubs used to call us the Cafe Latte boys, long before Starbucks were on every High Street, because property is so expensive in those Eastern Suburbs). But the fans had been starved of success for so long that they just went bananas. Banners were up in shop windows and outside schools, people would honk their horn if they saw us in the street – it was crazy. On the Thursday morning, we had the traditional Grand Final breakfast, which is a bit of a pain in the arse – both teams go along for a formal meal and presentation. But that aside, the week had a really good feel to it. Confidence was high. It was a quick turnaround from the semis a few days earlier, and unfortunately it was too quick for my family and friends to arrange time off work and come out. But from the constant flow of messages from home, I knew people were taking an interest in me.

The night before the game, Ricky kept everything the same. Instead of stopping in a flashy hotel, we stayed in the Ezron, and all of our pre-match routine was exactly the same. Ricky had been around long enough to know the importance of playing the game and not the occasion. And I was experienced enough to know my pre-match nerves weren't a bad thing. That the butterflies in my stomach would serve me well, help focus my mind, help maintain my concentration. There was no risk of me cruising if I was nervous. We had nearly an hour to get changed but I was done and dusted in 30 minutes. I sat on the bench and read the match-day programme, which had a nice feature about the English legends – Mal Reilly and the likes – who had been to Australia and won Grand Finals. It hit home the rarity of what I could achieve if we won. As it turned out, I wasn't the only Englishman involved in the Grand Final that day; Billy Idol headlined the pre-match entertainment, but the power went out just three words into his set, and never came back on!

The match itself started at breakneck speed. We scored first, but Stacey Jones replied with a gem of a try. Stacey was another half-back whose skills were always lauded much more than his toughness, but believe me he was hard, in spite of – or maybe because of – his girly name.

Soon after, Brad Fittler went to kick the ball, it went to ground and Freddie dived on it. And that's when the New Zealand forward Richard Villasanti, a big unit who'd had a great season, dived on top and head-butted him. It was a shitty act. Freddie was defenceless, lying on the floor.

As soon as he did it, I thought, 'Fuck you'. Freddie was our captain. From then on, every time Villasanti got the ball, he got clattered. I nailed him with a pretty good shot, which people talked about. But I didn't think it was that big a hit. And I certainly wasn't the only one who targeted him. All the lads wanted to smash Villasanti.

My one slight disappointment about the Grand Final win was that I didn't finish the game. Ricky brought me off before the end, which was an odd feeling when the final whistle went. I rushed onto the pitch to celebrate with my team-mates. Nick Politis, the club's chairman, came on and I hugged him. I was so pleased for him. It was a mad feeling – I was physically drained but I had so much energy, like a tired kid on a sugar-rush. I couldn't stop smiling and I couldn't get enough. Now, a decade on, my abiding memories are from the moments after the game. Bryan Fletcher pouring the Gatorade over Ricky Stuart. Lifting the Premiership trophy, and discovering how heavy it is. And the feeling of sitting back in the sheds with pure elation.

Townsville is a hot, dusty town in North Queensland, where the locals absolutely love their rugby league. Every time we'd play there, the pubs had billboards outside with signs such as 'Roosters – free beer' and 'Roosters, serve yourselves', so the boys thought it would be the perfect spot for our end-of-season trip. Paul Green, our half-back, had suffered a season-long injury, and said the only thing that kept him going was planning our holiday. Day one was typical carnage. We all arrived dressed as '70s tennis players, complete with dodgy wigs, tight shorts and the occasional porn star 'tache. Dave Kidwell looked the best, having managed to source an old, wooden racquet for the trip. They were mad affairs when we *hadn't* won a Grand Final.

On the third day, all rough as dogs' backsides, we jumped on a bus to Airlie Beach. After stopping at a bottle shop for some beers (another weird Australian quirk, they don't sell alcohol in supermarkets) we got back on it.

A few minutes into our three-hour trip, a familiar voice came over the loud speaker.

'Ladies and gentleman, this is your captain speaking.'

It was Freddie Fittler, sat in the seat next to the driver. Everyone cheered.

'I've got some important news – clothes are banned from this trip.'

We looked at each other.

'You heard me. Clothes. Are. Banned.'

He put the mic' down and started stripping himself. It was comical. The bus driver was in stitches. We were on a freeway, all stark bollock naked. Every so often, we'd pull over for a piss break, which drew all the honks from the cars that you'd expect from the sight of 15 naked men pissing on the side of the road.

The lads had gone to Bali in 2000 for the end-of-season road trip and all they did in 2001, my first year, was talk about how good it was. When we went to the Gold Coast, for my first trip, I thought it would be the end of it. Instead, they moaned that it wasn't as good as Bali. So in '02, I asked the lads if we could go to Bali. A few lads were with me, but some of the others wanted to go somewhere new, and we got overruled.

Out on Magnetic Island, just off Townsville, we got the news early one morning about the Bali bombing – an Islamic extremist terrorist attack. We gathered around a TV, and one of the lads recognised the pub and club which were targeted. They said they were in there every night on their trip two years earlier. Anthony Minichiello was really panicking. His brother Mark was out there. He rang home and eventually found out he was okay, which was a relief for everyone, but when I got back to Coogee I heard the stories of others who hadn't been as lucky. I'd linked up with the Coogee Dolphins – my local amateur club – during my time there. Five of their players died. I also later read a book by an AFL player, Jason McCartney, who got badly burned during the bombing. His story about how he came back from such horrific injuries is inspirational.

My season wasn't finished yet. I flew home the following week, and I couldn't wait to see my family. My dad told me we'd go for a real pint of Guinness as soon as we got back, but before we left he put the video of the Grand Final on and watched it through in its entirety.

'Watch this Aje?' he'd say.

'Dad, I was there.'

The reaction elsewhere was similar to my dad's. People seemed happy for me, proud of me; not many English players win a Grand Final in Australia, and it was a really nice feeling.

Many of the Warriors boys were in the Kiwi squad for a three-match series against Great Britain, and at the end we lifted the silverware . . . even though we only drew the series, which I thought was a complete farce. They'd introduced a new trophy which, they said, we'd get if the series was tied. It was embarrassing. We'd shown we were their equal, and after the stuffing

With dumb and dumber, my brothers Ste and Chris. I'm the cute kid on the right.

As a three-year-old, on the phone for some reason!

At primary school (back row, second from the left), with future rugby league international Carlo Napolitano next to me on my left.

Football was my real love when I was eight years old and I did pretty well at it.

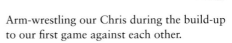

Arm-wrestling our Chris during the build-up to our first game against each other.

In my British Amateur Rugby League tracksuit, aged 16, shortly before signing with Leeds.

Raise a glass to that! Opening a Salford bar with, from left to right, our Chris, Brett Dallas, Terry Newton, parish priest Father Sean and Brian Carney.

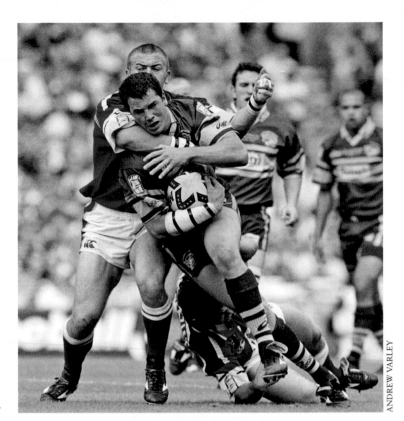

In action for Leeds against London Broncos in the 1999 Challenge Cup Final.

ANDREW VARLEY

SWPIX

Celebrating at Wembley with Barrie McDermott, his son Billy and Andy Hay after winning the Challenge Cup with Leeds.

My first year Down Under – playing for the Roosters against Newcastle Knights in 2001.

With my Roosters team-mates. From left to right: Anthony Minichiello, Craig Wing, Anthony Tupou, Craig Fitzgibbon, Chris Flannery, Braith Anasta, Joel Monaghan, Ryan Cross and Brett Finch.

A home from home – I loved life in Coogee, despite the sharks!

Naked cricket in Bryon Bay with Luke Ricketson and Brett Finch.

ANDREW VARLEY

Winning the NRL Grand Final with the Roosters in 2002 was one of the highlights of my career. I'm hiding in the back row, five in from the right.

GETTY IMAGES

Placed on report again for a high shot on Souths' Ben Walker in Round One, 2006.

Bradford treated me well and I have a lot of good memories from my time at Odsal.

Celebrating with the Bradford boys after winning the Grand Final in 2005.

Saying goodbye to the Roosters fans in 2006 – they were really great to me.

Playing for Great Britain in the 1999 Tri-Series brought me to the attention of the Sydney Roosters.

My lowest point – being sent off after 12 seconds in the first Ashes series Test in 2003.

Sending Australia's Jason Ryles crashing to the ground in 2004.

Tackling Ryles again the following year.
I loved playing against the Aussies.

Congratulating Sean Long after a drop-goal
in our 23-12 win against the Kangaroos in
Sydney in 2006.

Lifting the Albert Baskerville Shield, with Jamie Peacock, in 2007 after whitewashing
the Kiwis 3-0.

Taking the ball in hard against the Aussies during a disappointing 2008 World Cup.

We crashed out of the 2008 World Cup with a 32-22 semi-final defeat to New Zealand.

I always get goosebumps listening to the national anthem! Lining up with Jack Reed, Ben Westwood and Jon Wilkin to face the Aussies at Wembley in 2011.

Facing Jonathan Thurston in the Four Nations Final, 2011, my 50th cap for either Great Britain or England.

With Terry Newton – both of us feeling worse for wear at Leo's christening! I miss him immensely.

At Matt King's wedding in Melbourne, 2008, with Clare. It was love at first sight, for me at least!

The Morleys together again when Vicky came over from Australia in 2009. From left to right: Ste, Dad, Mum, Chris, Vicky and me.

Our children, Leo and Maya. Clare and I are so proud of them.

Clare, Maya and Leo, my world and my biggest fans, congratulate me for helping Warrington book a place at Wembley in 2012.

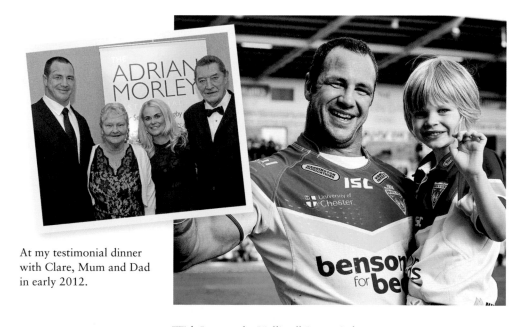

At my testimonial dinner with Clare, Mum and Dad in early 2012.

With Leo on the Halliwell Jones pitch.

I lifted the Challenge Cup with Lee Briers in 2009 – ending Warrington's 35-year wait for the trophy.

We defended the cup at Wembley the following year, beating Leeds 30-6.

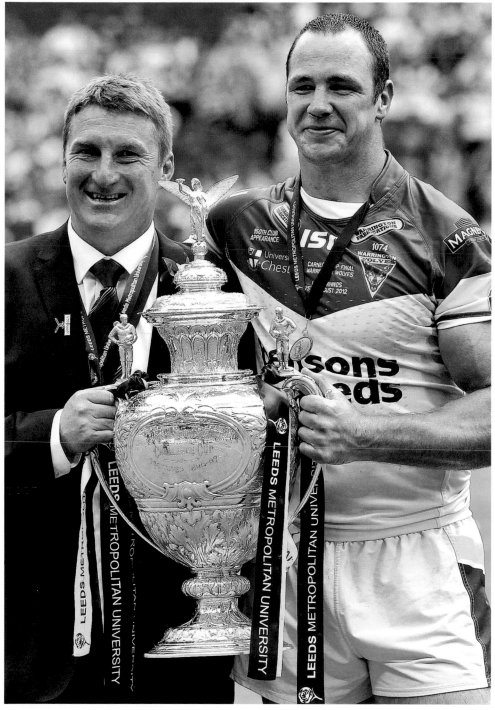

Celebrating the 2012 Challenge Cup success with Tony Smith. He has worked wonders since his arrival at Warrington.

A thumbs up after beating St Helens in the 2012 play-offs to secure Warrington a maiden Grand Final. Sadly, it didn't have the ending we wanted – but I was still proud of our effort.

GB had got in Sydney earlier in the year, when I was injured, that in itself was a decent achievement. I don't know why they pretended we were better than them. It was a weirdly uncomfortable feeling.

TRIBUTE: BY RUBEN WIKI (FORMER NEW ZEALAND TEST CAPTAIN)

I always thought it was funny how Adrian Morley and I became mates.

It was 2001, and I was sat in a Canberra hospital waiting room, prevented from moving my head by the rigid neck brace I was wearing, when a man came along and sat in the vacant seat next to me. It was Moz.

'Eh up, fancy seeing you here,' he said, in his distinctive, northern English accent.

He needed treatment for a broken forearm. We spoke briefly before the doctors called our names – it was the first time I'd spoken to him, other than a mumbled 'well played' during hand-shakes after a game – and we've been mates ever since.

But what makes the story funny is not that we met in a hospital waiting room, but the fact that it was Moz who put me in there! The Raiders were playing the Roosters, and it was my first contact with him since he'd left Super League to move to the NRL. I'd played against him before, of course. I was in the Kiwi side when Moz debuted for Great Britain back in 1996, and over the years he was a constant menace in the Test arena. A real tough nut.

When I took to the field for Canberra that day, I knew that Moz was a player capable of causing us damage. I didn't realise, though, just how much damage he would do to me! He drove the ball in, and as I went to tackle him he raised his forearm and whacked my head.

As soon as he hit me, I knew I was in trouble. Moz was, too. But we were both too proud to admit it. We got to our feet – Moz to play the ball, me at marker – refusing to accept that we were hurt. It turned out he'd broken his arm and I'd damaged my vertebrae (it took a few months for feelings in my left arm to return to normal). There was no drama there, injuries are an inevitability when you play footy. Besides, Moz is such a terrific fella, it's impossible not to like him.

We tussled a few times over the years – he nearly took my head off a few more times, too! – and we always had a mutual respect for one another. He never spoke much on the pitch and I didn't either, and we didn't need to – a look was all it took to know what we were thinking.

When I first came across him I was still a centre, but as I progressed to the back-row and then to prop, I got a new level of appreciation for the work Moz does.

I just love the way he plays. He has so much passion, energy and aggression. He plays the game hard and fast, the way it should be played. A rugby league game is won or lost in the front-row, and every time the Kiwis played Great Britain, we would assess their strengths, and he was one of the players we knew we had to deal with. If you give him a free rein he will torment you; if you try and close him down, he might still torment you. Playing against Moz is always physical, and our plan was to try and tire him out and take away some of his punch. But Moz has terrific energy levels and fitness, and taking him out of the equation is a helluva lot easier said than done.

It says a lot about the calibre of player that he is that he came over to the NRL from England and made a massive impact. I'll never forget the Grand Final in 2002, when Richard Villasanti hit Brad Fittler late. Moz then spent the rest of the game searching for Villasanti to get him back!

Moz is the type of player who leaves everything on the field, so much so that people probably see him as a tough man. But away from the pitch, he's a softie like me, spending his time with his kids and doing what his missus tells him to do!

I've few regrets from my career, but I'm pretty gutted I never got the chance to play alongside Adrian Morley. That would have been awesome, because I have so much respect for him, firstly as a person and then a player. The best gift you can give is your time, and that is something Moz will always give to you.

CHAPTER NINETEEN
FUNERAL DRUNK

I've been asked countless times over the years whether NRL teams take the World Club Challenge seriously. Or do they spend half the trip on the drink? From my own experience, the answer is yes. To both questions.

When the Sydney Roosters flew over to England in early 2003 for the annual match against the Super League champions, that was certainly the case. We landed on the Thursday – eight days before we were due to play St Helens. I met my dad and had a few pints with him. Then on the Friday, all the Roosters boys went out around Wigan. On Saturday we had a day off, so we were on it again. We trained Sunday morning, and Ricky Stuart was edgy. He told us to cut out the drinking. But we didn't. We had a few that evening as well.

Ricky got wind of it, though, and he was pissed off with us the following day. That's when we decided to knuckle down, and it worked – we dusted Saints 38-0.

I was excited to play in the World Club Challenge. It's a great concept, and it's a shame it's never been expanded into a top three or four, because I reckon it could be huge. I know the organisers would moan about fitting it into the season, but UEFA would never say, 'Sorry fellas, we've not got time for the Champion League'. It just wouldn't happen.

Saints had a great side that year, but our confidence was sky-high from our unbeaten run to the Grand Final the previous season. I even managed to get over for a try in the World Club, and it was a decent one, too. The ball passed through three or four pairs of hands, somebody broke through and I was on the inside to collect the pass. Even then, I had about 30m to the line, though by the time Leo and Maya have kids of their own that may have stretched to 90m! I later found out my family were sat behind the posts where I scored, making it extra special. I used to score a few for Leeds, but they'd dried up at the Roosters, as Graham Murray and Ricky Stuart both wanted me running at people, rather than into gaps out wide.

The Roosters had beaten St Helens 25-2 in the first World Club Challenge, back in '76. The late, great Arthur Beetson, who played in that match, was with us on the tour and he said to us, 'To be better than our team, you have to top that score.' Afterwards I said to him, 'There you go, that was for you,' which made him chuckle.

A great man, Beeto. I was sad when he died.

The fact we won so convincingly should have dispelled the myth that Aussie teams don't take the World Club seriously, which is the biggest load of crap I've ever heard.

Just because we went out on the piss early on, didn't mean we didn't want to win it. Anyone who says it's a game the Aussie teams aren't bothered about doesn't know rugby league players.

Players want to win everything they compete at. *Everything.* Very few players can reach first-grade level without having that competitive streak. Even fewer make it into a title-winning team. Whether it's golf or Monopoly, players want to come first. It's just the way they are. Admittedly, spending four days on the piss was not the best way to prepare for the World Club, but that was down to the boys being excited about coming to England.

Guys like Freddie Fittler had been over on countless Kangaroos tours, but for many of the lads, they'd never been over to Europe – they wanted to make the most of it. And I was happy to play the role of tour guide!

It was interesting for me, being the only Englishman in a team full of Aussies, seeing how much they liked it. Too many English people can fall into the trap of thinking Australia is so much better than their own country. They forget some of the things which make England so good, and being around the Aussies on that trip was fascinating.

They loved it. They loved the age of the buildings, the character of the towns and villages, the traditional pubs, the open fires, the pints, the low ceilings, the tiled floors – bars aren't like that over there. Even the freezing weather was a novelty for them.

Ricky Stuart let us have a few beers that Friday night, to celebrate the win, before we were due to fly back the following day. Over a pint, I asked him if I could stay behind an extra couple of days for my nephew's Christening, on the Sunday. Deep down, I think he knew I was bullshitting, but he let me anyway!

That night, in the Marriot, I'll never forget Brett Finch's face.

'How good's this?' he said to me. 'My first game for the Roosters, I'm on the other side of the world, I've just won the World Club Challenge – and best of all, it's a free bar!'

He was loving it. We'd lost Bryan Fletcher to Souths in the off-season, and it left a massive hole in our side. Fletch was a great player, but his personality outshone his ability. He was always the life and soul, and we missed him. We'd turn up at training, and he'd always be the one telling the stories. Thankfully, Finchy's arrival helped fill that hole. He just had so much enthusiasm, and he loved life. It's hard to take the piss out of him because he takes the piss out of himself so much.

The World Club was the only trophy we won that year. We started the year as the defending NRL Premiers, and it was a strange feeling – like we were on a pedestal. I knew other teams would find an extra gear against us, because we were the benchmark, but we had a frightening amount of confidence in each other. It wasn't cockiness, because we backed it up on the training pitch. We were smart enough to realise we'd won the Premiership by being so fit, not through arrogance.

Maintaining success is difficult, especially in the NRL, when the whole system is set up to even the comp out, and everyone's spending the same amount on players. But we were on fire. In our first game, we blitzed Parramatta 32-14, and we got on a roll. We only lost three of our first 11 matches – all by one score, no one battered us – and we finished the season really strong, with a seven-game winning streak.

It was my last year of a three-year deal. Halfway through the season the Roosters told me they wanted to extend it, and I was more than happy to. We were at the top of the table, we'd won the comp the previous season, I was settled in Coogee – I didn't even look anywhere else. The thought of playing for anyone other than the Roosters didn't appeal to me.

My mum and dad came over for three weeks at the start of the season. Even came up to Redcliffe with me for a friendly – or 'trial' – against Brisbane, where my dad enjoyed chatting to the legendary Tommy Bishop. It was the first time they'd been to Australia, and it was great showing them around, and doing all the touristy things.

It was a brilliant time in my life. I was 26, injury-free. I'd had a couple of suspensions but nothing major, and people were talking about me and writing about me. The fans' chants were getting louder and louder with each game.

'*Morrrr-leyyy, Morrr-leyyy . . .*'

As I've mentioned, fans in Australia don't sing like the English crowds, they're nowhere near as vocal. So hearing them chant my name – just two years after the rival fans were calling me a 'Pommie Bastard' and telling me to 'fuck off home' – meant the world to me. And it gave me confidence. I never cruised. I *wanted* to put a shot on, I didn't just do it because I wanted to hear them chant my name . . . but it was bloody great when they did.

We finished the regular season in second spot, but we were

playing like the favourites and that's how we felt. And after we hammered Newcastle 36-8 in the opening round of the play-offs, I think many pundits had us down as favourites, too. We played the Canterbury Bulldogs in week two, which was a huge game. They'd been stripped of their points the previous year, and some people tried to suggest our Premiership win was hollow because the Dogs weren't competing. That pissed me off. The reason they were stripped of the points was because they cheated the salary cap – had they played by the rules, they wouldn't have had as many good players. But that aside, I'd felt we'd beat anyone with our defensive pattern in 2002. The Dogs were a good side, but we'd have had them. And it felt so sweet to knock them out of the semis in '03, not only to take us through to the Grand Final, but to shut a few people up as well.

We expected to get the Warriors again in the decider but, surprisingly, Penrith beat them in the other semi. The Panthers were a solid side, but I thought we had the measure of them.

I was wrong.

The pace of the final was frantic, and they caught us cold. Anthony Minichiello hadn't dropped two balls all year, but he dropped a couple of regulation kicks. It was that kind of game.

We had a great chance to drag ourselves into the game when Todd Byrne made a break, but Scott Sattler came across and made a covering tackle. That tackle is on every Grand Final highlights reel in Australia, but look closely and you'll see that Toddy stumbled – if he hadn't, he'd have been away. Credit to Sattler, it was a decent tackle and he didn't ask for the coverage it generated. But the media can blow something into a key moment, to give themselves a talking point, a different angle, an opening line. In 2003, across the board, from start to finish, Penrith played very well and deserved the win. It wasn't all about Sattler's tackle.

The feeling afterwards was heartbreaking. I'd lost a Grand Final with Leeds in '98, but the concept was new to Super League back then. This was on a whole different level. I thought back to pre-season, and all those sessions that we'd worked our balls off. For a season to come down to 80 minutes, it's harsh and brutal for the losing team. But that's sport, and that's our sport, and I'd rather get there and lose than not at all. Sat in the sheds afterwards, I looked around at my team-mates, all sombre, all quiet, heads dipped. Drinking bottles of Crown lager as if they were obliged to, rather than out of choice. A year earlier, I'd been in the same room, drinking the same beer with the Prime Minister, John Howard, while blokes around me took pictures and passed the trophy around and sang and danced and hugged each other. But no one wants to hang out with the losing team. We'd had a decent season, but we didn't feel in the mood to celebrate. We went out that night and got drunk. But it was funeral drunk, not wedding drunk.

In hindsight, things started to go wrong with that Grand Final defeat. For the following few weeks and months, bad things just seemed to happen. I felt cursed.

When I flew back to England I was supposed to be heading to Lanzarote for a break with my brother Chris and my nieces. Only the airline or the travel agent or – more likely – my mate Butler, who had booked the flights, had messed up the dates, and I missed out. Then I played for Great Britain in a warm-up game at Headingley. No sooner had I heard the Leeds fans chant 'There's only one, Adrian Morley', than I had to leave the pitch with a knee injury. Then, of course, came my red card after 12 seconds in the opening Test of the Ashes series. I've seen that red card plenty of times since, and I know many people thought it was a harsh call – especially given it was the first tackle of the match – but I've never played the victim. Yes, if I was pushed, I'd say it was a hard call and that maybe it should have been placed on report. I've seen much worse go unpunished in Test matches, but I had no problem with Steve Ganson or the video official who was advising him. If you play the game on the edge, it's the chance you take. Straight after the Test match in Wigan, the players were going to the bar. Everyone expected me to head straight for the coach, but I went with them. I half-expected a few dickheads to mouth off at me and blame me for costing Britain the match. No one did. Or if they did, I had the blinkers on. I looked around for Clare and my brother, Steve, when I saw a familiar face near the bar.

It was Ellery Hanley.

I walked over to him and gave him a cuddle. 'What happened, did you catch him?' he asked.

Beating the Aussies meant as much to Ellery as anyone.

'Yeah.'

'Don't worry about it. Don't worry about it.'

I went to my mum's house but couldn't sleep. I stayed up to the early hours, replaying it in my mind. It was my nephew's Christening the next day (the one I'd told Ricky Stuart was back in February!) and no one mentioned it. I could feel – or maybe I was being paranoid – people's eyes burning a hole in the back of my head.

The judiciary was a Tuesday night. There were a heap of journos and camera crews outside Red Hall. Inside, there was an international panel, consisting of two English blokes and an Aussie, and they delivered a verdict of 'sending off sufficient', meaning I didn't cop a ban. I was later told the two English fellas looked after me. But to appease the Aussies, they hit me with a record fine of £2,000. Players received £500 a week for being in camp, so it was my entire earnings from the series. In truth, though, I never had to pay it. The RFL must have felt sorry for me, because they organised a few promotions down in London, and to compensate me for my time they paid me – yep – £2,000. When I told Craig Fitzgibbon, the Aussie back-rower and my Roosters team-mate, he couldn't believe it.

'You wanker,' he said. 'You got a record fine and they paid it for you.'

Fitzy was one of my closest mates, and still is. So I found myself in an awkward spot when he and Terry Newton had a few heated exchanges in the opening Test – Tez caught him with a really high shot – and then continued it in the press during the series. It was soon forgotten, though. All heat-of-the-moment stuff. I remember being with Fitzy in Sydney when Tez called me. 'Is that your mate Terry Newton?' he'd say, loud enough so Tez could hear on the other end of the line. 'Ask him if he's still got my chin on his forearm.'

The first game didn't have a bearing on the second Test, which we lost in Hull when the Aussies again came from behind to win. That was heartbreaking, gut-wrenching pain.

I've been in games when we've lost a player, and the team has been lifted. It happened for Leeds against Wigan in the Challenge Cup in '99 when Barrie McDermott was red-carded. We covered his loss. So who knows? Maybe my red card didn't matter. But it's a question which can never be answered, and we'll never know.

By chance, I saw Robbie Kearns in the Aussies' team hotel the following week. I was there to see a couple of the Roosters boys. I walked over to him and apologised.

'Moz, that's the game, it wasn't personal was it?' he said.

'Was it 'eck personal, no. It could have been anyone.'

'Well then.'

And that was it.

A couple of days after the third Test defeat, I got a call off a couple of the Roosters boys. 'Moz, we're going to Amsterdam, come with us.' Luke Ricketson, Fitzy, Craig Wing and Anthony Minichiello were all going along. I'd never been there before, but the idea of going out celebrating with the Aussie lads so soon after the series had finished didn't really appeal.

Fitzy sold it to me in the end. 'Mate, a game's a game – we're still mates,' he said. So I took off with nothing but my wallet, my passport, and my mate Butler for a few days in Holland.

Darren Lockyer and Danny Buderus were there too. I'd never really got to know them in Australia. One of the down sides of the NRL was the way home teams drove to their nearby leagues clubs after matches, and the away teams went home. So apart from a quick handshake, I didn't get to know opponents on a personal level like I did in Super League. In Amsterdam, there was one surreal moment when I was sat on a bar stool, facing Lockyer, thinking, 'You're the bastard who just beat us in the Ashes series'.

But he was so nice and so generous, it was impossible not to love the fella. As much as I enjoyed the trip, though, I was still on a downer when I got back. That's in no way an excuse to justify my drink-driving (and the fence-hurdling police chase that followed), because what I did was stupid. I look back on it now and I can't believe I did it.

The court fined me £2,000, which I didn't think was too bad, considering it was the same amount I'd been fined for high-tackling an Aussie prop a few weeks earlier. They also ordered me to do 40 hours community service.

Problem.

It was the week before Christmas, and I was booked to fly back to Sydney on 28 December. Thankfully, they allowed me to make an exception, so I spent the entire Christmas week carrying out the most tedious manual labour imaginable. I comforted myself with the knowledge that my arrest had not come out publicly. That was until Phil Clarke, the Great Britain team manager, called me up midway through my community service.

'Moz, I heard a rumour you've been done for drink-driving,' he said.

I lied to him.

'I was in the car when someone else got done,' I said. 'It was my mate, Butler.'

I felt embarrassed, lying to someone I respected. When it broke in the press, I later phoned him to apologise, and he was understanding. I think he realised my head wasn't in the right place after my sending off. Again, I'm not blaming anyone but myself.

I've learned to live with what I did. I've learned to accept that it might stand as my defining moment, and I'm okay with that. Brian Carney jokes that I ruined his Test debut and I've learned to laugh about it now. But inside it still hurts, and I don't think that will ever go away. I'm still shattered about what happened. Because to me, I cost us that Ashes series.

CHAPTER TWENTY
IT'S A KNOCKOUT

For a brief moment, I thought I'd killed Ricky Stuart. He was lying on the ground, motionless. Kangaroos legend and Grand Final-winning Sydney Roosters coach, out cold. He'd just been hit in the head by a heavy object at a fast speed. Worse, I was the one who had thrown it at him.

Ricky had introduced the heavy footballs to training to strengthen our passes. They were like light medicine balls, in the shape of rugby balls. We used to play games with them in training, when Ricky would stand in the middle, pass us the ball and then we'd take it and pass it straight back. He loved it.

One day, we were mulling around on the pitch, waiting for training to start. Ricky was chatting to assistant John Cartwright. Next to my feet was a bag of balls, so I picked up the heavy football, saw Ricky and thought, 'This'll be a laugh'. He was stood about 10m away, which was – I guessed – about the range of my passing with a weighted ball.

My plan was to throw him a pass, so he'd think it was a regular ball, and it would surprise him when he discovered it wasn't. Maybe it'd hit him in the gut, roll him back.

So I swung the ball and launched a pass his way. As soon as it left my hands I shouted, 'Ricky', expecting him to turn around. But I knew I'd passed it too hard. The ball was picking up momentum and arrowing straight towards his head.

'Ricky!' I shouted louder. Eventually he turned around . . . just as the ball hit him straight in the face.

THUD.

He dropped like a ton weight. Like he'd just walked into Mike Tyson's right hook. He just collapsed in a heap, no movement at all.

'Oh bollocks,' I thought. 'What have I done? I've killed him.'

He didn't move. One second. Two seconds. Three seconds. Then I saw a flicker. A movement. He tried to lift his head up, but failed. It was a small comfort to know he was alive. But he looked in a bad way.

John crouched down next to him and helped him sit up. His face had started to swell up. Ricky came around quickly. 'I'm alright, I'm alright,' he said. 'What happened?'

'Moz passed you a ball. A heavy football,' John told him.

Ricky seemed more embarrassed than anything. I got the impression he would have let it go, so it didn't help when Carty started giggling. Then all the other lads started laughing too.

I felt terrible. Not only could I have seriously hurt Ricky, but all the lads were laughing at him.

'You daft Pommie prick,' he called me, and he was right. But I will say, in my defence, that if I threw that ball again 100 times, I wouldn't get it on target with one.

Thankfully he can laugh about it now – in fact every time I see Ricky, he mentions the time I floored him with a pass.

The start of 2004 was tough for every rugby league player. When a 20-year-old woman was taken to hospital and filed a complaint of sexual assault against several of the Canterbury players in Coffs Harbour, a huge scandal erupted. It completely saturated the media, and shone a burning spotlight on players like never before. All of a sudden, every detail of our lives was being scrutinised. It didn't matter that no other club was involved, either. The case was eventually dropped, but while it was at its height it put the game under huge strain. I noticed it myself. Walking down the street, I dipped my head and kept myself to myself – I had nothing to hide, but there was always that tinge of, 'Are people looking at me differently?' The story was everywhere – all over the TV, the newspapers, the radio. I wasn't comfortable, feeling like I had to defend rugby league players and myself. I didn't change my life, I didn't have to; but for a few weeks, I felt ashamed to be a footballer. From a playing point of view, the Dogs were our main rivals as well. Everyone was tipping them to be our biggest challengers for the Premiership, so when we beat them 35-0 in Round 3 we were made up.

The salary cap in the NRL really has a huge impact on clubs, and makes balancing the squad a difficult task. And it's not uncommon to see teams yo-yoing, year to year. Maintaining success, in a fiercely strong competition and with a wage ceiling on players' earnings, is tough to do. The fact we'd beaten the Dogs so early in the season sent out a loud and clear message – our success over the past two years had not been a fluke. And we weren't about to fade away.

I was enjoying my day-to-day life in Coogee a lot. But I also saw a lot of Australia. If I had any chance to travel, I'd take it.

The Roosters were pretty good at going out, far away from Sydney, to different parts of the country to run coaching clinics and community events, and I'd volunteer for everything.

Anyone want to go to Northern Territory for a couple of days?

'Put me down.'

Trip to Perth, Cairns, Darwin?

'I'm your man.'

While the Aussie lads with families might have rolled their eyes at the prospect of two days in the middle of nowhere, I'd leap at the chance. I became the player who'd turn up everywhere. I reckon I've seen more places in Australia than most Australians have.

The trips to the bush were the best. Most Australians live close to the coastlines, but the bush refers to the small country towns away from the rural areas. A lot of Aboriginal communities are based in the bush. They're often very barren, dusty, hot places – small towns, spread out over inhospitable land, hundreds of miles apart.

A few times, I travelled to and from those Bush towns in an old, rickety three-seater plane, which was always exciting in an Indiana Jones kind of way. The people out there treated NRL players like celebrities, and I never tired of meeting them. I was probably the first Englishman many of them had met, and they had as many questions about my upbringing and home as I had about theirs.

I was enjoying Aussie life so much that I decided to apply for residency. And when I mentioned that to one of the journos, he asked me whether I'd like to play in the State of Origin. He put the idea in my head, rather than the other way around, but I was excited at the prospect of pulling on the Sky Blue jersey. In my first year at the Roosters, the Origin series was played on stand-alone weekends, rather than mid-week, and I made a point of going to all three matches. I loved them.

During the series, it seemed the whole of Queensland and New South Wales were gripped by the games. And what games they were! They were all ferocious, fast and fierce. I was desperate to be involved.

When the journo asked would I like to play Origin, I replied, 'So much so that I wish my great great-granddad had been a thief.'

I was proud of that one.

I supported Queensland when I was a kid, for no other reason than they always seemed to be the underdog. Even though I lived in New South Wales, I had no strong allegiance either way, so I ended up cheering for whichever side had the most Roosters players in their team.

Ricky Stuart was the New South Wales coach. I asked him whether I could play Origin, and he seemed as excited at the prospect as I was.

'If you want to play, I'll pick you,' he said. 'You're an Origin-type player'.

I made some enquires. Geoff Carr, the ARL chief executive, confirmed I was eligible to play if I got Australian residency, with one exception. I had to make myself available for Australia as well.

There was no way I was doing that. As much as I loved Australia, I could not play for them. I'm not Australian. I argued that Adrian Lam had played for Papua New Guinea and Queensland at the same time, but they wouldn't budge. Those were different circumstances, they said. A couple of New South Wales legends, David Gillespie and Steve Roach, were in the papers urging the ARL to change their stance. They wanted me to play Origin as much as I wanted to play it.

But once I took my blinkers off, I had no complaints. Carr was right. The Origin concept is a selection process for the Australian team – I had no right to be there. And if they picked me, then it would have cleared the way for half the Kiwi team to play for New South Wales as well.

Becoming an Australian resident made travelling easier, but that was the only reason I did it. I never considered getting citizenship, because that would have been cutting my ties with England, and I didn't want to do that.

While over there I met up with a few ex-pats; blokes who had gone over to Australia to play and never gone back – John Gray, Dave Eckersley, Phil Jackson and Cliff Watson. Dave Bolton had been over there for years and still refused to take out citizenship – as much as he loved the Aussie climate and lifestyle, he was still deeply proud to be English. I was too. And never was I more patriotic than during a sporting event.

When the Athens Olympics was on TV, I'd have digs at the Aussie boys every time we beat them at something, and vice-versa. But the biggest event, by far, was the Ashes cricket series.

I've never been a huge cricket fan, but it's impossible to avoid the sport over there. They love it. I met a couple of the England cricketers, Matt Hoggard and Michael Vaughan, when they came over for the series in 2002, and I even took them a signed Roosters jersey. They were good fellas. I went to watch their Test at Sydney and they were thumped, which I never heard the end of at training.

'Nice to see your motivational speech worked, Mozza,' they all laughed.

When the series was played in England in 2005, I had a bet with Ricky Stuart. A case of Crown lager for every Test our country won.

There was a little pub near to my house, the Duke of Gloucester, which was as near to an English pub as I could find. There were always some familiar accents in there. But for some reason I was in a different pub, full of Aussies, when I watched the fourth – and ultimately deciding – Test. When England won by three wickets, I ran around the pub screaming my head off!

In April, I was suspended for a week for a careless high tackle. The following month, I copped a three-week ban for the same offence. No sooner had I got back than I had to face the disciplinary again. Same charge, same outcome. I felt awful for the boys, as if I was letting them down. But Ricky was terrific. It's a really fine line between a great shot and a high shot, literally two or three inches, and being tall meant I could easily drift into high-tackle territory.

Ricky didn't want me to become a player who played it safe. He wanted me standing tall, intimidating players. When I lined up a target, I wanted to floor them. Sure, I could have tackled around the waist or made a copybook tackle, but that's not what I was about. I know how much of a lift it gave my team-mates when I knocked blokes down. And, more than anything, it also softened them up, making it easier for us to win the game. When I got banned at the end of the season, Ricky took a bit of heat from the media for saying it was okay because it meant I would be fresh for the play-offs!

The Penrith coach, John Lang, had pissed me off when he whinged about the 'cheap-shot merchants' after the Grand Final the year earlier. You didn't have to be a genius to figure out he was talking about me. But all the players who I'd spoken to didn't have a problem with me or my style, even the ones I'd hit high. And Ricky Stuart didn't either.

'I don't want to take the aggression from your game,' he said. But he did want me to stop getting banned, so he hit on an idea to help. A limbo stick.

After training at Wentworth Park, his assistant coach Dave Gillespie – great fella, even better nickname ('Cement') – would hold a tackle pad, and stand a yard or so back from a limbo dancing pole. I had to duck to hit the pad, or I'd smash my face into a piece of equipment I last saw at a crap wedding a few years earlier.

Michael Crocker and Stuart Webb did it too. It was a great idea, and I think it worked to an extent because I didn't get myself into trouble as much after that.

We finished top of the NRL and won the minor premiership, which was nice, even if – like in Super League – it didn't carry as much kudos as it deserved. I accepted the Grand Final system straight away, but I've always felt the league leaders deserve more credit for finishing top. A Grand Final is great but it's a Cup Final, 80 minutes of play. A team can be awesome all year and have a bad day on the wrong day, and their campaign is over just like that. And I'm fine with that, it's sport – but I still think the team finishing top deserves some credit.

We made it through the play-offs to reach our third straight Grand Final, against the Bulldogs. We'd been the two best sides all year, and the '04 decider had more hype around Sydney than the previous two finals. Everyone expected a classic. It wasn't. At least, it wasn't for us.

The conditions were awful, and there was a lot of dropped ball, from both sides. We took a 13-0 lead, but they pegged a try back before half-time. Even then we still felt in control. But in the second half they edged in front to set up a tense finish. Then came the moment which I'll never forget. Freddie hit Mick Crocker with a great ball to put him through the line. Time seemed to slow right down as he charged through. All he had to do was draw the full-back and pass to Chris Walker.

But Andrew Ryan, the Canterbury back-rower, came from nowhere to make a great cover tackle. He flicked his hand out and just caught Crock's boot, and the chance was gone. Even now, people talk a lot more about Scott Sattler's tackle on Todd Byrne the previous year, and even my hit on Richard Villasanti in '02. But for me, Ryan's tackle, when he must have been out on his feet, was a much bigger play.

The game hinged on that split second. If Ryan had missed Crock's foot, we'd have scored and won. But he didn't miss, and we didn't win. The final score was 16-13 to the Dogs.

That wasn't the only time that year I played in a final and ended up on the losing team. The introduction of the Tri-Nations was great. Great Britain, New Zealand and Australia playing each other twice, with the two highest-ranked sides meeting in the final. A slimmed-down version had been played in '99, with just one Test each, and I was gutted when that concept was binned.

Brian Noble had taken over from David Waite as Great Britain coach. I liked Nobby. He was a good forwards coach. Tactically he wasn't as strong as Waite, but he was terrific at motivating players, and at Test level that's exactly what you want.

We played well at Man City's new ground against the Aussies, who'd already played their two Tests against the Kiwis. Luke Rooney's try right at the death sealed the win for them, in typically agonising fashion. We regrouped and beat New Zealand 22-12 at Huddersfield a week later. The Kiwis had a really good side, too, but our forward pack was immense. Fielden, Newton, Peacock, Farrell, Sculthorpe. They were all at their peak, and with a good kid named Gareth Ellis on the bench. I loved playing with those blokes. That win gave us real confidence against the Aussies at the JJB, and for me it was a chance to exorcise a few demons after my red card the year earlier. I tried not to think about that in the build-up to the game, but it was playing on my mind as we ran out there; I made a concerted effort to keep my shots a little lower in that game!

It was a great Test match. All of our last four meetings had gone Australia's way, but the winning margin in each of the games was six points or fewer. And in all of them, we were in a winning position with a only few minutes to go. So when we were 18-12 ahead in that game, no one got carried away. Not until Keith Senior intercepted Scott Hill's pass and ran over to put us two scores in front. Faz joked afterwards that, after what had happened to us in the past four meetings, he expected a fan to come onto the pitch and tackle Keith!

We smacked the Kiwis in our last round-robin match to top the league, setting us up for a third meeting with Australia in the final at Elland Road, and I'd never felt more confident before a Test match. We'd had a great series. We'd beaten the Aussies by 12 points and beaten the Kiwis twice. Our only defeat was by 12-8 in our opening game, and we'd grown and improved out of sight since then.

Great Britain hadn't beaten the Aussies in a series for three decades and I was giddy at the prospect of making history. I even considered getting a tattoo to mark the achievement.

But we saved our worst performance for last. We just didn't turn up. We dropped passes, slipped off tackles, and to compound our misery the Aussies – the bastards – played the perfect half. And pulling the strings was Darren Lockyer. In that game Darren was at his peak. He always impressed me with his talent and patience and, combined with his exceptional pace, he was phenomenal. Once a team gains the ascendancy in a rugby league match, it's very hard to break them. Especially when they're the Kangaroos. But the way we caved in was really disappointing. They scored an average of a point a minute to make it 38-0 at half-time. I looked around the dressing room and everyone was just shell-shocked. Nobby walked in and said, 'Boys, I don't think you can win this Test match. But what you can do is give the people a reason to cheer for you, a reason to be proud of you.'

We scored a try each in the second half, but the damage had been well and truly done.

TRIBUTE: BY RICKY STUART (EX-SYDNEY ROOSTERS COACH)

When I took over the Roosters at the end of Moz's first year in the NRL, he had doubts about whether he was in my plans or not.

I told him straight away that he was.

I liked Adrian Morley from the moment I first saw him. He plays the game at an incredible intensity, but he also has extraordinary endurance. A big man who plays big minutes. That was an extremely rare combination among forwards back then, so much so that I would go as far as to say he redefined the role of the enforcer.

Moz had that intimidation factor about him – and he had it for 80 minutes. He wouldn't stop until the full-time whistle. Unless, of course, he was sent off!

I'll never forget his final game for the Roosters. It was against Canterbury in 2006, and before we ran out I told them to look out for Corey Hughes. Corey's a good mate of mine, but he was a real niggly player, so I said: 'If he tries any of his shit, someone job him.'

Moz did more than that – he had a brain explosion and kneed him in the head, and was red-carded. I said to him afterwards, 'Well, at least it's good to see you followed the coach's playbook!'

Moz played the game on the edge, and that's the way I liked it. I never wanted to curtail his aggression; that's what helped make him the player he was. If there is one Englishman who was made for State of Origin football, it's Adrian Morley.

He liked a laugh and he liked a beer, when the time was right, but like the rest of the senior players at the Roosters, he loved to work hard and rip in. He cared for the cause, he played for his mates. And never was that better illustrated than during our Premiership triumph in 2002. When the Warriors' forward Richard Villasanti hit our captain, Brad Fittler, while he lay defenceless on the ground, Moz took it into his own hands to settle the score by putting a terrific shot on him.

I'm sure Moz – to this day – will play down the massive role he had in our Grand Final victory that day. And he isn't just being modest; he just doesn't realise the huge impact his effort made. He typified, in one hit, the attitude that we were a team who looked out for one another. Stood up for one another. And it gave Freddie Fittler the inspiration to guide us home, knowing that someone was there, watching his back.

Moz doesn't need to say anything for people to know he's a tough man. Just like Ruben Wiki is, and Petero Civoniceva is. And just like those fellas, Moz is very soft natured person. The complete polar opposite to his persona on the pitch.

He's a loyal friend, he cares about people, and he'd never hurt you. Or, at least, he'd never intentionally hurt you! I still remember when he knocked me clean out with a 5kg training ball. He threw the damn thing right at my head. When I came around, he didn't know whether to cuddle me or run away! But even then, I couldn't be angry with him.

If English fans want to know what impact he had, I would say this; he made clubs over here all start looking for the next Mal Reilly. The next Bill Ashurst. The next Tommy Bishop. They all came over to Australia in the '70s and made a huge impact on the Australian competition. Of course, a few of Great Britain's best players came for short off-season stints in the late-'80s and early-'90s and did well. But no one had been over permanently and made the impact which Moz made. He showed people that – for all the vast changes in the sport – a player could come from England and take the Australian competition by storm. And within a year or two, all the club coaches and recruitment officers in the NRL began looking for the next Poms who could do that. I imagine the likes of Gareth Ellis and Sam Burgess, who've come over since, were inspired by the success Moz had over here – and I'm convinced the clubs were so keen to sign them for the same reason.

CHAPTER TWENTY-ONE
BIG HITTING

'Moz, two policemen are here to see you.'

I was in the Roosters gym, about to start training, when I was caught off-guard.

I'd not been in any trouble – at least, none that I could think of. And when I sweet-talked the girl giving me a parking ticket the other day, she promised she'd cancel it for me.

Think Moz, think.

'They're here for me?' I asked.

'Yeah. And they've flown over from England to see you.'

I walked through to meet the two officers. They identified themselves and told me they were from Merseyside. They'd flown to Sydney just to see me. Good gig if you can get it, I thought.

'Are you represented by Nick Fowler,' they asked.

He was my agent. Or manager, as Aussies call them.

'Yeah.'

'We have evidence to believe he has dishonestly obtained money.'

For a moment, I thought, 'Why are they telling me this? If he's been a naughty boy, what's it got to do with me?'

Then the penny dropped. Why they were here. Why they were telling me this.

'How much?' I asked.

They estimated it at around £110,000. I felt sick.

I phoned my mum and dad, and told them what had happened. I was so angry. I felt so stupid. I couldn't sleep that night, beating myself up about why I'd trusted him. I felt so . . . violated. I'd had my house burgled when I was younger and anyone will tell you it's a horrible feeling. This felt 10 times worse.

I'd signed with Nick when I signed my first contract – my Leeds team-mate Neil Harmon was with him too – and he seemed great. He set up a scheme where he took money from me for a pension fund, in case my career was ended by injury. I thought I was being smart.

It was money I had spare. Any extra cash I got, from bonuses and such, I gave to him to put into this fund. It was my life savings. Plus a good chunk of my monthly salary. I was putting a grand a month into the fund in my early days, which was a large part of my income. And I never had any problems with him.

Gary Hetherington, the Leeds chief executive, wasn't happy with negotiating with him, and Nick Politis, the chairman at the Roosters, expressed his concerns at times. But I just thought they were trying to get a better deal out of me, and ignored them.

I met with the officers again, gave an official statement, and handed over what wage slips and contracts I had with me in Australia. It took a while for the case against Nick to go to court. I didn't appear at the trial – I was still in Sydney with the Roosters – though my statement was read out in court. But I followed the case online.

It was revealed in the trial that he had also duped four pensioners out of their savings, producing forged documents to give himself a cloak of respectability. He was convicted of dishonestly obtaining nearly 200 grand, and jailed for two and a half years.

More than half that money was mine, but when I heard about his other victims I felt bad for them. At least I was in my mid-20s, and I was still in a position to earn some money. They weren't as fortunate – one of the victims was 76.

Nick phoned me from prison to apologise, but I lost the plot, called him every name under the sun and told him to get me my money. Days later, I appointed a solicitor, and he's still trying to reclaim as much as he can.

By the start of 2005, I'd missed 14 NRL games through suspension. I'd been banned on eight separate occasions, with all but one being for careless high tackles. But I'd never been sent off.

That changed when we played the Bulldogs in Round 6, when Paul Simpkins dismissed me for a high shot on Matt Utai. It was a penalty at worst. Thankfully, the Roosters won the game without me and I didn't get a suspension, but it got to me. I started feeling there was a bit of a witch-hunt against me. It got to a point where I only had to catch a player high and the ref would give a penalty. My team-mates were great, though, offering their support, and a couple of them even spoke about it in the media to say I was being treated unfairly.

We hovered around the play-off spots for most of the season. In the games we lost, we were never embarrassed, but at the same time in the games we won we were never really on fire. It was our first year without Brad Fittler, and we struggled at times.

When he was younger, Freddie may have got the captaincy for being the best player. As well as being obscenely talented, he was diplomatic, smart, a decent lookin' fella; the poster boy for a captain. But he grew into the role and became a real leader. He was tough, and he carried an aura about him. He could come up with the big plays when they were needed, and crack a game open. He was a freakish talent at times.

That's no disrespect to the lads who replaced him in the half-back roles that year, because Brett Firman came in and did a good job until injury, and Craig Wing and Brett Finch were great players in their own right. It wasn't their fault they weren't Freddie.

In Round 10, we travelled to New Zealand to take on the Warriors. In our last meeting the year before, their forward Awen Guttenbeil had floored Ned Catic with a great shot. But instead of walking away, Awen stood over Ned, mouthing off at him. We won the game, but afterwards Ricky Stuart blew up at us.

'If any player, from any team, does that to one of us,' he screamed. 'You fuckin' go over and chin him.'

That was in my mind as we took to the pitch at Mt Smart stadium. I thought, 'I've got a green light from Ricky to nail him'. Legally or illegally, he was going to get it. It was nothing personal, because Awen was a good fella, but he'd made 'the book' – my self-compiled list of blokes to go at. I didn't have to wait long for my chance. He came off the bench in the first half, got the ball early, I lined him up and cleaned him out. It was a sweet shot, and it was legal too. Out of all my shots over there – and the hits on Manly's Steve Matai and Jason King, in quick succession, the following year were pretty decent – that one on Guttenbeil was probably my favourite from my time in the NRL.

In the airport, waiting for our flight home after that match, Ricky pulled me to one side.

'You got a minute mate,' he said. I followed him to the bar, where he perched himself on a stool and ordered two large bourbons. The drinks arrived, we chinked glasses, and we downed them in one gulp. He didn't even say a word, and he didn't need to. It was his way of showing his appreciation for what I'd done, and it meant a lot to me.

Mid-season, when it appeared unlikely that we'd make the play-offs, news broke that Andrew Johns would be joining Warrington at the end of the year. His side, the Newcastle Knights, had no chance of making the top eight and – with the English season running later than the NRL, and the Wolves assured a play-off spot – he would be able to play in at least three games.

The idea that I could do a similar thing was already in my head when Brian Noble, the Great Britain and Bradford coach, called and asked whether I'd be interested in joining them for a similar stint.

'If you can square it with the Roosters, we'd love to have you,' he said.

My main concern was getting the Roosters into the play-offs, though, and Nobby understood that. After making the Grand Final for three straight years, I didn't like the idea of missing out.

I approached Nick Politis, the Roosters chairman. I felt really cheeky and awkward, because no matter how I dressed it up I was basically saying, 'If I can't play in the play-offs here, can I go to England and play in the play-offs there with someone else.'

With Joey Johns sealing a move first, at least there was a precedent. I liked the idea of playing in Super League again, even for a few games, and it would also help keep me fit for Great Britain at the end of the year.

Ricky Stuart wasn't too keen on the idea. My contract with the Roosters was up the following year, and he asked whether I'd agree to extend it if they let me play at Bradford.

I didn't like the idea of one having a bearing on the other.

'Look, I want to stay,' I said. 'But that's not how I do business.'

I also told them that my ideal situation would be not playing for Bradford, because that would mean the Roosters had reached the play-offs.

Reluctantly, they agreed. But before I phoned Nobby back, I called Leeds and asked to speak to Gary Hetherington. Bradford and Leeds are fierce rivals, especially back then when the Bulls were at the peak of their powers and Leeds were coming good. Leeds were my club for years, and I still had a strong affection for them. To this day, 'Rhinos' is part of my email address. I told Gary straight what was going on.

'Bradford want me to do what Joey's done, and come over for a few games,' I said. 'The Roosters are willing to let me, but I wanted to call you first in case you're interested.'

Gary said no.

He didn't think their coach, Tony Smith, would be interested in someone else coming in towards the end of the season, and that was fair enough.

'No problem, I just wanted to give you the option,' I said.

He phoned back a short while later.

'I've had a word with Tony and we'll have you in the squad,' he said. 'We can't guarantee you'll play and we can't give you any money . . . but come on board if you want.'

That was typical Gary. He always drove a hard bargain, but he didn't exactly give me a tough decision to make.

'Well, Bradford have offered me money and told me I will play . . .' I said. It was a no-brainer.

The Roosters carried on treading water mid-table, but five losses on the bounce really hurt us. I remember losing to our archrivals, Souths, 17-16 – my only defeat to them during my time there – with three games to go, and it really hurt us. Their loose-forward, Ashley Harrison, was outstanding in that game. If we'd won that game we may have sneaked into the play-offs; in the end, we finished ninth, one place out.

For some, that's a credible position, but for us it was devastating. As a punishment, Ricky kept the boys in and made them train up until the weekend of the Grand Final – even Braith Anasta, who had signed from the Bulldogs, for the year after! It was a shame we missed the finals, because I really felt we could have done something. We were never really out-played in the losses we'd suffered, and we had the big-game experience you need in the sudden-death encounters.

I went mad on our Mad Monday (the end-of-season celebrations), flew home on the Tuesday and landed at Manchester Airport on the Wednesday. From the minute I arrived, Bradford were terrific. They were up there with any of the clubs I've been at, in terms of looking after me. They arranged a car, a place to stay – everything was catered for. I turned up for training for the first time the following day. I already knew a few of the boys from the Great Britain squad – JP (Jamie Peacock), Stu Fielden, Paul Johnson, Leon Pryce – and my old mate Iestyn Harris was there. He'd sent me a text to say 'welcome aboard' when my signing was announced. But I was apprehensive about how the lads would treat me. I felt like an imposter. I convinced myself that the club wanted me there, yet I couldn't get the awkwardness of knowing I was taking someone else's spot out of my head.

Paul Deacon, Bradford's half-back, had said publicly he didn't agree with my joining them because one of his mates would lose their spot. He pulled me aside afterwards and said, 'I want you to know, what I said wasn't personal. I hope you don't have a problem with it.'

But the truth is, I would have felt the same. I actually respected Deacs for speaking out, because it would have been easier for him to toe the party line. The fact he risked a row with his club and his coach, to say what he thought, took real balls on his part.

He was right, of course. Me being at Bradford meant one of the blokes who'd toiled all year would miss out because of my arrival (it turned out Rob Parker and Andy Lynch both missed games to accommodate me). But from a selfish point of view, it gave me a chance to play in the Super League, to scratch an itch that had been growing since I'd heard about Joey joining Warrington, and it helped Great Britain by maintaining my match fitness. It was a bit awkward but that's rugby league; there's rarely any sentiment to selecting sides.

Parker and Lynchy were terrific, like all the boys were. And it was at Bradford where I got hooked on one of my big pastimes – poker. They'd play most days after training, just for £5 a tournament, until eventually it got more serious, though it was never for ridiculous amounts of cash. Rugby league players are extremists by nature; it's little surprise that the rush from poker appeals to them. In Australia, everyone gambles – they love it – but I was never into that. At least with poker, if you lose money, one of your mates wins it!

Three days after flying into England, I went to watch Warrington against Leeds. It was my first experience of the

Halliwell Jones Stadium and I loved it – it was a great atmosphere. Warrington had gone mad about Joey's arrival, and he didn't disappoint; he killed it, and deservedly got the Man of the Match award.

'Thanks for that Joey,' I thought. 'Now I'm under pressure to play well!' I'd like to say I killed it too, but the truth was I was average at best. We played Huddersfield, at Odsal, and as hard as I tried I just couldn't get into my rhythm. I went alright against Saints the following week in the last match of the regular season, though. It was an awesome game. We were trailing 18-6 going into the final 13 minutes but ran in five tries to run out 32-18 winners. It was one of the greatest comebacks I've ever been involved with. And the fact we'd finished so strongly gave us even more confidence as we went into the play-offs. We easily dispatched London (44-22) and Hull FC (71-0) in the first two rounds. The Hull game was Stephen Kearney's last match before he retired, and he was sent off early on, which was a sad way for him to finish because he'd had a great career.

That result set up another meeting with Saints, again at Knowsley Road, and it was nip and tuck all the way. Deacs kicked a drop-goal to make it 19-18, so we spent the last 10 minutes hanging onto our lead, before Shontayne Hape crossed in the last minute to put us 23-18 in front. It was a great feeling. I don't normally get cut, but in that match, I got cut twice – on my chin and above my eye. Bradford had two doctors and both were stitching me up in the dressing room while, all around me, the lads were going mad. We'd made it to the Grand Final.

Having just played in the NRL, those two matches against St Helens were up there in terms of quality and intensity, without a doubt. But in the games against London and Hull – play-off matches, remember – Bradford didn't need to get out of second gear. I was asked at the time how Super League compared to the NRL and I answered truthfully: the games between the top sides are up there, but the others just aren't. But I knew the final, against Leeds, would not lack in intensity. My last club game in England had been for Leeds against Bradford and now, five years later, I was with Bradford, playing in a Grand Final against my old club. To add even more spice to the occasion, it was Barrie McDermott's last game for Leeds.

I started the game on the bench, but within five minutes Paul Johnson was injured and I got the nod to go on. A quarter of an hour later, Barrie Mac came off the bench. I drove the ball in and Barrie didn't miss his chance – he whacked me, right across the face. The next thing I knew, I was staring at the spotlights, dazed, wondering how exactly I'd ended up lying on the grass. Then I heard Iestyn's voice.

'Moz get up,' he said. 'It was Baz who did it – you're going to get him in trouble.'

It was one of the most surreal instructions I'd ever had! There we were, in a Grand Final, and Iestyn was concerned about a mate on the other team being sent-off. Did he think I was acting like a footballer, and staying down? I gingerly got to my feet before Deacs kicked the penalty. Barrie stayed on the pitch, which I was glad about for two reasons – I didn't want his career ending with a red card like Kearney's, plus it gave me a chance to get my own back. We were 8-4 up – Leon had cancelled out Danny McGuire's opening try for Leeds – when I saw Barrie lining up, ready to take a carry. He collected the ball and, with adrenaline pumping, I shot out the line towards him, raising my elbow at the last minute. It whistled past his face. Half-an-inch to the right, and it could have cleaned him out. But the ref' didn't miss what I'd tried to do, and penalised me, giving Leeds the chance to close the margin to two points at half-time. As I cooled down in the dressing room, I came to my senses.

What the hell was I thinking? I'd just cost my side two points, trying to level a personal score.

I left it at that. Big Lesley Vainikolo thundered over for a try to put some distance between us in the second half, and when Deacs put us two scores ahead with a drop-goal I knew the game was won.

In the dressing room, everyone was smiling and celebrating. Everyone but Stu Fielden, that is. He was sat in the corner, sulking.

'What's up Stu?' I asked him.

'I didn't play well.'

That's how meticulous he is! Once he'd had a few beers, he got into the party mood, like everyone else, though. I had two invites that night – my brother Steve was in Prague for his stag party, and Clare was at her sister's wedding. But I missed both to spend it with the Bradford boys, celebrating the win.

I'm glad I went to Bradford, I enjoyed my time there and I wouldn't change anything. But the Grand Final win didn't mean as much to me as the other boys. They'd worked all year and toiled hard for it. I hadn't even suffered a defeat with them.

I still had a strong affection for Leeds. Just because they didn't want me back – or Gary didn't want me back – it didn't change anything. It didn't give me any more satisfaction that I beat Leeds, nor did I have any sympathy for them. That's sport.

But they were the club who gave me a chance, and I had – and continue to have – a real soft spot for them.

I had three Mad Mondays in 2005 – one with the Roosters, one with Bradford and then one with the Great Britain boys. Sadly, we didn't make the final but we weren't disgraced in the Tri-Nations. Paul Johnson got a hat-trick against the Kiwis in a defeat at Loftus Road, then we played the Aussies at Wigan and gave as good as we got, until Matt Cooper sealed their win. I scored a try in that match, Keiron Cunningham sending me over from close-range. My dad and brothers were at the game, and Ste told me my old man was in tears when I went over, which was nice to hear.

We whacked the Kiwis 38-12 the week later and would have made the final if we'd beaten the Aussies in Hull in our last match. We played pretty well and we didn't leave anything in the tank, but we ended up losing 26-14. Sometimes you've got to put your hand up and say you're not good enough. Still, I took small comfort from knowing we'd battered the Kiwis and they won the tournament. I was out with Clare, JP and his missus, Fay, in Leeds when the final was on TV. I had mates in both sides, but it wasn't about that – I was happy for the game that a different team had won. After the Tri-Nations, my brother Ste tied the knot. He asked me to be his best man.

'Aje, I've been to that many weddings when the speech has ruined it for the groom and best man,' he said to me. 'If you want to do one fine; if not, don't worry. I'm not doing one.'

Maybe he thought I wouldn't be funny enough. Or maybe, he wanted to make sure his wedding went off without any problems, unlike Chris's wedding!

He'd got married five years earlier, and had plucked up so much Dutch courage before his speech that by the time he got to the first dance he was off his head. He picked up my great Auntie Stella – who was in her 80s – on the dance floor. And then he dropped her!

Thankfully she was alright, but Chris wasn't. Ste and I ended up carrying him home at 9.30pm and tucked him into bed.

CHAPTER TWENTY-TWO
GREEN LIGHT, RED CARD

During a tough pre-season up on Coffs Harbour, I discovered that loving Bob Dylan and old music has its advantages.

It was a brutal camp. Ricky Stuart was still pissed off that we hadn't made the play-offs the previous year. The fact he'd kept the boys in training until the Grand Final meant they started back fitter than ever, and everyone really ripped in during our week-long spell at the beachside resort.

Ricky was loving it. 'Boys, you've all earned yourself a beer,' he said after one particularly hard day's training. 'But no going mad. Midnight curfew.'

Ricky was Old School in that way. And I loved him for it. I've learned enough about rugby league players over the years to know they bond far better and quicker over a beer or two than over a sober paintball or go-karting session. It's just the way it is.

Two schooners down, Ronnie Palmer, the Roosters conditioner, slid up to my side.

'Just be careful how much you drink there Moz,' he whispered, and walked off.

There was a midnight curfew, but it was only 10pm. I thought, 'Why would he say that? I've only had two beers.'

But I trusted Ronnie, and I knew he liked me. Good conditioners are like human lie-detectors. They know who's being honest and they know who's faking, and I think Ronnie respected me for the way I trained. I'd like to think I always gave my all, and I think that's one of the reasons he liked me.

The other reason, of course, was our shared passion for music. Whenever one of the Roosters boys put a crap rap or dance song on in the gym, Ronnie and I would only tolerate so much before we switched it back to the classic rock station. We even went to watch several concerts together in Sydney.

So I made my third beer last two hours, part-jealous as my team-mates ordered more beer, but part-anxious to know why Ronnie had warned me off the beers. We all made the curfew and were tucked up in bed five minutes later.

At quarter-past, there was loud knocking on the doors, and the muffled voice of Ricky and Ronnie yelling, 'Get your training gear on, we're going hill running.'

Everyone was pissed. Everyone, that is, but me. We hit the hills, and lads were puking up all over the place. I realised how drunk the players were by the abuse they were yelling.

'Ricky Stuart, you're a fucking prick.'

'Ricky you wanker.'

Everyone says things they regret when they've had a few beers, and I couldn't believe these lads – lads who'd grown up idolising Ricky – were mouthing off like that. But he took it in good fun – he knew they'd never say it to him sober. The day after, Ricky said to us, 'I did it for mental toughness . . . it'll serve us well for the year.'

My contract was up at the end of 2006. The Roosters said there would be a new contract if I wanted to stay, and I had no intention of leaving. But Clare falling pregnant in June changed all that.

I always planned to finish up in Super League, and the baby brought the plan forward a couple of years. When we sat down to weigh up all the pros and cons, being closer to our family swayed our decision. I didn't factor my disciplinary record into the move. I read several articles at the time suggesting I was being hounded out of the NRL, but that wasn't true. My bans were an irritation, but not a career-changer. It was the first year I'd gone with a new manager, Andrew Purcell, who I'd met years earlier when I was staying with Harvey Howard. I was walking past a restaurant one day when he rushed out, and said, 'I know what it's like being a foreigner abroad. If you want to catch up, give me a call.'

He wasn't a player-manager at the time. But we had a few beers in Coogee a few days later, and got on great. Managers are necessary evils, because it's hard to negotiate deals on your own, so I thought, 'If I'm going to pay someone, I might as well pay a mate', and went with Andrew. He's a wise old cat, and when I told him I was leaning towards going home, he flew to England to test the water.

Ricky was great. He told me that he'd take his Roosters hat off if ever I wanted a chat about my future. I told him why I wanted to go back to England, and he understood.

Going back to Leeds would have been the dream scenario. Denis Betts had done the same with Wigan-Auckland-Wigan, and I liked the idea of having one club Down Under, one back home. Admittedly, with a six-game spell at Bradford in between!

While Andrew was out there, I again phoned Gary Hetherington to see whether Leeds would be interested.

'You're not the player you once were,' he said.

I told him my manager was already getting four-year offers.

'Four years . . . I don't think you've got four years left in you,' he said.

I came off the phone feeling so deflated!

A couple of days later, the Leeds coach, Tony Smith, called me up. 'I know you've spoken to Gary, but if you want to negotiate I'd rather you did it with me directly,' he said.

In the end, Leeds didn't come to the table with a firm offer. It came down to Wigan and Warrington. They both offered me four-year deals. They both offered me similar terms.

I grew up disliking Wigan because they always won everything, so for that childish reason alone I was leaning towards Warrington straight away. The fact that Wigan were struggling against relegation at the time never came into it. When Brian Noble took over as coach and Stu Fielden joined, I knew they'd be fine. They'd already signed Trent Barrett for the following year, too, so I knew they would soon be on the rise.

But I was really impressed with Simon Moran's plans for Warrington. He told me they'd be spending up to the salary cap limit, and I spoke to Mike Forshaw, their conditioner, and he loved the club. Forsh' was actually quite instrumental in getting me over; as soon as I signed, though, he left to go to Wigan. But what eventually swung it was the memory of Andrew Johns's first game for the Wolves. I liked the Halliwell Jones and I loved the atmosphere inside. That game planted the seed in my mind – the more I thought about, the more I liked the idea of running out there.

I called Nobby and told him I was going to Warrington. He took it well.

'I hope you still pick me for Great Britain,' I joked.

'Don't worry about that,' he said. Nobby was as good as his word, and picked me in his squad for a mid-season, Tuesday night Test against New Zealand.

Nick Politis, the Roosters chairman, even agreed to let me have the weekend before off. But once our results started sliding, Ricky changed his mind. He picked me to play on the Sunday in Canberra – two days before the Test in England. 'You'll be alright,' he assured me.

My selection didn't make a difference, because we got stuffed. I flew out of Australia on the Sunday night, arrived Monday night in England, and played 24 hours later. It was a pretty tiring schedule, but at least I can say I played in two games, in two different hemispheres, in the space of three days. I bring that up every time I hear a player moaning about the congestion of fixtures over Easter.

Once I'd signed to go back home, I questioned whether I'd made the right decision. I loved my life in Coogee, the Aussie lifestyle, the Roosters. My exit didn't make me more determined to have a strong finish, but it definitely made me more aware that I didn't have too long left. We played Manly and lost, played Cronulla and won. Then we faced the Bulldogs in Round 20, and before we ran out Ricky gave us specific instructions. Nothing pleased Ricky more than beating the Dogs, his old team.

'That Corey Hughes is a cheeky bastard,' he said of their hooker. 'If he takes the piss, someone put one on his jaw.'

Sure enough, Ricky was right. Hughes was a niggling player, and I spotted him putting his knees in on the tackle. I waited for my chance. I tackled him, got to my feet. I was second-marker. Hughes got to his feet and shoved the first-marker in front of me.

A green light flashed. It's on.

I rushed at him, ready to clock him one, just like Ricky wanted. Trouble was, he hadn't seen me, and was bent over to play the ball. I had a brain explosion. Instead of just stopping, or waiting, or retreating, I carried on. And kneed him right in his head.

I thought it would start a brawl. I cocked my fist and braced myself for a flurry of punches from someone. But I looked around and everyone was looking at me with the same expression on their faces. An expression which said, 'What the fuck are you doing?'

I didn't know. The ref sent me straight off, and I had no complaints. I was so annoyed with myself. Hughes was fine, and why wouldn't he be? Seriously, it was the girliest knee ever. It was more of a shove with my knee, rather than a UFC strike into his head.

The media lapped it up. When I turned up for the judiciary, it was like something out of the OJ Simpson trial. There were camera crews everywhere. I pleaded guilty straight away, hoping they'd go easy on me. There were six games left and I was desperate to play for the Roosters at least once more. Willie

Mason, the Canterbury prop, even wrote and asked for leniency on my behalf, saying it would be a shame if I never got to play in the NRL again. I thought that was a great gesture, because I hadn't asked him to do it and we weren't really great mates. I sent him a text afterwards to thank him. The judiciary came back with their verdict. Seven matches. My Roosters career was over.

I was shattered. I couldn't believe that was it. I spent a couple of days beating myself up about how stupid I'd been, but the good thing about rugby league is that you're around your mates every day, so my mood soon picked up. I kept training with the boys for the final few weeks of that season. Ricky was the Kangaroos coach too, and would joke with Ronnie, 'Make sure you give him shit drills before the Tri-Nations.'

The Roosters won two of six without me, and finished 14th – the same position they were in after the Bulldogs game. With two weeks to go, Ricky was told he wouldn't be kept on at the end of the year. He broke the news to us after our penultimate game, against the Warriors in New Zealand. I was gutted for him.

Our last game of the season, against St George-Illawarra, was at the Sydney Cricket Ground.

I had a couple of beers before, while the boys were warming up, then I made my way down to the sheds. Before a match, we'd huddle in a circle just before we ran out. I had my suit on, but I joined in the huddle. I looked around at the boys, and it hit me.

I'm never going to be in this huddle again.

I started filling up. Once Craig Fitzgibbon, our captain, started talking, I couldn't hold back. I held onto them tight and cried my eyes out.

The boys went out and ended up getting beat 36-16. Amos Roberts scored two tries, Fitzy was terrific and Brett Finch played a blinder. But when Ricky hushed the players to present his final coach's Man of the Match prize, he picked me, because I showed so much emotion before the game.

The boys applauded, but Finchy was quick to take the piss.

'How unfair is that,' he said to me. 'I played my bollocks off out there – and you get an award for crying your eyes out!'

The Roosters fans gave me a final rendition of 'Mor-ley' at the leagues club. And in the days that followed, a lot of good people said a lot of nice things about me in the media, which was nice. I was invited onto *The Footy Show*, where Matthew Johns and Peter Sterling said I'd been great for the Australian competition. I was proud to play for the Roosters. They were my club and I loved them to bits, and they loved me, too. Even when I stepped out of line.

But of all the plaudits and praise I received, from legends and team-mates, the one that really hit me came from a fan. He was a Sydneysider who had settled in America. He approached me out of the blue when I was back in England and said, 'We've just had a baby, and I always promised I'd name my child after you.'

People had named cats and dogs after me at Leeds, but never kids.

'That's great,' I said. 'Thanks.'

'Only trouble is she's a girl. But we still named her after you.'

I felt obliged to say something nice. As if it was my fault the poor thing had been named Adrian.

'Well,' I said, clutching at straws. 'I suppose the girl in *Rocky* was called Adrian . . .'

'Oh no, we didn't call her Adrian. We named her Morley instead.'

Let me just say, on record, to the only girl in America named Morley: I am truly sorry.

The Tri-Nations was staged Down Under in 2006, which worked out great for me. Usually, I couldn't wait to get home at the end of the year to see my family and friends, but because I was leaving the Roosters I wanted to spend as much time as I could with my mates in Oz.

Brian Carney was over there, too. He'd spent the year at Newcastle and absolutely killed it. People say, 'Morley did well, Gaz Ellis has done well' – but they sometimes forget Brian was outstanding in his one year with the Knights. He was named Dally M Winger of the Year, and deservedly so. I spoke to him on the phone a few times and he seemed to be enjoying it, so I was as surprised as anyone that he decided not to stay in Australia with the Gold Coast Titans, as he'd planned.

I hadn't played in three months, because of my suspension and the Roosters missing out on the play-offs, but I used that time well. I trained hard, had a wrist operation to sort out a ligament problem and was good to go by the time the boys arrived. I waited at GB's team hotel in Manly to welcome them. I'd not seen Tez Newton for a few months, and he had a new mate in tow – Gaz Hock. Gaz followed him everywhere. I'd never met him before, but I got on well with him, and over a beer Gaz told me he'd looked up to me when he was a kid, which was nice. I liked the way he played the game. Full of fire – he really gave it to the Aussies and Kiwis during that series. Another player who announced himself on the international stage was James Roby. When I saw him arrive at the Manly hotel, I didn't know who he was. I'd never seen him before; the Super League was shown on TV late at night in Sydney, so I rarely caught any of the games. But as soon as we started training, I thought, 'This kid can play', and he backed that up in the Tests.

We played the Kiwis in our first match. Like the two previous years, they'd already played their two matches against the Aussies, and were battle-hardened. We were a bit scratchy, as you'd expect for a first game, but we improved and came home strong in the second half. We only just lost, 18-14, but in the end it didn't matter too much – the Kiwis were stripped of the two points for playing Nathan Fien. He didn't qualify through his grand-parents, as he'd said, and hadn't played in New Zealand for the three years he needed to qualify on residency grounds. There was even talk of awarding Britain the two competition points, but I was dead against that idea – it would have felt like charity. If anything, I thought docking the Kiwis the two points was harsh. It's not as if Fieny won the game single-handedly for them.

Our second Test was against the Kangaroos at Aussie Stadium, which was great for me because it was my home ground with the Roosters and I'd never had a chance to say farewell to the place.

In the build-up to the Test, Leon Pryce wrote a tour diary for the BBC and had a dig at the Aussies. He said Australia's 'not all it's made out to be. I'd much rather be back in Bradford. They can keep the country to themselves'. He then went on to have a pop at the Aussie people, saying they don't like the English. But the best bit was when he wrote, 'I'd rather be on Blackpool beach than Bondi beach'. The lads loved it. It was part comedy gold, part 'let's give a shot in the arm to the fans back home'.

There's a shred of truth in what Prycey said, too, because Bondi isn't even the best beach in Sydney. But I would say it is nicer than Blackpool!

The Aussies latched onto Leon's comments, and it erupted in the media. Over night, Leon became Public Enemy No.1. The Aussie journos are deliberately provocative – anything to cause a storm – and they're great at generating interest in the game. But the backlash to Leon's comments staggered me. A photographer snapped him leaving the team hotel behind me, and the headline in the *Daily Telegraph* the following day was 'Leon hides behind enforcer Morley'. There was footage on the TV news of Blackpool, in the pissing wet rain, run alongside footage of Bondi. We even had an undercover reporter, a good-looking girl, chatting up the lads outside the hotel to get an inside scoop. It was crazy. The marketing people at the ARL must have been loving it, because the Kangaroos were already guaranteed a place in the final, owing to their two wins over the Kiwis, so from their point of view it was dead rubber. By the time the Test rolled around, the intensity and anticipation was full on.

Brian Noble started with me on the bench, which I was disappointed about. I wasn't on the pitch when Willie Mason started throwing punches and dropped Stu Fielden. That was no slight on Stu's part – if you catch someone sweet in the right place, they'll go down, no matter who it is. There's no shame in that. It annoys me a bit that people still talk about that punch, because Stu was one of our best players for years. If anything, I wish people remembered the way Jamie Peacock waded in and nailed Mason with a flurry of punches. He stuck up for one of his mates, the same way Stu would have done had it been the other way around. Willie was lucky to stay on the pitch, especially when he cleaned out Sean Long off-the-ball a few minutes later. I was itching to get on and get involved. We were holding our own, but when Brian Carney went off injured and Greg Inglis scored, I thought, 'Not again'. It's so deflating to play well against the Aussies and lose. Longy was outstanding that day, and he created a try for Paul Wellens to draw us level at half-time. It was an awesome match. JP and Lee Gilmour scored to make it 18-12, but recent history had taught us to expect a strong finish from the Aussies.

It never came.

Gareth Raynor finished off a great move in the corner to make it 23-12 and seal the game for us. It was Great Britain's first win in Australia since 1992. Beating the Aussies is always special, and to do it in their own backyard, and at my old home stadium, made it even more special. That match is right up there in my top five from the 400-plus I've played in, easily.

Nobby was terrific, and he let us have a few beers the following day to celebrate. We lost to New Zealand a week later, but I felt the 34-4 scoreline flattered them. We weren't too far off.

After that game, a few of the senior players – JP, Longy, Terry and I – met with Nobby. We had to beat the Aussies the following week to reach the final. JP, our captain, said we needed to do everything right. No drinking, no short-cuts. 'We've got one chance left,' he said.

Longy was nodding in agreement. 'Definitely, definitely,' he said.

When we got to the airport to fly out from New Zealand the next day, Longy went straight to Duty Free, bought a bottle of Bailey's and poured it into his protein shaker. He fooled no one. I was playing cards with a couple of the reporters when he walked past. 'Eh up, Mozza,' he shouted. I could tell straight away he was drunk. I was already in a bad mood, because the Kiwis were in the airport at the same time as us, and a couple of their players were acting like pricks. I got on with most of them, but Steve Matai, the Manly centre, kept saying, 'Look at these doozers over here'. I didn't even know what a doozer was, still don't. But it sounded like 'loser', and the fact he was aiming it at us got under my skin. I went over to him and told him to shut up. There was a bit of pushing and shoving – I was ready to lamp him – but a few of the lads split us up, and he settled down. In fairness, I'm told Steve is a decent lad who just goes a bit mad when he's had a few to drink. Same as Longy.

He carried on during the trip back to Sydney, acting loud, acting the clown. Acting like a prick. I was sat next to Tez. Longy and Martin Gleeson – a terrific lad, if easily led – were in the seats in front of us.

Terry had injured Longy during a Super League game that year. He apologised at the start of the tour and everything seemed fine between them. But Longy didn't let it lie.

'Watch your cheekbone, Terry's about,' he kept shouting.

After a few minutes of it, Tez said to me, 'Moz, I've got to move or I'm gonna whack him.'

Longy's always been a free spirit, and a joker, but when there's booze involved he can go too far.

As soon as we got back to Manly, I popped home to see Clare, who was heavily pregnant. It wasn't until I got back to the hotel the next day that I found out Longy was going home.

My first instinct was, 'He's acted like a knob, he'll wake up, apologise, and we'll move on'. But he didn't. Nobby tried to talk him out of it, but he went through with his threat, and flew back to England. Longy claimed he was missing his missus and kids, but really, I'm convinced he just spat out his dummy after being bollocked for getting pissed on the flight from New Zealand.

His departure really pissed me off. He was our best half-back, he'd played great against the Aussies in our first meeting, and we needed to beat them again to reach the final. Walking out on your team is unacceptable. I'm sure he missed his family, like all the lads did. But I regarded playing for my country as the biggest accolade, the highest honour, and to treat it as cheaply as he did was out of line. My attitude was, 'Fuck him. We'll win without him.' But it wasn't enough. I'd known Longy most of my life, I'd been on holiday with him, but I was so angry with him that I avoided him for a while after that. We're fine now, but it took a few years for me to move on.

CHAPTER TWENTY-THREE
CHRIST

I first started talking to God when I was 15.

I'd been going to church, every Sunday, for as long as I could remember. My dad's a devout Catholic. I wasn't the only Adrian growing up in Salford, but I'm pretty sure I was the only one named after an English pope. I didn't mind going to church when I was younger, probably because I associated it with food! We'd all wake up and have porridge, then we'd go to church, and afterwards we'd have a cooked breakfast. But when I started playing rugby, my games clashed with morning mass, so I'd go in the evenings on my own.

It became a grind. Like homework, something I had to do. The prospect of going to church would loom over me all day. I'd play rugby, head home, have dinner, play with my mates – and then I'd have to head out to church on my own. None of my mates went. None of them had to go in to wash their face, brush their hair, clean their teeth, and make the five-minute walk to All Souls, near to Salford's old Willows ground. Chris stopped going to church when he was 16, and while my dad never put a time-frame on it, the common consensus was that, once we left school, it was our choice what we believed and what we did. When I got to 15, I thought I only had a few more months of it left.

No way am I going to spend my Sundays in here.

Then, one Sunday, for no reason, I started listening to the priest's words. I started taking in what was being said. It's not that I didn't believe in God until then. I was brought up a Catholic, in a Catholic household, Catholic church, Catholic school – religion was always there in the background.

But when I started listening, and when I started thinking about God, I got more and more into it – and much more out of it, too. I was fascinated by prayer. Still am, actually. I started to enjoy going to church. It was somewhere I could go and think about life, and the future, and all the other issues that lads that age think about. And I never felt like I was being judged. So when I left school, I carried on going to church – long after my dad expected me to. And I've been going ever since.

Most people are surprised when they find out I go to church. Team-mates throughout the years have raised an eyebrow. Until now, I've never publicised my faith. Reporters have asked me about it, but each time they've started that line of questioning I've quickly steered them off subject. I've never opened up about it.

It's not because I'm embarrassed about it. If someone wants to talk to me about religion I'll talk about it all day. But I'm not into people broadcasting their beliefs. I'm not bothered if someone is Muslim, Buddhist, Atheist or anything else. It's personal. Whatever they believe, I respect. And it irritates me when someone knocks on my door to try and persuade me to believe in something, or starts up a conversation over a pint and tries to tell me why there can't be a God because of a big bang. By the same token, I didn't want to be in a newspaper or on TV appearing to influence someone's beliefs.

The other reason I've shied away from discussing my faith publicly is I didn't want to be accused of being hypocritical. I could never claim to be holier than thou. I've done plenty of things that I regret. Had my scrapes, been arrested. Bought goods which may or may not have fallen off the back of a lorry. I'm not a bad lad, but I'm not whiter than white, either. If I appeared in the media claiming to be religious, it could come across as a hollow PR stunt, and I'm not into that.

For those reasons, I thought long and hard about including this chapter. But this is the story of my life, and my faith has played a big part in my life; for that reason alone, I decided to open up about it.

It's hard to explain why I believe in God. For me, it's not a case of wondering, 'How can there be a God?' but 'How can there not be a God?' Every time I look into my children's eyes, I'm convinced. They're little miracles. But even before they were born, I've always had that feeling that someone, a greater power, is out there. Looking out for me.

I don't want to say 'I go to church, I've had a great career'. Because many people don't believe in God and they have great careers, and I'm sure there are plenty who do have faith and fall on hard times. For me, that's not what God is about. I've had some testing times in my life. I've been in situations when I've worried for my career, and speaking to God has helped me cope with it. I once read a saying about God giving people the shoes to walk rocky paths – not smoothing the paths for them. That, for me, is so true. I feel that when I talk to God, he listens. He helps me. Since Terry Newton died, my faith has helped me a lot. Some people might think I'm daft for going to his grave and chatting to him, but I think he can hear me. I truly believe that.

One of my mates, Ian, called me up after his dad died. He was really struggling. He asked me about my faith, and so he came to church with me one Sunday, and then afterwards he had a brew and a good chat with Father Shaun, the Parish priest. It really helped him out.

With Facebook, Twitter and a million other things, some people think religion isn't relevant. But it is to me. It's made me happier, it's given my life a purpose and put it into perspective. It's also taught me to accept others and look for their strengths.

I've got mates who make their livings doing dodgy deals, doing what they can to get by. Buying and selling, wheeling and dealing. But they're not bad people and I don't judge them, just as I'd hate to be judged on the worst things I've ever done in my life.

Over the years, I've seen loads of pre-match superstitions and rituals. I've seen guys making themselves sick, psyching themselves up, putting on socks or tape in a particular way. For me, the best preparation for a game is to go to church first. It's good to have somewhere peaceful to go and have a place to think. It's easy to get bogged down by day-to-day jobs and stresses. For a sportsman, it can be hard to think of anything other than a game. Going to church gives me a chance to get away from that and think about my life more, and escape the pressures of life. A time to put things into perspective.

I like the Christian values, but I know some people will wonder how rugby players can be Christians and still whack each other. I can understand that. There are so many different types of people who play rugby league, so many different personalities. Blokes from different backgrounds, different countries. But there's one quality that binds them – if you play rugby league for a living, you've got to have a bit of a nasty streak. You just do.

A lot of lads, when they're growing up, love wrestling each other. Even though they know they might get hurt, they love that contest, that contact, that feeling of getting one over your opponent. Rugby league players are like that. They've just never grown up. They get a buzz from hurting someone, from knocking each other down. But you don't want to injure them – injuries are an occupational hazard. Hurt them yes, injure them? Definitely not.

Earlier in my career, I tackled Rob Smyth, the Wigan winger, and felt his knee go under my body weight. He needed a complete reconstruction and I felt terrible for him. But I didn't mean it, and I'd like to think he didn't hold it against me, just like I've never held a grudge against anyone who's injured me. People may be surprised just how many rugby league players are

Christians. In Sydney, I went to church at St Bridgette's in Coogee. I pointed it out to Brett Hodgson when we trained over there in early 2012, and he had no idea I was a Catholic. He is, too. We had a good chat about our faith. I also spoke to Ryan Atkins, another Warrington team-mate, before he planned to convert to Catholicism.

Matt King is a Christian, and until he left for South Sydney we'd go to church together many Sundays. I'm not as devout as many of the Islander boys, and credit to them.

By the same token, there are plenty of blokes who think it's all rubbish. I know that, as convinced as I am that there is a God, the next man may be equally convinced there isn't. That once you're dead, that's it. You're worm food. That's fine by me, each to their own.

There's no logic to faith. I've deliberately not read up on it too much, because if you're leaning towards faith you might pick a book that supports that opinion, and if you don't believe it, you'll read *The God Delusion* and it'll strengthen your Atheist views.

I believe in God for my own reasons, and I'm thankful to him.

CHAPTER TWENTY-FOUR
GUESS WHO'S BACK

My first impression of Warrington was one of an impressive and ambitious set-up. Their first impression of me must have been of a lazy sod who slept all day.

Days after arriving at the club, we were whisked away to Lanzarote for a warm-weather training camp. With a few new signings, Paul Cullen arranged a night for the lads to have a few beers and get to know each other. But I'd made a promise to myself not to drink. I realised my signing had generated a lot of hype and raised hopes for the forthcoming year, and I wanted to make a good impression on my new team-mates. Plus, Clare was due to give birth within a month – as unlikely as it was, I knew I could have got the call any minute to head home. Knowing my luck, that call would come after my eighth pint! She was already stressing because I'd left her in a home with little furniture and no fridge (we kept milk on the step outside to keep cold) while we waited for a container with our belongings to arrive from Australia.

So while the other boys headed to the bar, I stayed in, playing poker with two or three of the lads. And I was doing well, too. Martin Gleeson wasn't drinking, either. Midway through the night, he took some tablets out of his pocket.

'What are they?' I asked.

'Sleeping tablets. D'you want one?'

'Yeah alright.'

I'd never been hugely into them. They're readily available in most dressing rooms after night-games, simply because it can be hard to get to sleep with the adrenaline flowing. I never had a problem, though. I always slept well. But we weren't due to train until 2pm the following day, so I thought I'd have a good lie-in with a little help from the pills. Gleese took two, and so I did, thinking they would take effect within half an hour and I could go off to bed for a nice, early night, ready to rip into training the following day.

Two minutes later, I was seeing double. My mind was hazy. I abandoned my poker chips and just about made it to my bed, before collapsing on top, fully clothed.

I was shaken awake.

'Moz, get up,' the voice said. 'Training's in 10 minutes.'

I looked at my watch and it was 1.45pm! I couldn't believe it. The pills would have knocked out a horse.

I managed to dress myself and stumbled downstairs. I'd had no breakfast, no lunch, nothing to eat.

We started with a weights session, and I tried to go through the motions, but I couldn't concentrate. I just wanted to go back to bed. Cull, realising he'd let the lads have a few beers the previous night, then took us for a five-a-side football game – part team-building, part training. On the way over, I'd told a few of the lads how I used to play football as a kid, and I was pretty good. Which only made my feeble efforts on the pitch even more embarrassing. My eye-foot reaction was like a satellite link-up. The ball would whizz past me, and half a second later I'd try and kick it! Thankfully, Cull saw the funny side.

I recovered a couple of days later, and I trained pretty well for the rest of the camp. I was still in the mind-set of wanting to make a good impression. The Warrington fans were terrific. The short-term signing of Andrew Johns the year before had shown them that the club had real ambition, and I think they saw my arrival as further confirmation of that. For years, they'd seen a lot of the best players go to St Helens, Wigan, Leeds or Bradford. But not any more. They were full of excitement, and I was too.

We played Wigan in our first game, at their place, and I was desperate to make a big impact. They'd recruited well in the off-season, particularly with Trent Barrett joining, and the fact I'd chosen Warrington over them made me even more determined to have a good game. The last thing I wanted was any of the Wiganers thinking, 'I'm glad we didn't get him.'

We led the first-half 12-2, but I just didn't feel comfortable. I did okay, I carried the ball well, I didn't drop off any tackles. But I didn't smash anyone, either. And Warrington hadn't signed me to be a functional forward. As we went in to the dressing room at half-time, two thoughts crossed my mind. Firstly, I was sat in the same spot where I sat when I'd been sent off in the Test match in 2003. And secondly, I was going to clean someone out.

This time the journos up there in the press box, and the commentators perched in their seats, will be talking about one of my legal hits on this pitch.

Early in the second half, I saw Eamon O'Carroll lining up to take a carry. Short, compact, he was easy-pickings. He took the pass and I sprinted out at him, standing strong, ready to knock him flying. But at the last minute he jinked – when, by the way, did props learn to step? – and I hit the top of his head flush on my cheekbone. Instantly, I heard the noise of bone gnawing together inside my mouth, followed by a sharp, screaming pain down the side of my face.

I ran back into the line on autopilot, as every rugby league player is bred to do, and even made a couple of tackles. But the physio had seen me struggling and took me off.

The lads ended up winning 16-10 and, as I held an ice-pack to the side of my face in the dressing room, they celebrated around me. But I didn't feel like celebrating. I knew I'd broken my cheekbone and, to make it worse, my eye resembled a purple water bomb. The day later, I went to see a specialist who popped the bone back into place, but I knew I would be out for a few weeks to allow the bone to knit together. I was pissed off like you wouldn't believe. One game back and I was out.

In a way it worked out well because a week later Leo was born, so it gave me some time off with him while I recovered. But I couldn't wait to get back out there and play. I did a lot of extra training with Paul Darbyshire, the conditioner – his favourite was stair-running at the Halliwell Jones – to make sure I was up to speed once the doctor gave me the nod. I travelled with the squad to Perpignan as 18th man, which was great because it was my first experience of the Catalan Dragons and I loved any excuse to go to the south of France. I've always loved it down there, since we used to go camping as kids.

I returned to face Hull KR, only to break my cheekbone again on Paul Johnson's big horse head, and after another lay-off I returned to the side for a match at Bradford, which was perfect for me, because I'd won a Grand Final with them 18 months earlier and two of my best mates – Iestyn Harris and Terry Newton – were there. I gave away three penalties from being over-excited – one of them was a deliberate high tackle on Tez – and did okay.

We smashed my hometown club Salford a week later in the unlikely setting of Cardiff's Millennium Stadium – I was a fan of the Magic Weekend concept, despite its modest success – and I slowly began finding my feet, even winning a Player of the Month award. Without excelling against the big sides, we were cruising along pretty well with some decent results.

During the season, injuries had really taken their toll – I hate using that as an excuse, but it was true. We lost some matches – against Wakefield, Harlequins and Catalans – which we should have done better in. Realistically, we needed to beat Saints to keep alive our hopes of reaching the play-offs. It was a really frustrating game. I knew Warrington had an awful record there, and we were only down 18-10 at half-time. The frustration got the better of me, and during the second half I whacked Paul Clough high. I didn't think it was too bad, but Ashley Klein sent me off. It was my first – and to date, my only – red card since returning to Super League. When I was given my marching orders, the Saints player, Jon Wilkin, started waving at me in a child-like 'bye bye' way. It was poor form on his part. I was so angry, I was tempted to run up to him and smash him. But I thought the better of it, turned, and jogged off the pitch. Keiron Cunningham patted me on the back as I ran past him. I thought that was a lesson, right there, in class.

I went to the judiciary and got a one-game ban, ruling me out of the last match against Salford. The lads won without me, but it didn't matter. We missed out on the play-offs, which I was gutted about. I genuinely thought we had a chance of competing for silverware, but that season showed we were still behind St Helens, Leeds, and Bradford, who beat us in all of our meetings. Coupled with that, I hadn't been thrilled with my own form. I wanted to set Super League on fire, I knew I'd returned with a big reputation, and for a spell I even began doubting my ability. My dad said, 'Remember your first season in the NRL. That didn't go as well as you'd hoped.'

And he was right.

Mid-way through the season, the new Great Britain coach, Tony Smith, phoned me up. He called me and told me he was resting a few senior players – including skipper Jamie Peacock – for the mid-season Test against France. He'd planned to rest me, too. But I'd missed 10 weeks with my broken cheekbone and I told him I'd love to play. He agreed.

The day later, he phoned back.

'Adrian, I'd like you to captain the side,' he said. I was elated. I phoned my mum and dad, and my brothers. They were all happy for me. It was a great honour, a great feeling. I felt eight feet tall.

A couple of days later, Chris sent me a text.

'Get the *Daily Star*.'

I picked a copy up on the way to training, expecting a nice article. I was wrong. Garry Schofield had done a piece saying I wouldn't have been in his 17, and then he questioned my leadership qualities.

I was livid. I can take criticism, and if he was questioning my form I wouldn't have minded. But questioning my leadership? I'd played with him when I was 17 or 18. How did he know what kind of leader I was?

'You prick,' I thought.

What really irritated me was the fact I'd defended Schoey so many times over the years. When I came back for Test matches, many of the Leeds lads used to tell me how pissed off they were with him, for his criticisms in the media. Even people in Australia slagged him off for being a 'cat' – Aussies like using that word. It basically means the same as 'scaredy cat' – and I always, always, told them Schoey was a belting bloke.

He was an incredible No.6, one of the best that this country has ever produced, and I was proud to have played alongside him. I wouldn't let anyone say anything bad about him. So when he turned his guns on me, it made my blood boil. He was an ex-team-mate, and I thought he was a mate.

It was the best week of my life, and to be brought down to earth by a person I'd always respected was gutting. I scored a try in the Test and played pretty well, and I was tempted to do an Andy Farrell and thank 'big fat Garry Schofield' in the media afterwards, but I didn't.

He had another pop at me the following year, during the World Cup, but it didn't bother me. By that point I'd lost all respect for him as a bloke. I've come to realise that's his game. He likes being colourful and controversial. Good luck to him, if that's what he wants to do. I'm still proud to have played with him, because he was a phenomenal player. I'd still say hello to him if he walked into the same room as me, but that's it for me. And I know a lot of players feel the same way.

Being in the Great Britain squad was my first involvement with Tony as a coach. I liked his approach. As a coach, he ticks most boxes, and I like his ethos of trying to improve players as people, too. But I wasn't a huge fan of his decision to call up Maurie Fa'asavalu. Maurie was born and raised in Samoa. He's a terrific fella, but three or four years living in England did not make him English, in my view. Tony explained it was an exceptional case because he'd never played rugby league anywhere else, and I understood his reasoning. It never really sat comfortably with me, but he was the coach. I just got on with my job.

Before the series, I played in a Northern Union match against the All Golds – a commemorative game to mark a century since the first international tour. Ben Westwood was in the squad and was due to play for us. But he was rooming with Gleese . . . and he didn't learn from my mistake! Two nights before the game, he took one of Gleese's sleeping pills and was completely zonked. He came down for breakfast the following morning and fell over a couple who were eating breakfast! He was full of apologies.

Tony Smith heard about it, and he went to see Benny and told him he had to prove his fitness. We were only doing basic passing drills, but Benny was really sloppy – I felt sorry for him, because I knew exactly what he was going through. Tony said, 'I can't play you,' so Sam Burgess got his chance against the All Golds, blitzed it, and kept his place in the side for the first Test against New Zealand, at Huddersfield.

Sam put on some monster hits in that game. It was one of the best debuts I'd seen by anyone, not just from an 18-year-old. He was a big boy, tough, and he could play. On top of that, he was grounded, a great lad.

We got the win, and I immediately sensed the series could be ours. I'd never won anything with Great Britain, and I'd been playing a decade. I'd been desperate for success. When it came, it came easier than I expected, with the Kiwis folding in the second Test at Hull. To win a series felt amazing, and it was even better to do it in style.

Before the last Test at Wigan, Tony pulled me to one side and asked, 'It's dead rubber, the series is won. Do you want to play?'

'Damn right,' I said. 'I want to finish the job.'

We completed the series whitewash. And what made it feel even more special was that it was the last as Great Britain, before the team's switch to the England name. It felt good to put the jersey to rest with a win.

I didn't like the decision to ditch the Great Britain name. When I hear England, I think of the football, cricket and rugby union sides. Apart from the Olympics every four years, Great Britain belonged to rugby league. That's how I saw it, anyway.

I'm sure, over the years that mentality will change, but I grew up cheering for Great Britain. Even the jersey's iconic. When I hear 'Great Britain', I picture Jonathan Davies scoring in the corner at Wembley, Ellery Hanley leading the team out, Henderson Gill doing 'a bit of a boogey'. And no image is more distinctive than the TV footage of Mike Gregory, blond locks flowing, racing towards the line in a Test match in Sydney, in 1988.

I'd seen Greg when the Lions held a dinner for him before our series against the Kiwis. By that point, motor neurone disease had really taken a grip of him. I kissed his head and cuddled him. The first thing he said was, 'How's your kid?'

They were at St Helens together, and got on great. That, for me, was the measure of the man he was. There he was, confined to a wheelchair, his body failing him, and his first thought was for my brother. He was so thin and weak, yet there wasn't a shred of self-pity about him. He was still thinking of others, and he was still smiling. That same, toothy, lob-sided smile.

I was devastated when he died a few weeks later. Motor neurone disease would later also take the life of Paul Darbyshire, my conditioner at Warrington. It was such a tragedy to lose two great, great men to such a horrible disease.

CHAPTER TWENTY-FIVE
BANGED UP ABROAD

As soon as I read the text message I began panicking.

'What have you been arrested for? It's all over the news.'

I was in Lanzarote with the rest of the Warrington team for our pre-season training camp. It was the same spot we'd been to the year before. Only this time, on our designated night on the drink, I decided I'd have a few beers with the rest of the lads – there was no way I was going to risk the episode with the sleepers again! Matt King and Michael Monaghan had joined the club that season; if there's a better way to break down those new-boy boundaries than over a few beers, I've yet to find it.

So on our one, designated drinking night, we had a few scoops in the bar at the complex, and had a good time. Too good, actually. So we decided to carry it on in the nearby town, Puerto del Carmen. We were all a bit giddy. We were asked to leave the first bar we were in, for clowning around. Someone suggested we do what we were told, before the police arrived and arrested us.

That planted the seed in my drunken head.

'Imagine us in a Mexican stand-off. The Warrington players and a group of us against a few bushy-'tached coppers.'

That thought was bouncing around my mind as I walked outside, and spotted a parked car. Without thinking, I rolled across the bonnet, and shot up onto my feet, clutching an imaginary gun and telling the lads to put their hands up. It was the best Starsky and Hutch impression I could manage after eight San Miguels. The lads were in stitches. And when a taxi driver nearby started mouthing Spanish obscenities at me, it only made them laugh even more.

We went into the next bar and got back on it. A few minutes later, I saw the driver coming down the street towards us – with two policemen with him. We left our pints and legged it. As soon as they saw us, the coppers ran after us. Lee Briers and Rob Parker got caught, but their Spanish was as bad as the coppers' English, so they let it go. And when we all met up back at the complex, we had a giggle about it.

The following day, Paul Cullen asked me, Jon Clarke, Monners and Kingy for a chat. It's not unusual for coaches to use a small group of senior players as a sounding board.

'Boys, this is serious,' he said. 'The police are on their way. It seems there was an incident last night. I know it won't be any of you in this room, but someone in the team has messed up.'

Before he could say any more, I interrupted.

'Cull,' I said.

He looked my way, waiting – presumably – for me to say I knew about it, or I'd seen what happened. 'It was me who screwed up.'

He looked crushed. A week earlier, before flying out, he'd asked me to be the team captain – an offer I'd enthusiastically accepted. It was a huge honour, and really flattering that he felt I was the right man to lead his team.

I felt awful. Cull had given me the captaincy and how had I repaid him? By kicking him in the balls. I didn't know what to say to him, he looked so dejected.

'Moz I can't tell you how disappointed I am,' he said.

'I'm really sorry,' I said. 'I'll sort it out, I'll pay whatever they want.'

I just wanted the problem to go away, so I could begin making it up to Cull. I'd only rolled across a car bonnet after a few beers, but it was unacceptable. I didn't want to be one of those 'Do as I say, not as I do' captains – I wanted to lead by example. And what example had I set? I just wanted to pay the fine, explain what happened, and make the problem go away as quickly as possible. But when the police arrived, they cuffed me, threw me in the back of a van and drove me away.

'They're teaching me a lesson. Trying to shit me up. Why else would they use handcuffs? Unless they'd heard of my legger from the coppers in Yorkshire in 2003, which was unlikely.'

We got to the station, where they booked me in.

One of the coppers could speak waiter-standard English.

'We're taking your phone,' he said. 'Do you want to call anyone first?'

A dilemma. I'd called Clare every night since I'd been over. If I called her and told her I'd been arrested she'd go mad at me. But if I didn't call her and she couldn't get hold of me, she'd also go mad at me.

'No, it's alright,' I said, expecting to be kept an hour or two. Three at the max.

The cell was freezing and damp. And to make it worse, someone had written on the ceiling with mud. Only, there was no mud in there and prisoners weren't allowed shoes.

It dawned on me that the mud on the ceiling must be a previous occupant's own shit. And seeing the Spanish equivalent of 'Jose was here' written out in shit was a sobering thought.

I was desperate to get out of there. But the afternoon rolled into the evening and, after a few hours, I realised I was in for the night.

The morning after, they took me out and put me in an interview room. When they handcuffed me to a radiator, I half-expected one of the coppers to whisk off his hat and reveal himself as the MTV fella who tells celebrities they've been Punk'd. But I wasn't a celebrity, certainly not in Spain, and the seriousness of the coppers' faces told me they were taking it very seriously.

I went through what I'd done in my mind. Rolled over a car bonnet . . . that was it!

The lead policeman, the one who spoke English, told me I'd need to pay 800 euros to repair the car. Which was rubbish, because I can't imagine I left a dent. And even if I had, how much did it cost to repair a bonnet? The car itself couldn't have cost much more.

'Right, no problems. I'll pay it,' I said. I couldn't stand the thought of going back to the cell, and the cold bed, and the shit on the ceiling.

'There's also a fine for criminal damage,' he said.

'How much?'

'40 euros.'

Finally, a break. I'd expected them to take me to the cleaners.

'No problem, I'll pay it now.'

'It's 40 euros a day. For 30 days.'

I was always pretty good at maths. It only took me a few seconds to work out that 40 times 10 is 400. Times three and that's . . .

'1,200 euros,' the policeman interrupted.

I bit my tongue. I wanted to scream out, 'You robbing Spanish bastard!' – it was hardly a coincidence the damage and the fine came to a round two-grand. But they had me by the balls. There was nothing I could do.

'And you must pay before you can leave the island.'

I signed the paperwork and hurried out of the police station. When I saw Cull waiting for me, I ran up to him and felt like hugging him. I apologised again for what I'd done.

I turned my phone on. I had a load of missed calls and texts from Clare, so I phoned her straight away and told her I'd messed up.

'Adrian, you dickhead,' she said. She seemed more upset about the fine.

I trained with the lads that afternoon. Before the session, I gathered them together.

'What I did was unacceptable,' I said. 'And I'm going to make it up to you.'

A few of them started giggling. I knew something was up. Then from nowhere, someone threw a black-and-white-striped top – like a convict's uniform – in my direction, and they all started laughing.

Cull then addressed the lads.

'We want this to stay in-house,' he said. He'd told me in the cab he'd spoken to the club's bosses about me, and they were happy for him to handle it. He'd fought my corner, and told them I'd already been stung in the pocket, so they agreed to fine me two grand, and suspend it.

'We don't want this getting out – please keep it to yourselves,' he told the players.

The club had considered releasing a statement to the press, but had decided against it, which was a massive relief. I was already embarrassed about it, the last thing I needed was everyone else knowing. And so, that evening, when my phoned buzzed in my pocket, and I read the text from Terry Newton, I was stunned.

How the fuck is it in the news? How's it got out that I've been arrested?

I phoned him straight away.

'Tez, what've you heard? What are people saying about me,' I said.

'Who is it?' he asked. I was confused.

'You just texted to ask why I had been arrested.'

Apparently, my team-mate Paul Rauhihi had told his missus what had happened. She'd then told Glenn Morrison's wife Robyn, who'd told Glenn, who'd told some of his Bradford team-mates, including Terry. Somewhere along the Chinese whisper chain, my name had been lost. All Tez and the rest of the Bulls players knew was that it was one of the Warrington lads.

'I fuckin' knew it was you,' Tez said. 'I thought you'd grown up, you dickhead.'

He had called my bluff, and I'd given the game away!

Thankfully, the story had died before I returned, and the lads were terrific in keeping it to themselves. So much so, that – a few weeks later – when we went out for dinner with Kingy and his missus, Clare mentioned it during the conversation.

Kirsten – Kingy's wife – didn't know anything about it.

'Did Matt not tell you?' Clare asked her.

Kingy looked at me, smiled, and held out his fist for me to punch.

'Solid to the cause, Moz', he said. 'I'm going to get in trouble with the missus now'.

We got off to a solid, if unspectacular, start to the season. My first game as captain was against Hull FC, and I remember it well because my old Roosters team-mate Peter Cusack led the opposition out. It was a nice moment. We won the game 32-20 and, though we lost to St Helens, we pulled off some good results, beating Catalan, Hull KR and Wigan to climb to second in the ladder. By the end of March, we'd played eight, won six.

Then it all went wrong.

Harlequins – the daft name that London had taken – narrowly beat us 8-6. We told ourselves it was a blip, but a shock defeat can easily create nervousness. Especially when you're not sure why things had gone wrong in the first place. We were cagey, edgy. We lost to Wakefield a week later – we didn't even score a try – and then lost four of our next five matches. Those defeats weren't to any old mugs – Leeds, St Helens and Wigan – but the club had spent cash to compete with those sides, to break up the big-four monopoly, and losing to them just put under sharper focus the fact that we weren't there yet.

Our next game was at home to Castleford. A few days before it, I had a meeting with Cull – we'd frequently have captain-coach chats – and he told me that if we got beat by Cas' he was a goner.

At the time, I was struggling with a knee injury. The physio told me to take a couple of weeks off, but I told him I was going to play. I needed to.

It was my first season as captain and the first time I'd had such a hard period. I tried to remain upbeat and positive and say the right things; I kept what Cull had told me to myself. We scored a few points against Cas', too, but our defence was shocking that day. We were in an arm-wrestle when Luke Dorn plucked the ball out of the air, intercepting one of our attacks, and set off towards our line. I saw it in slow motion, and the reaction to that was huge. I was crest-fallen. I knew there was no way back from that. I knew Cull was gone.

In the changing room immediately afterwards, no one said a word. Cull wasn't there. I wondered whether, as captain, I should say anything. But there was nothing to say. I knew what was coming. A few minutes later, Cull came in. All the lads turned to face him.

'Boys, I've just had a meeting with the board,' he said. 'That's it. I'm gone.'

That was it. I felt fucking horrible. All the lads did. We weren't performing as a team, and because of us, a bloke we all liked and respected had just lost his job.

I remember Ricky Stuart saying to me, 'There are two types of coaches. Those who have just been sacked and those who are waiting to be sacked'. Anyone going into coaching knows that. It's a harsh, cruel, results-based business. When things are going wrong, the clubs want to make changes and they can't change the playing personnel. I'd been at clubs before when coaches had been sacked, and even when they're not likes mates, even if they're not your cup of tea, they're still people losing their jobs. And I had a lot of time for Cull. He's got integrity, and I like that.

Jimmy Lowes stepped up from the assistant's role, and everyone bucked up their ideas. It wasn't because of anything Jimmy changed; more because of the way we all felt about Cull being sacked. The year before, we'd had an horrendous run of bad luck with injuries. This year, we'd been okay. We had no excuses.

A few players were struggling to find their feet, including Kingy. While Chris Hicks had come in and done terrific – he was my type of winger, eight out of 10 every week – Kingy just couldn't catch a break. He worked really hard, but when your confidence takes a dip it can be tough. It didn't help that my old mate Schoey branded him the worst signing in Super League history – what a tool that made him look like. Kingy lived near me at Salford Quays and I told him, 'Sydney didn't go well for me at first, keep with it.'

Jimmy told us he wanted us to play with smiles on our faces. And for a time, it worked. We won seven of our next eight games, including beating Leeds 22-12. They had been trampling over everyone that year. We should have beaten Saints, too, a week later; we were level at the break and six points ahead a few minutes later. But they just had that mental edge on us, and they levelled before Sean Long popped over the winning drop-goal. I was shattered afterwards.

That Saints game took a lot out of us. Everyone said the right things and did the right things in training, but we weren't the same. Saints took more than two points off us that day.

We lost all of our next three games, against sides we should have beaten. Hull KR, Castleford, Huddersfield, all decent sides, but we felt before that run we had the measure on them.

It was my first year as captain, and it was a stiff learning curve. I felt an obligation to speak – I thought back to how Brad Fittler handled tough runs, and what Andy Farrell did after Great Britain had lost a Test match. But I wasn't like them. At least, not yet. I was confident with what I could do on the field, but I wasn't a confident, natural speaker like they were. Cull always said he wanted me because I led by my actions, and not my words; I was quite shy, when I was sober. And I was grateful that other lads in the team stepped up. You don't need a 'C' next to your name to be a leader, and Mick Monaghan and Briersy were terrific. We made the play-offs quite comfortably but our form was shocking, and one thing I knew from my time in Australia was that momentum was far more important in finals football than a team's league position. I'd played in every round that year and we did the worst thing possible – we limped into the play-offs. Catalan whacked us 46-8 in the first round. Our season was over.

Our first duty under the new 'England' banner was the 2008 World Cup. As Great Britain, we'd whitewashed the Kiwis the previous year and we travelled over to Australia under pressure. There were real hopes we could cause an upset, and no one had higher hopes than me. As soon as lads became available, when their teams were knocked out of the play-offs, we started training with England. Our first game was in Townsville, in northern Queensland, and to help us acclimatise to the hot and humid conditions we rolled exercise-bikes into saunas and trained there. No stone was left unturned. Tony Smith said publicly that we were the best prepared team in the tournament, and I could believe it. We flew out there in first-class (the Irish boys were at the back, in economy). We were really well looked after.

England were placed in a 'super group' with Australia, New Zealand and Papua New Guinea. Three teams qualified for the semi-finals, so we knew that if we beat PNG, there was a good chance of us going through. The format came in for a bit of stick, but I liked it; it created competitive matches in the other two groups and, while PNG got the rough end of the stick, they should have been flattered that they were considered the fourth-best team in the world.

And credit to them, they gave us a huge scare in our opening game. They were always going to give it to us. Rugby league is massive in PNG, and with plenty of their fans cheering them on they were as fired up as anyone, and were even ahead at half-time. Enthusiasm can take you a long way in rugby league, but so often not until the 80th minute. Usually, the full-time athletes come out on top. It's just the way it is.

Still, we weren't exactly bouncing off the walls with our 32-22 win. We had to be at our absolute best to beat the Aussies, and we weren't. Worse still, they were white-hot. They'd thrashed the Kiwis in the opening round, and they hammered us in Melbourne, too. Some of their backs were phenomenal. Billy Slater and Greg Inglis each scored hat-tricks but, as good as they were, we were embarrassed with our own performances. Those kind of players were good enough without us helping them out. I don't know whether the big stage got to us, or whether we struggled to handle the expectations, but we just didn't perform. We improved a week later against the Kiwis and still lost; they beat us in the semi-finals the following week, too. Both those matches were competitive – we lost both by two scores – and we bowed out to the eventual tournament winners, New Zealand, so it probably wasn't the disaster everyone seemed to suggest. But that provided little comfort. I was really disappointed with the way we performed, and our results. In the public post-mortem that followed some players blamed a split between the St Helens and Leeds players. Those two clubs had provided the bulk of the squad, and rightly so because they'd both been terrific that year. Apparently, there was a divide between them in the camp, which was to blame for our poor World Cup.

For me, that was bullshit. As long as I'd been involved in representative teams, players tend to stick with their own club-mates. I'm nomadic, I've got mates at every club, but other players can be shy about mingling with those from different teams. During that World Cup, there were times when the Saints lads were at the front of the bus, the Leeds boys at the back. It didn't mean they didn't like each other. And it didn't mean there was a problem. It was an excuse, and a pretty lame one at that. I'd have much preferred it if players had put their hand up and admitted they hadn't performed, rather than put the blame elsewhere.

TRIBUTE: BY MATT KING (FORMER WARRINGTON TEAM-MATE)

S itting in my seat at the MEN Arena in Manchester, I looked over at Adrian Morley stood in the corridor a few metres away. Singing. Dancing. Throwing his bulging arms around so wildly it was a miracle no one was seriously hurt.

Is this guy for real?

I'd arrived in England days earlier to take up my contract with Warrington. When he'd invited me to a Take That concert I thought it was a wind-up. A gee-up. Some kind of 'let's trick the new bloke' initiation I had to go through. But no.

Moz, his girlfriend, Clare, and quite a few of the other players and their partners were there, all enjoying watching and listening to England's favourite grown-up boy band. And leading the way was Moz, giving it his all, throwing out his moves, belting out *Relight My Fire* on cue.

Is this the same player who terrorised the NRL?

When I first saw Moz play, back when I was a reserve-grader at Melbourne and he was at the Roosters, I thought he was a madman. Since moving Down Under, he'd wasted no time in compiling an impressive highlights reel of bashing blokes, with the ball or without.

And when I came into first-grade and played against the Roosters for the first time, I don't mind admitting I was frightened. The Roosters had such a dominant and aggressive pack, led by Moz. Throw in the fact that one of my heroes, Brad Fittler, was their stand-off and it made for quite a daunting experience.

It had been such a long time since an English bloke had come over to the NRL and made the same kind of impact as Moz, so he became an easy villain. Whenever he got banned, it was never a case of 'Morley's been suspended', more like 'It's that bloody mad Englishman again!'

During my first Origin camp, I was chilling out with Craig Fitzgibbon, mucking around on our guitars, trying to master the chord progression of *Relight my Fire* (that's a joke), when Fitzy took a call from Moz.

When he'd finished, I asked him what Moz was like; he couldn't speak highly enough of him. Like many fans, I imagine, I had an impression in my mind of what Moz must be like, and it was the complete opposite of the bloke who Fitzy described.

When I arrived at Warrington in 2008, I discovered for myself that Moz the player is a complete contradiction to Moz the person. As a prop he is aggressive and nasty and doesn't give an inch. As a bloke, he couldn't be more different.

It's no secret it took me longer to settle into England, and Super League, than I anticipated. But Moz, and Clare, his parents Leo and Mary, his brothers, his mates . . . they couldn't do enough for my wife, Kirsten, and I. He'd invite us around for dinner and – when I found out he's a Catholic, like me – I'd see him at church as well. It was nice to have that connection with him.

He's an incredible bloke, full of life and generosity, and as a player I don't hesitate to say he's the best front-rower I've ever played with. And I've played with some awesome props with Melbourne, New South Wales, Australia and now at Souths.

With age, he's become wiser, more level-headed. But he still makes a big impact in matches, and that was best illustrated during my final year with the Wolves. It was September, and Moz hadn't played for several weeks because of an eye injury. He had double-vision, and just couldn't get the problem sorted out so he could come back. Some people were actually questioning whether he'd come back at all.

He finally found a surgeon who agreed to operate. It just so happened that we had a game against Wigan a couple of days before his surgery; once Moz was told the injury could not get any worse, he put his hand up to play. Only, he didn't just play, he had a stormer – he was inspirational, setting the tone with his aggression and enthusiasm, even though he hadn't played in several weeks.

That's what makes Moz the inspiration he is – it's not the words he speaks, but his actions on and off the pitch.

CHAPTER TWENTY-SIX
THE FANNY'S
IN THE CUP

As I walked up the Wembley steps, I laughed to myself.

The night before, I'd wondered what I'd think about if I got this chance to lift the Challenge Cup. Maybe I'd think about my hero, Ellery Hanley, doing the same thing at the old place years earlier in those cup finals I'd watched on TV as a kid. Maybe I'd reflect on the years that had passed since I'd won the cup with Leeds a decade earlier. Or maybe think of all of those Warrington fans who had never seen their team lift a piece of silverware.

It was a proud moment. But as I dragged my tired legs up the steps, as I led my team towards a trophy that had eluded Warrington for 35 years, all I could think about was something Doug Laughton used to say before Challenge Cup matches at Leeds.

'Lads, just remember,' he'd say. 'The fanny's in the cup.'

I'm not sure whether he meant the feeling was like sex, or that winning the cup would land us plenty of girls, or both. But as I walked towards the silverware, shaking hands with the various dignitaries on the way, aware the BBC cameras were beaming my image to millions of people, for some stupid reason I couldn't get his words out of my head.

'The fanny's in the cup.'

For a team that won the Challenge Cup in 2009, we couldn't have made a worse start.

We didn't go to Lanzarote for pre-season. Instead, we went to Lilleshall, a little village in Shropshire. I'm sure it's a lovely place. But in January, in the mud, in the freezing cold, it was nowhere near as enjoyable as a trip abroad. All the lads took the piss out of me, of course, saying it was my fault we'd stayed home because I'd been arrested the year before! It was Jimmy Lowes's first pre-season and he took it all back to basics. Jimmy's an intense, mean-looking fella, but he has a lighter side, too. He even organised a *Britain's Got Talent*-style event for the squad (for the record, the props – myself, Gaz Carvell, Paul Wood and Mike Cooper – impersonated Take That, and won. Not the biggest accolade on my CV, but still).

We had St Helens first up. Our defeat against them at the end of the previous year had triggered a downfall that lasted until the end of the season. We were desperate to beat them and, 8-0 up at half-time, I thought we could. But they came back strong and ended up winning the match. Once again, losing to them really deflated us. Catalan and Wakefield smelled blood and put big scores on us, and that's when Simon Moran announced that Tony Smith would be coming in.

Simon made his money running SJM, a hugely successful promotion company, but he's poured more than his wealth into Warrington. He's the perfect person to be involved in rugby league, because he's got the enthusiasm of a fan but he's got business acumen as well. Too many in rugby league have the intention to do well, but not the know-how.

Simon didn't get involved in the day-to-day running of the club, but he made the big calls, and after three games, and three losses, he felt he needed to make changes.

It was a bit awkward because Tony's arrival meant Jimmy had to step back down to being assistant. It was a kick in the balls for Jimmy, but he handled it well. When Tony arrived, he didn't change anything. Not straight away. For the first few days, he let Jimmy keep in charge of the side – he wanted to watch us, to see where we needed to improve – and we trained well all week before our game with Leeds. After three straight defeats, it was always going to be tough, but we were holding them 14-14 until they scored at the end.

Tony took charge the following week, but our results got worse, not better. Harlequins whacked us 60-8, and the mood in the changing room afterwards was the lowest I'd ever known. No one said a word for five minutes. It was the worst feeling of my career. I was totally demoralised. An awful, awful feeling.

Tony stood up and broke the silence.

'Remember this feeling,' he said. 'This is rock bottom. There's only one way for us to go, and it's going to need a lot of hard work.'

It was a soul-searching moment. On the bus home, Matt King told me he'd given some fans the V-sign as he walked off the pitch. He was frustrated with his own form, like we all were. But as a big-name recruit and a former Australia international, he copped it from the fans much more than the rest of us. He shouldn't have done it, and he knew that, but I could understand why he did. He was as angry about the whole situation as anyone. The losses, the booing. It's a horrible feeling for a player when things aren't going well, because often it's down to a lack of confidence, not effort, and that is hard to find.

Tony didn't work miracles. His big skill was his attention to detail with every individual. His logic was that just a small improvement with every player can have a huge effect on the team. We beat Hull KR and Crusaders, but our form still wasn't quite there. It was a gradual work in progress, and no one realised that more than Tony himself.

In hindsight, the Challenge Cup was our best shot of silverware that season. The beauty of the cup is you only need to win four matches to reach Wembley, and if you get lucky you can play lower-league teams in the first two of those.

We got lucky.

We beat York and Featherstone to book us a place in the quarter-finals, against Hull KR. It was a fantastic game in scorching heat, and my first experience of the golden-point over-time system. Lee Briers is the master of the drop-kick, but that day he missed with his first, then missed again. I was thinking, 'Bloody hell, Lee, just get it over.' When he finally nailed one to win us the game, 25-24, I couldn't speak. I was so drained, I had to be scraped off the pitch.

We were one game away from reaching Wembley. Our Super League form had picked up marginally under Tony, and although we still weren't firing on all cylinders we knew we had the talent in our side. On our day, we could compete with anyone. Our semi-final at Wigan took place at Widnes, and when I pulled up in the car park I thought, 'This is our day'.

I closed my eyes. I wanted a minute to myself.

'Don't think of the prize, think of the game. Focus. Focus.'

Suddenly, my self-meditation was interrupted by a bang on my window. It was a steward.

'You can't park here,' she said.

I wound down the window. 'Love, are you having a laugh?' I asked.

'No, you're not allowed to park here. You'll have to move your car.'

Another jobsworth in a bright yellow jacket was walking towards us.

Reluctantly, I started the car up, left the car park and drove around until I found somewhere to park. Nearly a mile away. I had to run back to the stadium, weaving my way through the Wigan and Warrington fans, who all cheered me as I went past.

By the time I got to the ground, I had a full-on sweat. I daren't look at the jobsworth steward as I crossed the car park towards the players' entrance, for fear I'd say something I'd regret. Besides, I had a job to do.

Tony did a great job on breaking down Wigan and finding their flaws. Rugby league is a ruthless sport. Every week you look at your opponents' weaknesses – anything that can be exploited. Halfbacks will be told which wingers are soft under the high-ball, centres know which opponents wedge in, props know who tires, who offloads, who steps. That's just the way it is. And we tweak it during a game, it's not all premeditated. Michael Monaghan is great at spotting players who are flagging. He'll look at their body language and say, 'he's rooted', and we'll blitz that person until they cave. We might even make it the goal on the set. It's one of those intricacies the fans probably don't notice – Eddie and Stevo might be saying, 'So-and-so has made X amount of tackles', but he might not have had a choice, because the team with the ball ran everyone at him. That's why, during training, I'm really strict on body language. I'm a real bitch about it, the lads say. If we're doing fitness sessions, players aren't allowed to put their hands on their heads or their hips, no matter how tired they are. If you do it in training and you get used to it, you'll do it in a game and show your opponents a chink in your armour. Against Wigan, our plan was to target Feka Paleaaesina. The big prop is a real handful, a powerful runner in attack. But we knew he'd tire easily so we ran at him all afternoon, made him tackle, made him work, and watched his energy just drain away. He looked like he had just come out of a tumble-dryer at one point.

They opened the scoring, but we ran in five on the bounce before half-time. Somehow, though, they got it back to one score and I was thinking, 'please no'. That's when panic and nerves can creep in. We stalled. Wigan got on a roll. Thankfully, Briersy kicked a drop-goal, and as soon as we went back two scores in front we knew the game was over. Wigan did, too. Chris Riley added a late try, and our fans were going mental. Many of them had never been to Wembley. Or at least, not to watch their club.

Later that night, I sent Paul Cullen a text message: 'You assembled the side and you played a massive part, you should be proud', which he was thankful for. He was really happy for all the lads. If there was any bitterness over his split from the club, he never showed it.

By a quirk in the fixtures, we had Wigan in Super League the week later, which we lost. Then, the following week, we lost at home to Wakefield. It was embarrassing. Tony came into the dressing room and said, 'What can I say?', and just walked out.

I stood up and gave few home truths. I told the players we'd been soft, and that if we played like that next week, in the Challenge Cup Final, we'd be humiliated in front of the country.

Later that night, our Kiwi prop Paul Rauhihi, who I got on with but who I wasn't particularly close with, sent me a text: 'Well done, it needed to be said'.

One positive from our back-to-back defeats had been the form of Tyrone McCarthy, who had debuted against Wigan. Tony said he couldn't be dropped, and left Rauhihi out instead (on the end-of-season trip, Rau had too much to drink, phoned Tony and gave him an earful. Fair play to Tony, he called him back, but Rau didn't pick up). I thought that was a really gutsy move by Tony. Tyrone's third game was a Challenge Cup Final, and it came at the expense of a player who had captained his country and played in an NRL Grand Final.

Our enthusiasm all week was top notch, which you'd expect. But our final session, the day before the game, was so sharp, and not a ball was dropped. I started sensing it would be our day. Everyone was focused on what we had to do. When our pre-match meal didn't turn up and we ending up eating sandwiches on the coach, like a school packed lunch, no one moaned. Not even Michael Monaghan.

Before kick-off, Tony sat us in a group and asked, 'What could possibly happen in this game for it to go wrong for us?'

Every time someone gave an answer – nerves, injuries,

penalties – Tony had a response. He got all the premeditated excuses out in the open and got rid of them. It was a great ploy, because not everyone in the team had played in big matches before. Only a few of us – myself, Micky Higham, Paul Johnson – had won the cup elsewhere.

We made a blistering start with a Richie Mathers try and were 18-6 up after 20 minutes. We exchanged tries in the next 40 minutes, but it had become an arm-wrestle, and I knew that if we hung on in there, Huddersfield wouldn't break us. They certainly wouldn't score three tries. At the final whistle everyone went nuts. Like winning the NRL Grand Final, or beating the Aussies, it's one of those great feelings I wish I could bottle up and share with my family and friends.

As we were celebrating on the pitch, I walked up to Lee Briers. 'Mate, will you lift the cup with me?' I asked him. I'd thought of the idea the night before. He'd been captain for so many years before I got the gig.

He was so made up, he nearly started crying. So I made the long walk up the steps, thinking of the fanny in the cup, with Lee right behind me. And when we lifted it up together, the Warrington fans went mental. I moved over and passed the cup along the line.

One of the tallest in the team, I had no problem reaching the corrugated metal ceiling above my head. I started belting it with my fist, others joined in, and we gave the loudest and proudest rendition of our winning song I'd ever heard.

> *Oh Warrington, Oh Warrington,*
> *Oh Warrington is wonderful,*
> *It's full of tits, fanny and the Wire,*
> *Oh Warrington is wonderful.*
> *The Wolves, the Wolves, the Wolves are on fire.*

I don't know who thought of it – they'd been singing it long before I got to the club. Briersy always leads it after every win.

He always gets his cock out, and bangs his boot on top of the drinks bottles. Singing it at Wembley was the first time I'd seen him doing it without being completely naked.

As our bus inched through traffic on the way to the hotel, I left my seat at the back and walked down to the front. I needed a minute to myself. I was drained and proud and happy. I checked my texts, replied to a few, then phoned my mum. Listening to her voice, I could tell she was proud as punch of me. My dad had been down to the final. He goes every year with his local pub, and didn't have a mobile. There was a free bar inside the hotel, but I just couldn't get drunk. I was on such a high from the game, the beers just wouldn't go down until the following day.

When Tony came in he outlawed drinking on the coach. We didn't do it often, but on trips back from Hull and London it wasn't unusual to have a few cans. So we thought there might be a problem.

Briersy said to him, 'Tony, are we having some beer on the bus?'

'You're damn right we are,' he said.

The wives and girlfriends went on a different coach, and I'd told Clare I'd be alright to drive home when we got back to Warrington. I'd said it at the time when the beers weren't going down.

Within an hour of the ride home, a photo of me topless, holding the cup, having beer poured into my mouth had been sent to one of the girls.

The first I knew about it was when Clare text, 'Why am I seeing you naked? X'

'It's the magic of the cup,' I replied.

She told me to enjoy myself, and I did. When we got to Warrington town hall, after an open-top bus ride from the HJ, I was asked to say a few words. I took the mic' and thanked the fans. I thought I got through it pretty well, too, until I saw a picture a few days later of Jon Clarke, Gaz Carvell and me together on the stage, and none of our pupils were pointing in the same direction!

CHAPTER TWENTY-SEVEN
TEZ

I'll never forget the words that changed my life forever.

'*Moz, I think Terry has hanged himself.*'

It didn't hit me at first, because it sounded so . . . wrong. As if the sentence meant something else and I'd misheard it.

What do you mean hanged himself?

My mind was overloaded. Overwhelmed.

What the hell is going on?

Then the severity of what Brian Carney had just told me began creeping into my mind.

Please, no. Not Tez.

I'd only spoken to him 24 hours earlier. I was in Magaluf with some of the Warrington boys on an end-of-season trip, when Tez called Paul Wood, our prop. He was sat alongside me in the hotel, as we were waiting to be collected and taken to the airport.

'Woody,' I heard him yell down the phone. 'Why's that knob-head Moz not answering his phone?'

I'd lost it during the drunken trip. Woody laughed, and passed me his phone.

'How you doin' you dickhead,' I said to him.

Tez and I always greeted each other with insults. It's just what we did.

We chatted for a few minutes, and he told me he was having a family day at his pub, the Ben Jonson, in Wigan later that day.

'Bring Clare and the kids round, it'll be good to see ya,' he said.

That was a Saturday. But by the time I got home, I just wanted to chill out and see the kids. I'd drunk so much over the last few days, the idea of tagging one on the end didn't really appeal to me. I'll go over in the week instead, I thought.

The following day, we went over to Yorkshire to see Clare's family. I was driving, and Clare was sat next to me when her phone rang. I saw from the screen it was Brian.

I'd played with Brian for Great Britain. As well as being a good mate, he was also Warrington's welfare officer. Clare answered.

'Brian's on the phone,' she said. 'He sounds serious.'

We were only a few minutes from Clare's parents' home, so she told him I'd ring him back soon.

Truth was, I didn't want to take the call with Clare next to me, because I thought he was ringing about a bullshit rumour that some of the Warrington lads had landed themselves in trouble in Magaluf. Coach Tony Smith had called Lee Briers about it as we left Manchester Airport – presumably he'd tried, and failed, to get through to me too, not knowing I'd lost my phone. The story wasn't true, but in an era of internet messageboards, bullshit stories about misbehaving players were more commonplace.

When we arrived, I went into a room on my own and returned the call.

'Brian, I know why you're ringing.'

'You've heard have you.'

'Yeah, and mate it's not true. Me and the lads were all good as gold . . .'

'Let me stop you there. Moz, I think Terry's hanged himself.'
'What?'

'Mate, I think Terry's hanged himself. I don't know the full story. I'll call you back when I know anything.'

I just sat in the room, alone. Numb. I couldn't believe it.

A couple of minutes later, Clare walked in to check I was

okay. I told her what Brian had said, and she came over and held me tight. Then a text came through on the phone.

It was Brian.

'Moz it's true. I'm sorry.'

And that's when it hit me. I started to cry. I couldn't stop. I'd lost my grandparents – two when I was a kid, and two when I was older – and, as upsetting as that was, it was almost expected, because they were old. I'd never known someone so young to die unexpectedly. Tez was in the prime of his life. He had everything to live for.

I couldn't get my head around the fact Terry Newton, my best friend, was dead. I needed some answers, so we left Clare's parents and drove straight over to Terry's pub. His father-in-law, Keith Holden, was there. I looked at him and asked if it was true. He gravely nodded his head. I went home, my head a mess. I just couldn't believe that the same mate I'd had a laugh with on the phone would end it all less than 24 hours later.

Why d'you do it Tez? Why didn't you ring me instead?

The next day, the Monday, was the Man of Steel dinner. I'd been shortlisted for the main award, but that's not why I went. I wanted to be around people who knew Terry as well as I did. Rugby league is a close-knit community, and Terry had friends at every club. I spoke to Barrie McDermott and Terry O'Connor, two of Tez's close mates, and they were as stunned and devastated as I was.

Over the next few days, I went to see Terry's wife Stacey. We cried every five minutes – she was absolutely devastated. We held each other for what seemed like a lifetime, both of us so numb. When I spoke to his parents, Tony and Val, my heart went out to them. They had been inundated with messages from across the country, and Australia. People telling them how much they loved Tez, how much he'd be missed. Tony asked would I carry his coffin, which was the strangest and saddest honour I've ever had.

The turnout for his funeral was incredible. Rugby league fans packed the church grounds, and as we took the first steps towards the church doors there was a roar of spontaneous applause. It was a surreal scene, plenty of sadness but plenty of love and pride, too. The mass itself was a blur to me. I remember thinking how sad it was for Tony, Val and Stacey. I remember thinking how brave they were. I remember thinking just how well Brian did holding it together, when he read a eulogy to a man he loved and respected as much as I did. And I remember leaving, heading off towards the airport for a flight Down Under for the Four Nations, still asking over and over again the question I'd been asking for the last few days. *Why?*

I love the way Brian described Terry in the foreword to his book: 'He's one-third pantomime villain, one-third loving father and friend, one-third cage-fighter, and one-third Del Boy . . . and that sums up Terry's mathematical skills for you.'

Fans knew he was a pantomime villain on the pitch. They had a pretty good idea he could handle himself, too! I discovered soon after meeting Tez that he had hands of stone. I invited him on a night out around Salford with a couple of my mates. He was only 17, maybe 18, so I felt I had to watch his back. But when my mate Carlo got into trouble with a group of bouncers, I discovered just how tough Tez was. He was dropping blokes – big, hard blokes – with his windmills. From then on, I always felt he had my back. And I can't tell you how glad I was about that.

Over the years at Leeds our friendship grew and grew. We used to hang out all the time. We were similar in many ways – he liked a laugh, he loved life, and he didn't take himself too seriously. Early in our Leeds days, the five lads from the North West – George Mann, from St Helens, Phil Hassan, Tez and Mike Forshaw from Wigan and myself – met each morning at Birch services, on the M62, and travelled over in one car. We had some great times on those journeys, just talking crap and acting like idiots. Forsh' was older than us and the ultimate professional, so Tez and I looked up to him and tried to emulate what he did.

Tried.

But I remember when Leeds presented the players with McDonald's complimentary cards, we made sure they were put to good use. All we had to do was show the cards at McDonald's and we could claim a free meal. It was limited to one per person per restaurant per day, which worked fine for us – we'd get one in Leeds for the drive home, pick up another at the services and Tez, the fat pig, even had a third in Wigan some days! All the while, Forsh would be sat in the passenger seat, eating his fruit out of a container, shaking his head in mock disbelief. This was at a time when my mum and dad had just moved out to live in my grandparents' house, after they had passed. I must have been the most malnourished first-team player in the competition!

My diet of endless Big Macs and Filet O' Fishes was complemented by plenty of ale from my frequent nights out with Tez. We weren't bad lads but we were mischievous, and occasionally we'd get ourselves in trouble.

One time, after a night out around Leeds, we called for a curry on the way home. Jamie Field, a team-mate at Leeds, was with us. Tez was always hilarious in an Indian, because he'd do the typical bloke thing of ordering the hottest curry he could! He'd goad the waiter into making it as hot as possible, and then when his order came he'd spend the next 10 minutes panting, moaning, gulping and sweating his way through every mouthful. That night, Jamie didn't even get a meal. Two curries, three beers – the bill came to about £18. I looked around and could only see two blokes in the place – the old guy serving us, and the cook we could see through the hatch in the kitchen. Jamie got a fiver out, and put it on the table. Tez looked at me, and I looked at him. We both had the same knowing smile on our face. Full of ale, we bolted from our chairs and raced for the door.

'You bastards,' Jamie yelled. He was right behind us. I don't know why we thought it'd be hilarious to do a runner – too much beer, I guess. We got 50 yards down the road, but we could hardly run for laughing so hard. We were in stitches. We stopped and looked behind us to see if anyone was chasing. No one did. Then, we saw a figure come out the door and point our way. Then another came out.

We started laughing again. We knew there was no way the old fella and the fat guy from the kitchen could catch us, drunk or not. Both of them looked our way, so we gave them a wave.

But then another figure came out the door. Then another, and another . . . I don't know where they all came from, but nine or 10 bodies poured out of the door! Then they did what I feared the most; they started running in our direction.

'Oh bollocks,' I said. 'Split up.'

They caught Jamie first. The poor sod ran down a dead-end – he had no chance. He got a £20 note out, he later told me. One of them took his money, and then chinned him, before walking away.

I ran up a hill, and darted into a small park. I burrowed through a bush, so I had a good view of the road. I was pretty confident that, with little street lighting, I couldn't be seen. I looked down at my feet and cursed to myself – I'd ruined my new Rockports.

A few minutes later, I saw the silhouette of a man walking up the road. I knew straight away it was Tez – he had a distinctive strut. No grace at all, just a clumsy, caveman stomp. I waited for him to get closer, and then whispered him over.

'Tez. Tez, it's Moz.'

He stopped, looking in my direction. 'Tez, over here. In the bush.'

He walked over. The fact that he was walking, so openly up

the street, gave me confidence that he wasn't being chased, so I climbed out from my hiding spot.

'You alright?'

'No I'm fuckin' not,' he said.

'What's up?'

He looked absolutely fine. But then he twisted his back towards me, revealing a definite outline of a footprint on the white shirt he'd bought that afternoon. 'They steamed me,' he said. 'And they took my gold chain, too.'

And all for £18. It was a lesson learned the hard way!

Another time, we'd finished training at Leeds, and were heading home along the M62. It was a gorgeous day.

'You fancy a pint?' I asked. It was a rhetorical question – Tez always fancied a pint. So we went into Manchester for one. Then one turned into two, two turned into a few, and the next thing I knew it was 2am when we stumbled into my place in Salford.

The following morning – or later that morning, technically – we drove over to Leeds for training. We were both nursing monster hangovers and, to make it worse, we had a field session scheduled. Worse still, it was a full-on fitness session, full of shuttle runs and sprints.

'You know what'll cure your hangover, don't you?' I said. 'A couple beers.'

'Shut up you dick'ead.'

'Tez it's proven – it's hair of the dog.'

He didn't believe me. By chance, a mate, Warren, had done a booze cruise to France a few days earlier, and a couple of crates were on my backseat. So I reached over, grabbed myself a bottle – one of those small, stubby green lagers – unscrewed the top with my teeth and started drinking. It tasted awful, but the fact I continued drinking it convinced Tez I was telling the truth. So he twisted around, grabbed a beer, and started drinking too. Then I reached over for a couple more, and we both had another.

Tez reached back for a third.

'Mate, I better bail – don't want to be over the limit. But you go ahead.'

So he had a third, then a fourth. Then when we reached the training ground, I parked at the furthest corner on the carpark, and we each polished off two more.

The carpark was next to the training pitch, with a building off to the left which housed the physio room and coaches office.

We got to the edge of the pitch, and most of the lads were already there, stretching, chatting, waiting for the session to begin.

'Right mate,' I said to Tez. 'Have a good 'un. My back's still not right, so I'm just having a deep massage today.'

I tried my best to keep a straight face but failed miserably. I was in hysterics.

He shot me an expression which said, 'You absolute wanker'. I had my massage – which had been arranged the day earlier – and, best of all, through the window I could see Tez training while he was leathered!

That was the only time I got him. Usually, he was the wind-up merchant. Tez may not have been the brightest academically, but he's one of the sharpest people I've ever met. Nothing got past him, and he never missed an opportunity for a laugh. Whether it was a prank phone call, or loading porn onto a coach's laptop, or pretending to be asleep when the conductor came along on the train, he never stopped. He was unrelenting.

Brian mentioned a Del Boy side to him – Tez was a real wheeler-dealer. He was like a magpie, always on the lookout for something he could pillage and sell. No matter what you wanted or needed, Tez could get it for you. And if he couldn't, he knew someone who could.

Terry was quite a shy person; his brash personality was a

mask, to some extent. He was never comfortable in big groups, but you could never tell. He was a walking one-liner, always on guard, always taking the piss. Once he got to know you, though, he would do anything for you. If ever anyone needed help, he'd be there. No fuss, no moans. He was a true friend. When I got banned for drink-driving, he thought nothing of driving to Salford to pick me up for training in Leeds, even though it added many miles and minutes onto his journey. That's the kind of bloke he was. Nothing was too much for him.

We stayed close mates even when I left for Australia. He was there for me when I was sent-off against the Kangaroos, and when he got banned for taking HGH I was there for him. I drove to his house, gave him a cuddle and told him he would get through it. At the time, I honestly thought he would.

I've thought a lot about Terry since he died. I've retraced conversations and events, asking myself if I could have done more to help him. Maybe if I'd gone over to his pub that day, I'd have stayed with him, and things would have been different. But maybe not. I don't know.

I knew he had issues. I knew his ban had affected him, despite the brave mask he wore. Clare was chatting to Stacey on Facebook, soon after his ban, and she asked would I keep an eye on him. She was worried about him. Tez's ban didn't just take his rugby league away from him, it took his discipline. But more than that, it took away the one thing which defined him. Even players who have finished on their own terms have struggled to cope with life after rugby league.

Shane Webcke wrote about it in his book. Kris Radlinski, too. They were depressed when they retired and really struggled to come out of their dark places. For Tez, such a proud man, that feeling must have been amplified by the fact his career didn't end on his terms, but because he was caught cheating.

Through the State of Mind scheme, which was set up after his death, I've got a greater understanding about depression and mental illness. Rugby league is probably the most macho team sport there is. We spend our careers pretending not to be hurt when we are, and players take that mentality into their lives.

Anyone who walked into training, moaning and kicking stones, would find very little sympathy.

Thankfully, through State of Mind, players are becoming more tolerant and aware of these kind of issues. Most of them now have a greater understanding. The scheme is trying to drum home the message that the harder man will open up about his problems, not bottle them up. More and more clubs are appointing welfare officers, and the issue of dealing with retirement is being taken more and more seriously.

Before I really understood depression, I struggled to understand how anyone could take their own life. But I learned that there's no rational thought when someone is depressed. Tez loved his kids as much as I love my own, he was a great father – he really was. He loved his girls to bits. I hope, when they get older, they understand that their dad died because he was ill. I'm just sorry that nothing could be done to prevent it, and that he's not here to see them grow up.

A few days after Terry's death, Clare took a phone call. It was one of her mum's neighbours, a psychic. She's a nice lady, but I must admit, I'd always been sceptical about psychics and their powers. She phoned Clare to ask whether one of my family members had died.

Clare told her about Terry.

'He wants Adrian to stop blaming himself,' she told her. 'He doesn't blame anyone.'

I know a cynic would say she'd seen the news and put two

and two together, but I was convinced. I still find myself in situations, from time to time, when I can't help think, 'Terry would have loved this'. Seeing old mates, nights out, occasions like that. It's horrible to think that his illness blinkered him from the fact that he was so loved, by so many. I miss him immensely and I think about him every day when I say my prayers.

CHAPTER TWENTY-EIGHT
CLARE

Referees have got a funny knack of playing big parts in my life. Steve Ganson sent me off for Great Britain, and another whistle-blower – Steve Presley – introduced me to my partner, Clare.

It was Boxing Day, 1999, and I was in the Skyrack in Leeds. It's a cracking pub. Leeds had played their traditional Boxing Day friendly, and I'd gone in with a few of the lads to celebrate. I saw Elvis – that was Steve's nickname, for obvious reasons – across the room with two girls. Clare, and one of her friends.

How the hell has he pulled them?

I fancied Clare immediately. Quite small, blonde, my age, gorgeous. Far too hot for Elvis. I went over to chat to them and, thankfully, discovered that Clare was just a family friend of Steve's. We started talking and we hit it off straight away (that's me and Clare, by the way, not me and Elvis, just to be clear). But she had a boyfriend at the time, so we couldn't do anything about it.

I saw her again a few months later, on a night out in Leeds, and I asked her out. We went out a couple of times. Her relationship was coming to an end, so we agreed not to rush in to anything.

Before I left to go to Australia, at the end of 2000, I went to watch Leeds's Boxing Day friendly at Headingley. I met a few of the lads afterwards.

'Come on Moz,' said Barrie McDermott. 'We're all going to the pub for a farewell drink.'

'I'm flattered.'

'It's not for you, it's for Damien McGrath.'

Damien was our assistant coach, who was leaving the club.

They were heading to the Skyrack, the same pub where I'd met Clare exactly 12 months earlier. I kept my fingers crossed that she would be in, that she'd be single, that maybe I'd even strike lucky. Two beers later, and I was stripped down to my underwear while a girl provocatively peeled her clothes off for me. But it wasn't Clare.

The place was packed with Leeds fans, when Barrie Mac walked over to me.

'Mate, I want you to know how much you'll be missed,' he said.

'Thanks mate, I'll . . .'

'So as a gesture, a few of the lads have thrown in for a going-away present.'

He then moved out of the way, and a Chinese stripper – complete with revealing clothing – was stood behind him. I looked for McGrath, who'd made a sharp exit. She sat me down and went through her act, with hundreds of fans in the pub cheering her on!

One advantage of being in the first team so young was that I was recognised when I went out around Leeds. I know that helped attract girls, but a down-side was I never felt I had a real girlfriend. Someone I could really open up with. I'd go out with a girl and have a laugh and the rest of it, but I always felt I had to keep up an act. I was never really myself with anyone.

I started going out with a Kiwi girl, Lynell. She even went over to Sydney with me when I moved there at the start of 2001. (When I told Graham Murray I was bringing a girl over with me, he said, 'Jeez Moz. That's like taking coal to Newcastle.')

Lynell was a nice girl, but we weren't right for one another, and it soon fizzled out. All the time, I kept in touch with Clare.

There was just something different about her. I emailed her from Australia, to see how she was doing, and to try and keep her interested in me. I was coming home at the end of the year, and the last thing I wanted was her hooked up with a new boyfriend by the time I got back.

And that's how it carried on for about two years. It was pretty tough trying to start a relationship with a girl when I lived in Sydney and she was in Wakefield (it said she was Australian on Wikipedia; not true). We caught up at the end of 2002, when I came home to play for Great Britain, and then when I returned for the World Club Challenge in February the following year. I invited her out to Australia to see me, and she flew out in August for three weeks. That's when we officially got together.

I really enjoyed showing her around the place, and introducing her to my mates. She got on with them great. Being with her was just so easy. She'd make me laugh without intending to. Like the time I took her to the beach. Clare hates sharks, and wouldn't go into the sea.

I told her there hadn't been a shark fatality in Coogie since the 1940s.

'There's a shark alarm, too,' I told her. 'If there's a shark in the water, the siren goes off.'

She was still sceptical.

'In all the time I've been here, I've honestly never heard it.'

It was the truth.

So she went into the water and – just my luck – within two minutes, the alarm started ringing! I couldn't believe it. She's not been in the water since. When I came home for the Ashes later that year, we spent a lot of time together. Throughout the whole red-card saga, the drink-drive charge, the community service, she was terrific. I knew then that we were the real deal. A few months later, she moved out to Australia and spent three years living with me in Coogee, before we came home when she fell pregnant with Leo.

I feel too old to call Clare my girlfriend. It sounds too casual. We've been together for years, we've lived together in two countries, we have two beautiful children together. We're practically married anyway.

So why haven't I popped the question? Timing.

When we came back from Australia we had a new house to furnish and settle into. Then we had Leo. Then soon after, Clare was pregnant with Maya. Plus, rugby league players usually get six weeks off at the end of the season, but I've never known when my season was going to end because of the play-offs and the international matches.

I realise that may sound like a lame excuse, but with mates on both sides of the world I want a time when I can really relax and have a good time. I don't want getting married to be something I squeeze in and stress about. Trust me, it would have been easier to get engaged and get married by now, because everyone expects us to. But I've been to too many weddings when close friends have not been able to drink because of an upcoming game, or on some occasions missed out completely, and I don't want that happening to me.

Luke Robinson had to call his wedding off when he got picked for England, because he'd planned it not expecting to get the call-up. His mates had all paid for their trip, and still went on his stag do to Vegas without him. If there's one downside to rugby league, this is it.

We will get married one day, probably when I've hung up the boots. I joke with Clare and say, 'If we go two months without you calling me a name we'll get married', to which she usually tells me where to go! I like the idea of marriage and I'm looking forward to being able to introduce Clare as my wife, because that's how it feels. I know she's the one for me. 2013 will be our testimonial – a decade together.

Clare's not only a great partner but a great mum. Our two kids – Leo and Maya – are amazing. Leo, our eldest, came early into my first season back in Super League in 2007 (they were both born in February. Just a coincidence that's nine months after my own birthday!).

We'd trained hard during the day, and in the evening I was feeling tired. I was ready to hit the sack when Clare said, 'Adrian I think I'm having this baby'. We went to hospital, and a rush of adrenaline kept me up all night, until she gave birth after dinnertime the next day. It was a bad delivery – a crash team was called for the late stages because Leo had turned into an awkward position, so it was a frantic final few minutes. The doctors and nurses were rushing around. They weren't panicked, but they moved with such pace and efficiency, I knew something was wrong. I felt so helpless, and poor Clare was going through a white knuckle ride of emotions. But when Leo came out and I heard his cry, I started crying myself.

'Is he okay?' I asked the midwife. She was friends with Paul Deacon's wife, and we got on great.

'He's absolutely fine,' she said, presenting me with my son.

I cradled him with Clare and that moment, as I looked at his little face, and his little fingers, I felt a feeling I'd never had before. Every man who has been through it will know exactly what I mean, and every man who hasn't been through it could never know. It was instant love and elation and pride, all rolled into one.

By chance, one of my best mates growing up, Neil Farrow, had become a dad for the first time a day earlier, to a little girl called Phoebe. We met when we were nine, before we even started fancying girls, and there we were, years later, both celebrating becoming dads together at the same time. We went straight to Eccles Rugby Club, I met my brothers and my mates and I didn't stop smiling all night. And it wasn't because everyone was buying me drinks.

Paul Cullen, the Warrington coach, gave me some time off when Leo was born and I loved spending time with him. I even didn't mind the feeds in the middle of the night – I felt I bonded with him, and it was really fulfilling.

I love being a dad. I love seeing the wonder in my kids' eyes when I show them something new. The honesty of their hugs, the way they love me for being me. I love having one of each, because they're so different. I love wrestling with Leo; he's my little man. And when I went to Australia for pre-season training in 2012, I told him he was in charge while I was away. He loved it. He's started to realise now that not all dads play rugby league for a living, that not all dads have people asking for pictures or autographs, which is cute. Clare wanted 'Leo' and, with it being my dad's name, I was made up. My dad was, too. My little girl, Maya, is my princess. I wouldn't dream of wrestling with her! It definitely feels different having a girl. She likes doing girly things, playing with dolls and baking cakes. I feel blessed to have them, and I'd love a big family. I've told Clare I'll have as many as she'll give me, but I get the easy part. I think she's content with two, and after what she went through – what every woman goes through – I completely understand. If we don't have any more, I'll still be more than happy with what we've got.

CHAPTER TWENTY-NINE
WINNING WOLVES

Clare stared at me quizzically and, for a second, she thought I was taking the piss.

'Are you really going?'

'Yeah,' I said. 'I've got a game to get ready for.'

She'd always been so supportive of me during my career. Every training camp or trip away I've been on, every wedding and Christening she's been to alone because I've had training or a match, she'd never once moaned or groaned.

Not until that cold Sunday morning in February 2010.

'But Adrian,' she said. 'I've just had a baby.'

She had been due on the day of our first home game of the season, against Harlequins. But we'd had reservations about going the full term because of the complications with Leo's birth, so had asked for Clare to be induced. It was better for her, as it stopped her worrying, and better for me because we could pick a convenient day. We arranged to go in on the Friday, two days before her due date, but that morning the hospital phoned to say they couldn't fit us in. Come the next day, they said. Instinctively, selfishly, my thoughts were on rugby – I would have to miss the final training session. We went in on the Saturday morning, the doctors did their thing, and after four hours nothing had happened.

'We'll come back in another four hours,' they said. I had no idea it would take so long. The afternoon rolled into the evening until, around 10pm, her contractions started.

Clare was brilliant. She went through the night, and at 6.30am on the Sunday morning she gave birth to my beautiful, precious princess Maya. We'd found out the sex of the baby, yet when she arrived I was taken aback how different it felt having a daughter, to having a son. It's impossible to explain – but it is definitely a different feeling. By the time we'd got from the labour ward to our own room, it was approaching mid-day. I hadn't slept in 36 hours and I wasn't tired. Not one bit. I was on a natural, emotional high that I'm sure only new dads can understand.

And that's when I told her I had to leave. It went down like a pork pie in a synagogue.

'What, you're leaving me? You're seriously leaving me?' she was shocked, to say the least. She knew no athlete would dream of taking two-weeks paternity leave after a baby, but at the same time she couldn't contemplate me leaving.

Her mum was on the way, so I knew she'd be okay. And she was. In fact, I phoned her straight after the game and she was already home, which I was a bit gutted about.

Outsiders looking in have said Tony Smith tackled a booze culture at the club. Warrington were renowned for it. Long before I got there, I'd heard stories of how the Warrington lads were animals on the beer.

From my own experience, I never saw any truth in that. To be honest, when I got there, I thought they were quite tame compared to the Roosters! Lee Briers is called Lee Beers, but only because it rhymes. I can only imagine they got the reputation because Warrington had underachieved for so long, and when a club underachieves fans look for reasons. And what better reason is there for under-performing than too much drinking? Sure, the boys might enjoy a few every now and again, but that's the same as at any other club.

But Tony knew he had a perception to tackle, if not a problem, so we had a meeting and agreed that drinking in Warrington was banned. Tony knew that with Twitter and internet message-boards, a ban was the best way of stopping any rumours. That's not to say lads can't go out if they've got a good reason. Drop Tony a text, and he's usually fine. He's a disciplinarian, but he's fair. After the World Cup, he didn't want any of the England lads staying in Australia for a holiday. But Clare and Leo had come over to watch me, and I was going to stay on for a few weeks with them. I told Tony after the tournament that I respected his wishes, and that I was prepared to fly back to England, then straight back to Oz, if he wanted me to. But he realised that was stupid, and let me stay.

The older I've got, the more I've realised how much impact the little parts can have on a team. Training habits, time keeping, good kit . . . they all contribute to the culture of a club. We earned a lot of praise for the way we blitzed teams in 2010. But we weren't the finished article. We still had a step to take, because – while we posted some big scores against lesser opposition – we struggled to beat the better sides. We lost all of our Super League matches against the previous year's Grand Finalists, Leeds and St Helens, and that year we had another top team to contend with – Wigan.

Michael Maguire had replaced Brian Noble as coach, and he did a great job in making them into a well-oiled, fit, slick machine. A few opposition coaches moaned about the wrestling tactics which Madge brought in. Actually, that's not true. It had crept in gradually over the previous seasons, but Madge's former club Melbourne had mastered the art.

Rewind to the start of my career at Leeds, and it was a case of 'tackle made, job done'. Now, the contact is only the start. After that, it's a wrestle to twist the ball-carrier onto his back. Trouble is, he will be using every muscle and sinuous strength to ensure he isn't twisted. It sounds technical, fine-line stuff, but if a player lands on his front, he can get up and play-the-ball quicker, the opposition defence isn't set in place and it helps his team get on a roll. It can have a huge bearing on a game, which is why players are put under pressure to 'win the ruck'. Credit to Wigan, they became really good at it, and for all the complaints from other quarters I never had a problem with it. Anything to get an advantage. My only problem was their use of tactics like the 'cannonballs' – when a player is being held up, defenceless, and an opponent dives in around the knees. Tommy Leuluai did it, Jeff Lima did it. I saw Sam Tomkins do it on Keiron Cunningham when he'd just come onto the scene. Keiron looked at him with an expression which said, 'What the hell d'you think you're doing?' Sam was only built like the man from the Peperami TV adverts back then, rangy and thin, so there was no harm done, but Lima's a unit – if he dives at knees, he could cause real damage.

Sam really flourished that year. He was great to watch – all lightning bursts of speed – but I'd seen other players burst onto the scene to a load of fanfare and fuss and bow out just as quickly. When he came into the England squad for a mid-season Test against France, I realised straight away he was the real deal. As talented as he was, he was also tough, hungry, and a great trainer – qualities which you don't see in the 'flash in the pans'.

Wigan and ourselves duelled for top spot all year, which they edged, and having finished the season in third we dropped out of the play-offs with a home defeat against Huddersfield.

But it was certainly not an unsuccessful season – we managed to defend our Challenge Cup trophy. We smashed three Super League clubs to get back to Wembley (Bradford, Huddersfield and Catalan) to set up a date against Leeds in the final. As an experience, it wasn't quite as memorable as '09 – simply because we knew what to expect. But as a result, it was a bigger achievement; no one could accuse us of having luck on our side.

Tony kept the routine the same as the previous year. We travelled down at the same time and stopped in the same hotel. I've still got a reminder of Wembley week, scorched onto my back – I burned myself on a wall light as I was climbing into an ice bath!

We had a terrible record against Leeds, but we really turned up with our A game that day. It's amazing how much energy you can draw from everyone being on their game. Leeds hammered us early on and we didn't fold – from that point on, we grew in confidence. Chris Hicks finished with a hat-trick, but Briersy rightly got the Lance Todd Trophy. Over the years I'd heard people question why he had never won more than one Test cap. Until I joined Warrington, I was sat on the fence – but once I played with him and realised how gifted he was, and just what an astute rugby brain he has, I couldn't help ask the same question. He's certainly got a maverick quality to crack a tight match open, something you need in a Test match. Like many of the top half-backs, he appeared to have so much time on the ball, and against Leeds that day he was so assured. I'd lifted the cup with him the previous year, and after the full-time whistle (we won 30-6) he walked up to me and said, 'Moz, lift it yourself this year.' I hadn't even thought of sharing the honour again, but at least he made sure I avoided a prickly situation!

The club owner, Simon Moran, organised a great function for us after the match, and he even brought a special guest along – Gary Barlow. The poor bloke was mobbed by the players' wives and girlfriends. Clare still has a picture of her with the Take That singer on her Facebook page. Tyrone McCarthy's mum is a huge rugby league fan, and she made me laugh when she said, 'You've just won the Challenge Cup – who's this Gary Barlow?'

But a few of the players seemed excited by his presence, too. I'm sure I saw Matt King go over for a picture. Afterwards, I had a beer with Gary at the bar and he seemed like a really nice fella.

That Challenge Cup win was a really significant moment. It really announced Warrington as one of the genuinely big sides. For years, the Big Four had been Wigan, St Helens, Leeds and Bradford. But Bradford's slide coincided with our rise, and the fact we'd lifted trophies in back-to-back years, beating Leeds in the final – and finished third in the Super League – really cemented us in that cluster of top sides. For me, it was the day we took the next step.

I was happy with my form throughout the year. I'd made the Dream Team in 2009 – the line-up adjudged the best by the press – and I knew I'd lifted a notch on that. Warrington were only too happy to offer me an extension until the end of 2012. 'You old bastard, how did you get that,' was the text from Jamie Peacock. He doesn't look it, but he's six months younger than me. For the last few years we've had a running battle about who will continue the longest.

My performances during the season earned me a place on the shortlist for the Man of Steel. I'd been nominated in '98, with Iestyn Harris and Henry Paul, and again in 2009 along with Brett Hodgson and James Graham. That year, two Wigan players – Pat Richards and Sam Tomkins – were also up for the prize and, given the voting system had been changed so the players across the league decided who won, it was hard to predict the outcome. Personally, I thought my team-mates Michael Monaghan and Ben Westwood had played better than me that year. For what it's worth, both Pat and Sam had killed it that year, but I thought their skipper, Sean O'Loughlin, was a more deserving candidate. When it came to announcing the main prize, Eddie Hemmings lapped it up.

He'd done it the previous year with Hodgo, the eventual winner, and myself.

'Your Man of Steel has won a Grand Final in the NRL.'

We both had.

'He has led his side out at Wembley this year . . .'

I think he'd been watching too much *X-Factor*. Like '09, I can't say I was upset to miss out. I had no moans – Pat'd had a great year.

Just to be shortlisted was an honour in itself.

CHAPTER THIRTY
OLD

Before I'd hit 27, I felt like an old player. One of those nostalgic old farts, reminiscing about the glory days, and I had to stop myself from saying things like, 'It wasn't like this when I was a lad.'

I still do it now, and I can't help it. I look at some of the young players and I feel detached from the way they live their lives. The way they need new trainers, the latest iPhone. The way they obsess over who killed who on *Call of Duty*. At their age, all I needed was a ball and a new pair of boots every six months. And when I say 'new', I meant new to me. I used to think I was cool wearing my brother's stuff! It just seems a different world now, and I'm still living in a different era. More and more, I feel like the odd one out.

Take tattoos, for example. There are 14 clubs in Super League, all with 25-men squads. That's 350 players. And I'd bet I'm one of only a handful who doesn't have a tattoo somewhere on his body. Unless I go through a midlife crisis, I don't plan any either. A few of the Roosters boys had tried to convince me to have one done after we'd won the Grand Final – they had 'Roosters '02' inked on their bodies. But then I thought, 'I didn't have "Leeds '99" after Wembley, so why should I?' My boring logic is that phases, fads and fashion change all the time, but tattoos can't.

Most of my mates are covered in them. Paul Wood and Lee Briers are. Every time I see Sam Tomkins I say, 'No more for you.' My mate Butler had one on his shoulder, a Bulldog with the words 'Great Britain Rugby League' underneath.

It looked really smart. Only, Britain was spelt 'Britian'. He got so much abuse, he had it covered up with a different design.

My mate's dad is a tattoo artist and, out of curiosity, I once asked him to give me one without ink, just to know what it felt like. It bloody hurt, too. The lads always call me a dinosaur, but I don't mind. When I ask them whether they regret having them done, a lot do.

It's the same with my black boots. Always worn them, always will. When I first played for Great Britain in '96, Terry O'Connor got hammered for wearing white boots. Now, everyone wears white, or purple, or orange, or other outrageous colours. I refuse – and I'm determined to finish my career with my black boots.

Most of the lads in Super League are on Twitter, but I still don't get it.

Sure, if you were a sports fan and you wanted to follow Man United or Wayne Rooney or BBC Sport, or something like that, I'd understand. But it's not like that. Clare's shown me some of the things the boys have written, and it's crap. Like a text message, only one which can be read by thousands.

'Let's go to Starbucks. Let's meet at Nando's . . .'

Why would anyone want to reveal that, and why the hell would anyone want to read it? I've known Twitter to cause frictions at other clubs, when players have revealed whether they've been dropped or called-up – information which can be used by opponents – and also when lads have written about girls, causing blow-ups. It amazes me that Jamie Peacock and Brett Hodgson, old blokes like me, are on it. I just don't understand why players would open themselves up to abuse from random fans. Anyone can be tough as nails behind a keyboard.

I have an iPhone, so in that sense I've moved with the times. But truth is, the library of songs on it is full of Bob Dylan! I'm a self-confessed Dylan fanatic, and I have been since my mate, John McFadden, stood up on an open-mic night in a Leeds pub and started playing, *Don't Think Twice It's Alright*.

He then played, *Carina Carina*, and I thought, 'I'm in the presence of a future music legend'. I had no idea they weren't his songs. When he told me afterwards, I went out and bought every Dylan CD I could get my hands on. And an acoustic guitar.

I have about 50 albums now. *Blood On The Tracks* is my favourite. I have the songs on shuffle, and listen to them when I'm driving. They're so laid-back, so lyrical, so incredible. I do my best to try and spread the Dylan gospel, too.

Terry Newton was into his dance music. Once, we were in my car, listening to Dylan.

'Will you turn this shite off,' he said. But I told him to listen to the words, and he actually started liking it. And when Martin Gleeson started learning the guitar, I leant him a few of my Dylan albums, and within a year he'd mastered a raft of them. I'm not the greatest guitarist, not by a long shot, but I can knock a tune out, and maybe if I had a better voice I'd have the confidence to play in public.

At the Roosters, I used to make the lads listen to WSFM101.7, which played classic rock. Sadly, most of the Warrington lads listen to dance music, including the conditioner Chris Baron, so I've learned to have selective hearing and blinker it out!

Of course, rugby league has gone through some major changes over the years. The only ice baths in the dressing rooms when I started my career were filled with beers. Even at the Roosters, until the day I left, there were always beers in the dressing room after a game.

Brad Fittler even smoked in the toilets as soon as a game had finished during my early years there, and he certainly wasn't alone.

During my Leeds career, I used to go out most nights. Leeds had student offers on somewhere every night, so it wasn't uncommon for us to go out Sunday, Monday, Tuesday, Wednesday and Thursday. I'd give it a rest on a Friday, if we were playing on a Saturday. I don't know if it was my genes, or my age, or the difference in standards between now and then, or maybe a combination of them all, but I got away with it.

Now, players may go two or three weeks without a few beers. The Wolves players are banned from drinking anywhere in Warrington. The professionalism has gone through the roof, and that's not a bad thing. But sometimes, I do feel a bit sorry for the young players coming into the team, that they don't get a chance to live and socialise like I did. They just couldn't get away with it now. Things are much more professional. Young players are ripped. They're athletes. They generally live their lives to good standards, in terms of beers and diet and going out.

But somewhere along the way, something was lost.

Respect.

I didn't like the segregation at Leeds when I was coming into the team, but it helped give the first-team players an aura that they were untouchable. As a young player, I held them up on a pedestal. And when I did get to train with them, I didn't say a word to them. I felt I had to prove myself first before I was accepted. These days, many young players don't have that. They're too cocky for my liking. I've no problem with confidence, but there's a fine line. And when I see academy lads saying, 'Moz this, Briersy that, Monners this . . .' – I don't like it. I would never have dreamed of acting like that with Ellery Hanley when I was a teenager.

Ellery, of course, was one of my idols. They say you should never meet your heroes because you'll only be disappointed, but he's a great bloke. And he still has the same aura about him as he did when I was a teenager.

Dylan's one hero of mine who I've never met. But I think I've met all the others. I was invited to a dinner in London to celebrate sport under Labour, and Sir Alex Ferguson was on the next table. As a lifelong United fan, I wanted to say 'hello'. I'd seen him a few months earlier in Puccini's, my all-time favourite restaurant which is near to where I live, but I didn't want to interrupt him.

At the function in London, I waited for a break after the meal, walked over and introduced myself. I told him I'm a rugby league player and I've always shouted for United, and we had a good chat. He was a really nice fella. I respect him enormously. And when I read in the newspaper, a few months later, that he'd told his players to forget Twitter and to go and read a book instead, I smiled to myself. It's nice to know I'm not the only dinosaur with black boots.

CHAPTER THIRTY-ONE
FIFTY CAPS

Midway through the 2011 season, I sat down with Tony Smith and told him I might be finished. I'd had an eye problem for the past few weeks, which wouldn't go away. Wouldn't improve.

'I think this could be the end,' I said to Tony.

It was hard getting the words out. Every player knows their day comes at some point and, at 34, I should have been ready for retiring from the game. But I wasn't.

'Let's hope it's not,' he said. He told me not to give up hope that I could find a cure to my injury. I'd been suffering with double vision ever since playing against St Helens in June, when I'd driven my head into the chest of my former Roosters team-mate Chris Flannery. Visits to three different eye specialists had all proved futile. They'd all said rest would solve the problem but, after eight weeks, it was showing no signs of improving. I was miserable. Hard to talk to. I must have been a nightmare to live with.

I could see perfectly looking straight ahead, so I was able to train and – with no knocks or niggles – I was flying, as fit as I'd been in years. But that only added to my frustrations of not playing.

Tony was great with me; but he didn't bullshit me either. As a player, that's all you want. Even if it's bad news. He told me he was going to keep a look out for props for the following season in case my eye didn't get any better. We'd been knocked out of the Challenge Cup by Wigan earlier in the season and so, with no trip to Wembley at the end of August, Tony suggested that I take the family away on holiday.

We flew to Lanzarote. Typically, I made the most of the all-inclusive restaurant, but I kept on top of my fitness with daily visits to the hotel gym, and the steep 60m hill outside was perfect for shuttle runs – even if it did draw the occasional raised eyebrow from the staff and guests.

One morning, a fella recognised me.

'You're Adrian Morley', he said, in a London droll. Rugby league may be largely confined to the north, but I've been recognised by enough southerners over the years to realise its appeal certainly isn't.

When we got back home, I took a call from our club doctor. He'd found someone who he thought might be able to help with my eye.

Two days later, I was sat upright on an examining table, waiting for the specialist's verdict. Over the next few seconds, he helped save my sanity. He explained that I'd had a squint from birth, which one eye had compensated for. The bang to my head had knocked my sight off line, and it could be corrected with a simple procedure.

'We'll get you in next Monday,' he said.

I was intrigued about the operation he had planned.

'We have to get behind the eye and put a tuck in the muscle,' he said.

Get behind the eye? I didn't ask whether he would need to take the eye out of its socket. I already knew the answer, but I wanted to blank the thought from my mind. Like all players, I'm hardened to injuries and operations, but there are some things which I'm still squeamish about.

Besides, there was only one question I really wanted to ask.

'When can I play again?'

'Play this week if you want,' he said. 'You can't make it any worse.'

I was thrilled. Eight weeks didn't really qualify as a long layoff, but it was the frustration of not knowing when I could play again – no goal to aim for – which had eaten me up.

As soon as I left his office, I phoned Tony with the news. He was as pleased as I was; he didn't need any convincing I could play against Wigan that weekend.

They'd won the Challenge Cup at Wembley a couple of days earlier, and our Super League game against them – at home – was effectively to decide who would win the League Leaders' Shield. They were one point ahead of us, with two rounds remaining.

I burned off what holiday excess I needed to during the week. The excitement and adrenaline carried me through the sessions and, when it came to the game, I felt great. I couldn't have scripted it better than to come back for such a big game against a team that had been on fire all season. I'm a fierce critic of my own performances, but that day I knew I'd played well. None of the Wigan forwards had dominated me – Jeff Lima got a bloodied nose for his efforts – and I caught my old mate Brett Finch with a couple of high shots, which he was quick to give me abuse for!

He never took anything personally, Finchy, even when his mates were trying to remove his head – most players are like that. The following year, I nearly caught Sean O'Loughlin with a head-butt. It was genuinely accidental – I swung my head back in the tackle but literally missed his face by a couple of millimetres. Had it connected, it would have smarted a bit. Lockers blanked me after the game, but I saw him a couple of days later and said, 'Are you still my mate?', which made him laugh. Even earlier in the 2011 season, we played Castleford in a match which was being shown on Sky television, and their Australian full-back Ryan McGoldrick stood on my hand as I got up to play the ball. When I was younger that would have been a green light for a punch, but I'd matured and mellowed since then. Or so I thought.

Almost instinctively, I lashed out and jabbed at him, catching his chin with a sweet one.

'McGoldrick's gone, run at him,' said Lee Briers to the forwards, and we did, as he was all over the place after I hit him. Thankfully, the Sky cameras and the RFL missed the punch and I got away with it, and credit to Terry Matterson and McGoldrick, too. They could have complained, but they didn't. They had a word with Tony, he rightly gave me a ticking off – giving away penalties while you're in possession of the ball is a big sin in his book – and it was all forgotten. No hard feelings.

But there are exceptions.

Like in that Wigan game, when Gareth Hock gouged the eyes of my team-mate Ben Harrison late in that match. I'm no angel, but gouging is a real shit-house tactic. He'd missed out on Wembley and in the heat of the moment he must have had a brain explosion, but it was out of line. And Gaz knows it, I'm sure.

We won the game 39-12, edging ahead of Wigan in the ladder and completing a full house of Super League doubles that year against our closest rivals, having also beaten Leeds and St Helens home and away. I had the operation two days later, and we duly secured the top spot by beating Hull FC the following week to get our hands on the league leaders' shield. Or the hubcap, as fans call it.

I'm a huge fan of the Grand Final concept but more should be made of finishing top of the regular season. If the team that comes top of the league can't be called champions, at least give them something else. I realise it must be a hard balance to strike to celebrate finishing top without taking away the gloss and ceremony of the Grand Final, and I don't know how the RFL could build that kudos. Prize money, maybe. But we were proud to finish top of the ladder and, personally, it was something I'd never done before. It was another honour ticked off.

We blitzed some of the poor teams that year, putting 60 past

Crusaders, Salford, Bradford, Harlequins and Wakefield. Around that time, the Manchester United legend Roy Keane was invited to speak to the boys, and he had us hanging on his every word. I had a half-hour chat with him and he was engaging company, so frank and funny.

Michael Monaghan was killing it at hooker for us. Everything was going his way, but he still found things to complain about. Thankfully, that year, he had someone who'd listen to his sour moans.

His younger brother, Joel, had joined the club that season. Canberra hadn't taken kindly to Joel putting his todger in a mate's dog's mouth during a Mad Monday drinking session – especially when the picture hit the Australian papers – and fired him. That's the problem with camera-phones; they don't just take pictures, they can be sent to anyone, anywhere. By the time you've woken up and sobered up, everyone can know about what you've done. In a country where league players' indiscretions are pounced on by the media, it's a dangerous combination. I'm not defending what Joel did, it was a bad joke, but I will say this – I've seen just as bad things over here in the past, before camera-phones, message-boards and Twitter.

All the boys realised what Joel had done was a drunken prank, nothing more. Of course, that didn't stop them ripping into Joel with dog barks when he arrived, and the fans did the same. When we played Leigh in a pre-season friendly, one supporter gave Joel a bag of dog-biscuits after the match! But he took it on the chin. It's a measure of the man that he has moved on.

As well as being a tabloid target, Joel was also a Kangaroos winger, and it showed. He scored 30 tries that year, including two in our opening play-off game against Huddersfield, when we slaughtered them 47-0. More than any other side, Huddersfield were the one who you turned up to play against wondering what sort of side would turn up. They could either be on fire or not. There seemed to be no in-between with them.

That win earned us the dubious advantage of the 'ClubCall',

allowing us to choose our semi-final opponents – either Wigan or Leeds. Some people weren't too keen on the idea, they thought the ClubCall was too gimmicky, but I could see its logic; sometimes the lesser-placed side are in better form than those above them. The entire squad had a meeting with Tony to talk about who we'd select. We had the mentality of 'We can beat anyone' and, as such, chose Leeds simply on the fact that they'd finished lower down the ladder. We also knew Wigan and Saints would knock seven shades of you-know-what out of each other in the other semi-final, softening them up for the final.

Leeds went toe-to-toe with us. It was a ferocious match, and it was a shame it came down to my old mate Steve Ganson's whistle. At 24-24, I was preparing for extra-time, when Ganson blew up. He penalised Richie Myler for offside. From 35m out, I'd have bet my mortgage on Kevin Sinfield kicking the penalty.

It was probably the right call, but it was a tough call. And it was certainly a hard way for our season to finish. Warrington had never been in a Grand Final and we all believed that it could be our year. In the dressing room, it was like there had been a death in the family. No one could believe it.

We were that confident in our ability we just didn't expect to lose. No one had even planned a Mad Monday. We met the following day and ended up going out on the lash around Blackpool, but it was a miserable mood. I was so disappointed. A few boys were leaving that year, including Matt King, one of my closest team-mates, who was heading back to Australia.

Kingy had worked in a bar and been a bin-man before his rugby league career took off; I'm convinced that helped make him the grounded, well-rounded person he is. I'm not saying most players don't live in the real world, because their salaries certainly aren't Premier League football standard, but some of the kids could do with a reality check now and again. Maybe go and do some hard graft on work experience, to make them realise how lucky they are to be paid to train every day with their mates and play on weekends.

I only did two years of an apprenticeship earlier in my career, but at least it gave me an appreciation of real life. Still does, to be honest. It helps me feel blessed for the career I've had.

When I thought I would have to hang up the boots, I began reflecting more and more on my career, and the way the game had changed. I watched a video of an old Leeds game and couldn't help laugh at some of the play – it was terrible! There were holes in the defence, the marker play was slack, tacklers bounced off to allow the play-the-ball – fundamentals that kids are taught now.

But back then, when I watched videos from 15 years earlier, we laughed then about the way those fellas played it. And it certainly makes me wonder how much the game will have evolved by the time I'm 50. I'm not saying it will be better, or the players will be better – I'm firmly of the opinion that great players would shine in any era – but I'm sure there will be a change to the tactics and the styles of play.

I've out-lived plenty of fads and phases – shoulder pads, nasal strips – and seen some big changes over the decade-and-a-half. Hookers have got smaller. Loose-forwards have got bigger. Shoulder charges – the technique which helped launch my career – have been demonised into virtual extinction. Corner posts were once out of bounds, now they're in. The number of allowed substitutions has ranged from two to unlimited, with several numbers in between. Off the field, I've seen some massive moves as well. I've seen expansion clubs come and go. Paris, Gateshead, south Wales, north Wales.

Rugby league is a great game and Super League is a great product, and I don't like being too critical. But as a player it's been extremely frustrating, tolerating the short-sightedness and lack of common sense of some of those who run the sport. Every time something goes wrong, it seems no one is accountable. I welcomed the move to licensing and the financial stability it would bring, but then what happened? Three clubs hit the wall.

They've retired the Great Britain name when everyone wanted to keep it – it might take years for the England name to have the same magic – and signed a cash-free sponsorship deal with Stobart which no one wanted.

The competitiveness of the Super League has improved, no doubt. When I started there was one team to beat; by the time I'd moved to the NRL there were three or four, and in 2012 there were five clubs who were genuine trophy contenders. It's great to see Catalan in that mix. I know Hull FC have big ambitions, cash to burn and a great set of fans – Widnes are the same – and I expect them to get better and better. But there is some way to go before it can match the week-to-week intensity of the NRL.

That doesn't mean Super League is bad; many leagues in most sports in the world have a handful of top sides, a few nearly-men and the bottom clubs. The Premier League, for one. In many ways, the NRL is quite unique in its competitiveness. But the NRL has to be the yardstick which Super League aims for, and that's why I liked Jamie Peacock's idea of a 20-team Super League split into two divisions – 10 in the top, 10 in the bottom with promotion and relegation between them. I think that would be a great competition. There would be enough quality in the top tier to make it strong, with tough games every week, and those in the second tier could get their house in order and aim for promotion.

But I don't expect it to be even discussed because – just like when I started – no one seems to care what the players think. I just wish, at times, the organisers would listen to the players' views more. Hopefully, with the formation of the 1eagu3 union, they will.

On my first Great Britain tour in 1996, our squad had one player with an Australian accent (Tulsen Tollett). By 2011, our national side had several more. Jack Reed and Gareth Widdop had emigrated Down Under as kids; Chris Heighington got in to our squad by virtue of his English mum. Then there was Rangi Chase, the New Zealand-born, Australian-schooled half-back who had played for the Exiles – the team of Super League's best overseas players – against England earlier in the season. He qualified under the residency rule of having spent three years in the country. His selection was met with some fierce criticism, and I could see why.

But do those fans expect England to use a harsher selection criteria than the Aussies and Kiwis? When we're trying to catch them? New Zealand have been fielding Australians for years, and vice-versa. Even in State of Origin, one of Queensland's best players – Greg Inglis – is from New South Wales. They do it all the time. I read that one in 10 of Team GB at the London Games wasn't born in Britain. I've learned to accept that it's part of modern sport; those are the rules.

There were two things no one questioned about Rangi Chase. He had the coolest name in the squad, and he was talented. And with the players we had in our team, I genuinely thought we had a good chance of winning the Four Nations. We'd reached the final in 2009 in Tony's last year as national coach – were the better team for an hour, too, before the Aussies' superior class came to the fore – and, with more players joining the squad from the NRL, we had real strength. Our pack was typically strong and we had some backs to rival the Aussies and Kiwis. Previously, our backline had lacked fire-power; that's not a criticism of the blokes who have filled those roles. They all tried their best. It wasn't their fault they weren't as good as Andrew Johns and Billy Slater. But in Ryan Hall, Tom Briscoe and Sam Tomkins, we had a back three as good as any, and they proved that in our Test against the Kangaroos at Wembley, when we were edged out 36-20. Hally, especially, was awesome.

The week earlier, we'd easily disposed of Wales; I'm not sure who my brother Chris was supporting! We played the Kiwis and, after beating them convincingly 28-6 to set up a final date against the Kangaroos, I went into the match as confident as I'd ever been. Certainly as confident as I was in 2004. It was my 50th cap for my country, either in the Great Britain or England guise; a special moment for me. I'd already surpassed the record for the longest Test career, in terms of years between my first and last internationals, and to become my country's most-capped player was overwhelming. A huge honour. Coach Steve McNamara asked me to present the lads with their jerseys – usually legends of sport are invited in to carry out the task – and I spoke to the lads about believing in one another. They then presented me with a special commemorative cap (in rugby league, players only get one cap, on their debut) and a framed picture listing all my games, and a montage of pictures.

By the time I took my seat, I had to hold back the tears.

Had it really been 15 years since I was sin-binned in New Zealand?

The Four Nations final was also a big game for another player, Darren Lockyer. I'd first come across him in '97 and he had been a constant thorn in our side ever since. Obscenely talented, he seemed to play the game at his own pace, and was always capable of conjuring up something special.

It was his final game before he hung up the boots, and it was no comfort whatsoever that he got the send-off his career deserved; we sold ourselves really short and they beat us 30-8. When it mattered the most, we just didn't turn up.

I congratulated Lockyer afterwards; a top bloke, it was a privilege to be involved in his final game, even if it was a defeat. Two weeks earlier, I'd made a beeline for him after our Test at Wembley and asked could I swap jerseys with him. I figured he'd want his last-ever shirt; his penultimate one would just have to do!

I'm not really into collecting shirts – I only have half-a-dozen or so – and when I have gone to the trouble of asking a player, I've been a forwards man. Craig Fitzgibbon, Ruben Wiki, Jamie Peacock, Gorden Tallis. I've got Matthew Ridge's too, though I feel bad about obtaining that! It was in 1996, after my second

Test for GB, and the Kiwi kit-man popped his head into our dressing room and asked could Ridge swap his Kiwi No.1 with the GB No.1 shirt. Ridge was a legend back then, a real gun full-back. I was 19-years-old, and I sensed an opportunity; I folded my number 16 shirt so you could only see the number 1, and handed it over!

I also swapped shirts with Keith Senior. Throughout my career, Keith was always one of the best and most durable players. He was also one of the tightest. He's the kind of bloke who won't enter a round with you in a pub if you're drinking lager, because he drinks bitter and it's 20p cheaper. So maybe I shouldn't have been surprised when, a couple years after we'd swapped shirts, a mate texted me to say I must be hard up if I was selling my shirt on eBay. I looked, and it was the one I'd given Keith! I followed the auction and he earned £300 from it.

The next time I saw him, I couldn't help tell him what I thought.

'You wanker,' I said.

'What?'

'Putting my shirt on eBay.'

He didn't reply, so I carried on my rant.

'You can have yours back, I don't want it.'

He pricked up then. 'Oh please Moz, that'd be great, then I could se . . .'

'Like hell,' I said. I was livid. 'I'd rather burn it in front of you.'

But I've still got Keith's. I calmed down, and there's no grudge there. I know he's just a tight Yorkshireman!

CHAPTER THIRTY-TWO
NEARING THE END

We were playing around in the surf, trying our best to blend in with the locals. My Warrington team-mates have more than their fair share of muscles, tattoos and scruffy haircuts, which would normally qualify them as typical beach bums. But, having flown from an English winter to an Australia summer just a few days earlier, their pale white skin gave them away for what they were – Brits abroad.

It was new territory for the team's English lads, but I was on familiar turf. Back in my old town, back in Coogee.

'Moz, I don't know why you ever left this place,' said Ben Harrison. We were in as deep as our shoulders, bobbing up and down. I scanned the landscape, looking for a reason to disagree, and not finding one.

'Yeah, it's pretty nice, eh?'

We were halfway through our pre-season camp for the 2012 season and, more specifically, at the end of the day's training. Our dip in the ocean was doubling as a recovery session. I turned to Ben and, as I did, I saw something on the horizon which triggered a memory. A promise.

'You see that?' I said to Ben, pointing out to the sea. 'It's Wedding Cake Island. Six years I lived here, and I always said I'd swim to it. I never did.'

'Yeah,' he said. 'You fancy it then?'

Compared to Aussies, who are brought up on the beach, most British players can't swim very well. Ben was an exception – he'd swum for his county, Cumbria, in his youth, and he could cut through the pool like he had an outboard engine on his back.

'Yeah, go on then,' I said.

So we waded in deeper and set off, without telling anyone our plan. We kept to an easy pace, chatting all the way.

After what seemed an eternity, I looked ahead. The island didn't appear to be getting any closer.

Maybe this wasn't such a clever idea.

I was already pretty tired from that morning's fitness session and my shoulders were beginning to ache. I kept my mouth shut and motored on. Finally, eventually, we got to within about 50 metres of the shore.

Then I heard a noise behind us. I craned my neck. A jet-ski was slowing towards us, a lifeguard on board.

'What are you doing, you idiots?' he asked.

'We're swimming to the island,' I said. 'Are we not allowed to?'

'Yeah you're allowed to,' he replied. 'But there've been 10 shark sightings here in the last week. Jump on.'

We grabbed onto the long surfboard dragging along on the back, Ben one side, me the other.

In fairness to the lifeguard, before turning around, he took us to the island and let us plant our feet on the rocks – at least we could say we'd achieved our goal – and then we hopped on his jet-ski and he brought us back in. As we neared Coogee's shore, the lifeguard cut the throttle. He turned his head towards me.

'I'm a Souths fan,' he said, twisting his arm around his body to shake my hand. 'I should have just left you to the sharks!'

News travelled fast. A few days later, a few miles away, we were training on Maroubra Beach. I knew one of the lifeguards from my time at the Roosters, and afterwards he showed me a picture on his computer.

It was a three-metre-long shark.

'We pulled this out last week,' he said.

If he intended to shake me up, it didn't. It just gave me and Ben something to brag about to the lads. As far as we were concerned it was Poms 1, Sharks 0.

Being back in Australia for a few weeks made me realise how much I loved the place. And how much I missed it. I caught up with my sister and my old mates from Coogee, Bryan Fletcher, Kris Smith, Ricky Stuart and Brad Fittler. Our hotel was in Coogee, my old town, and I was amazed at the welcome I got. Every time I walked down the street, it seemed someone would honk their car horn, or stop me for a chat, or an autograph, or a photo. It was like I'd gone back in time seven or eight years; the only difference was no one had camera phones back then. It was really touching.

While over there, the Roosters' Nick Politis – the guy I'd borrowed a car off all those years ago – and one of the club's directors, Harry Phipps, took me out to lunch. They floated the idea of me returning to the club when I retired from playing in England.

'That'd be great,' I said. 'But the way I'm feeling, I think I've got another year in me.'

They mentioned the possibility of me playing for them again. They didn't so much offer me a deal, as much as ask me to keep them informed if I fancied another crack at the NRL. In my mind, I wanted to go back. I caught up with Sam Burgess and Gareth Ellis, who had both killed it at Souths and Wests respectively, and I was envious.

I went to see Tony Smith, and asked could we have a chat. His brother Brian was coaching the Roosters, and the last thing I wanted was their interest to filter back to him. Plus, Tony and I have always been honest with each other. I told him about the conversation I'd just had.

'I'll take my Warrington hat off,' he said. 'If you want to move to Australia and start a new life for your family, I'll support you'.

I asked him the one question I'd not stopped asking myself – did he think I could still hack it in the NRL?

'You played for England last year and you weren't picked on your previous record,' he said.

Before we parted, he added one more thing.

'Just remember,' he said. 'If your form's good this season, I'd like to talk about another year.'

I spent most of the flight home weighing up the pros and cons in my mind, before talking it over with Clare. We decided that the kids had settled into school and all my family – and Clare's family – were at home. We were happy where we were. But I would like to return to Australia in the future. I suppose a lot will depend on whether I stay in the sport once I retire.

Midway through 2012, I started thinking more and more about retirement. I didn't want to hang up my boots. But after a bright start to the season, my form nosedived to a depth I'd never been before. We travelled to Perpignan to play Catalan in early April, and I had a shocker. I gave away penalties, I slipped off regulation tackles . . . it was one of the worst performances of my career.

A few days earlier I'd started experiencing pins and needles in my arm. I was already still playing with my eye problem – the previous year's operation had made it much better, but my peripheral vision on my left side was still washy – and now I had another injury, too. I didn't make a fuss, nor did I use the injury as an excuse.

I told the physio the pins and needles were getting worse, so I was sent for a scan and was told that the tubes carrying my nerves to my shoulder had been worn down. He was confident rest would be enough. And it was.

Within a couple of weeks I felt better. I couldn't wait to get out onto the pitch again. That old adage about a player being 'only as good as their last game' is true – and the memories of my awful display against Catalan were gnawing at me. That enthusiasm to play again was amplified by the fact that it was my testimonial year and around that time I went to a dinner in Manchester. I had decided to drive to the event, and I had our Chris, Dad and Clare in the car. I picked up my other brother, Ste, and the three blokes squeezed up on the back seat, which was a sight as they were wearing dinner suits.

I set off along Ste's street, chit-chatting, joking about my brothers looking like bouncers, when suddenly – SMASH!

A car ploughed straight into the side of us. I went into auto-pilot. I asked how everyone was, got out of the car, assessed the damage – both doors were caved in – and went over to the car that had bulleted straight into us. There were two lads inside, who were maybe 20 or 21. Instinctively, I asked if they were okay. They nodded. Then I gave them a barrage of abuse along the lines of, 'What the bloody hell were you playing at?'

I looked again at the road, double-checking the position of my car. I'd had the right of way. I was on the main road, and they'd failed to stop at the end of their street. Or, more precisely, they had stopped – but only after smashing into the side of my car.

I walked back to get my phone. I'd done the whole insurance thing before and knew the value of taking photographs for evidence and . . .

'Aje!'

It was Chris.

I turned to see my brother dart from the passenger seat. Ahead of him, I could see the two lads – they had done a runner. Without thinking, I took off after them. Within a few seconds, I was nearly level with Chris, about 40 or 50 metres behind the lads. Chris and I were both wearing tuxedos and smart black shoes, but we still got up to a decent pace. One of the lads quickly looked back. He knew we were making up ground, and fast. So they detoured to the left, leaping over a fence into a back garden.

Chris carried on down the road, to cut them off. I followed them over the fence. I leapt, cleared the top, and landed on the ground. And that's when I knew I was in trouble. My heel landed awkwardly on the ground. It wasn't a bolt of pain, more a twist, an instant ache that told me something wasn't right. I surrendered the chase, and the two lads got away.

The following day, I told Tony my heel wasn't right. I told him I'd stumbled while running. I left out the bit about me being dressed in a tuxedo.

A few weeks later, at the end of May, I was back to full fitness and I returned for the Magic game against Widnes, at Manchester City's ground. I felt refreshed, back to my best. The Wolves players are given a score by the coaching staff after each game – a culmination of tackles made, metres made, quality of runs, effectiveness, that kind of thing. I'm not big on statistics generally, but that score usually seems to reflect my own opinions of how I've played. That day, I scored 160, one of my highest. Against Catalan, my score had been 48.

My body felt good. My heel was fine and the pins and needles had all gone. Over the next couple of weeks, I felt I was inching close to my best as we lost at Hull KR and then won at home to Leeds.

Then the England coach, Steve McNamara, did something I never expected. He dropped me.

'It's a tough one Moz, but I can't fit you in,' he said, when he rang me up. 'You've had your injuries, and I don't think you've been playing well enough.'

I took it on the chin, thanked him for the call and wished him well. Part of me thought, 'I'm Adrian Morley, I never get left out' – my pride was hurt. I'd been a part of the international set-up every year since I broke through in 1996. But I soon realised Steve was right. I didn't deserve a call-up.

England's game against the Exiles was on a weekend with no club fixtures, so I went to the hospital for another operation on my eye. Within a couple of weeks, in late June 2012, I was ready to play again and – my pride still stung from being left out of the England team – I couldn't wait to get back on the pitch. I wanted to prove I belonged in the England team. But in my first game back, against Salford, I started doing stupid things I wouldn't normally do. I started looking to impress. I wasn't trying the Superman plays exactly, but I stopped focusing on my job. We got smashed 48-24 and, worse, I had another shocker. I was awful. Possibly not as bad as I'd been at Catalan weeks earlier but, I told myself, I had had injury problems then.

Not now.

My mood was really down. I chatted to Paul Wood, my fellow front-rower, and told him my confidence was low.

'I go through that three times a year Moz,' he said. 'You'll come around'.

I don't want to sound big-headed, but it was a new experience for me. All of a sudden, I started doubting myself.

Am I too old?

Am I past it?

I was 35 years old, and I'd already exceeded my own expectations by playing beyond 30. Back on tour in '99, Denis Betts told me to make the most of my career because, as he put it, 'You'll be finished at 26 with the way you play.' I could see what he meant. I was all about collision. If I'd carried on like that, I'd never have reached 34.

But my game had evolved – a little bit consciously, mostly from maturity – so while I didn't have the same edge, I felt I was effective in other ways. Tony once said to me, 'If you'd carried on with the hits, one in three would look awesome. But another might miss, and the other might get you suspended'.

He preferred to use me for my size and my engine, which – combined with my good genes – had no doubt prolonged my career. I hadn't been dropped since I was a teenager at Leeds, but I had played that badly against Salford, I thought I'd given Tony no option.

A few days before our next match, he pulled me to one side.

'I've had to make a few tough decisions,' he said. 'And the

toughest one was keeping you in the team. You probably don't deserve to play this week – but I've got faith in you.'

Those words were a shot in the arm. And Woody was right. Within a few weeks, I had come around. I started focusing on doing the basics right, on making sure I wasn't a liability to my team-mates, and I got better and better. I played well against Castleford and Bradford. I helped the team pull off back-to-back wins against two of our biggest rivals, St Helens and Wigan. Between those fixtures, I took up Tony's offer of a new one-year deal for the following season. I called up Harry Phipps, one of the Roosters directors, and told him. He was terrific and completely understood.

As I warmed down after a field session, Tony came up to me. It was a Tuesday, four days before our Challenge Cup Final date with Leeds.

'Moz, I'm not 100 per cent sure about my team yet,' he said.

I gulped.

Please tell me you're not dropping me?

'I'm thinking of benching you this week.'

I felt a cocktail of emotions that didn't normally go well together. Relief and disappointment, rolled into one.

'Do you still want me to lead the side out?' I asked.

'Of course. You're still our captain,' he said. 'Look, I know you're disappointed – but there are lads who haven't even made it into the 17. Things could have been worse.'

The fact we'd been to Wembley twice in the last three years did nothing to dilute the excitement of our return to the capital. I loved the build-up and the hype.

I went on Simon Mayo's drive-time show on Radio 2 with Leeds' Jamie Peacock. A dinosaur like me, JP was just as thrilled as I was about it.

'We've not made it yet Moz,' he said to me. 'We've only made it when we've been on Jeremy Vine.'

I mentioned JP's remark to the lads, and they had never heard of Jeremy Vine. Some had never heard of Radio 2. I was definitely getting old.

The day before the game, Tony Adams came in and presented us with our shirts. He spoke about his memories of the finals with Arsenal, the dozens of games he'd played at Wembley, his drink problem, his rehab – he made us think and laugh at the same time.

That night, shortly before I hit the sack, one of his former opponents – Ryan Giggs – sent me a text to wish me well. Similar messages came in from mates at home and Down Under.

Leeds had played in the previous two Challenge Cup Finals, and lost both. We'd reached Wembley in '09 and '10 and won both. We were expected to win and, in truth, we expected it ourselves.

The training all week was fluid. Everyone was switched on. And on the morning of the game, there was a sense of something special. There was an excitement and an edge to everyone – I was confident we were going to perform.

Inside the Wembley changing room, I got the call to go to the tunnel and do the coin toss. Only this time it wasn't the referee throwing the coin, but a special four-year-old boy –

Jack Johnson.

He was there with his mum and dad, Alex and Andy, as part of rugby league's backing of the Joining Jack charity. A wonderful couple, Andy and Alex had learned Jack is suffering from Duchenne muscular dystrophy a few months earlier, and thrown themselves into raising money for research into the condition. I'd holidayed with Andy 15 years earlier, when he played for Wigan, and liked him immediately. We'd lost touch in recent years, simply because we'd both got families and he'd got a 'proper' job, but I told him I'd support the charity in any way I could. A few weeks later, he asked me if I'd play for his team in the Dubai Sevens. I didn't hesitate to say yes.

What's special about Wembley is its size. Not just the stadium, but its history, its name, the images it evokes. Every event that takes place there is huge. Whether it's a Champions League Final or an NFL game or Live Aid, there's a magnitude to it. I got the same goose-bumps as I always did as we walked out.

By half-time we were 12-10 up. We'd outscored Leeds two tries to one in the first half and I felt we were in control. The rain eased off in the second half but Leeds didn't. Early on, Kylie Leuluai – he's harder than his name suggests – caught Brett Hodgson with a shoulder-charge, leaving our full-back flat out on the deck. The ball came loose, and Brett Delaney scooped it up to cross. Being on the pitch, waiting for a video referee's decision, is a lonely place. Like the fans, we've no inkling as to which was a 50-50 call may go – viewers at home at least get the insight of commentary; we're left to guess, and second-guess, what the official may be looking at. This time, the try was ruled out by the video ref.

It could have gone either way, and it was cited afterwards as a turning point. But honestly, even if Leeds had scored, I'd still have been confident of finishing the job. One 'no try' decision alone doesn't halt a team's momentum, certainly not a team of Leeds' quality. We smothered Rob Burrow each time he got the ball. Limiting his involvement had been high up on our to-do list. We didn't have as much joy containing JP – he was outstanding all match, and would surely have been a contender for the Lance Todd Trophy for Man of the Match had Hodgo not recovered from Leuluai's tackle to score a try and create two more, to steer us home to victory.

Hodgo doesn't look like a rugby player. In a dressing room of Buzz Lightyears, he looks like Mr Burns from The Simpsons. But what he lacks in physical presence he more than compensates for with his tenacity, composure and intelligence.

The beer started flowing the minute we walked into the dressing room. It was the same feeling I'd experienced after our previous cup wins – emotionally overloaded, physically drained but a bit hyper. Juvenile, carefree.

And when our conditioner, Chris Baron, left the room and walked back in a moment later, I gathered that everyone must have felt the same. He was wearing leather pants, with a big hole in the back, allowing his arse to prod out.

Next to him was an Indian. And a policeman. And a cowboy. Then the music started.

'Yo-ung man . . .'

Their outstretched arms started waving across the room in harmony. Either they'd practiced their routine or, worryingly, Chris and the staff all knew the YMCA dance routine very well. Either way, it was hysterical.

After the Challenge Cup win our Super League season was written off. Not by us, but by the critics, who said it would be impossible to do the double. I got tired of hearing that no team had done it since St Helens in 2006.

But when we lost our first play-off match 28-6 at home to Saints, I think even some of our own fans had doubts we could reach the Grand Final. We recovered to beat Hull FC, and in the semi – against Saints again – Tony told us we didn't want to sell ourselves short.

We didn't.

We won and, what's more, the win set-up a Grand Final date against Leeds – a rematch of our Wembley Final – who'd edged a nail-biter with Wigan the day before.

It was my third Grand Final at Old Trafford. Incredibly, it was Warrington's first. It had a different feel to the build-up of the Challenge Cup Final, but the fact our players had been exposed to that level of interest before certainly helped.

I had a chat with JP at the media conference early in the week. He told me he'd put his name down for the Liverpool marathon later that month, but he couldn't make it. 'I'll do it for you,' I said. I'd always fancied giving it a try. 'Unless I'm picked for England.'

But the following day, Steve McNamara phoned to tell me I was back in the national team. I'd never felt such elation at a call-up since my first one, in '96.

Credit where it's due, they do the Grand Final right. The build-up, the pre-match, the 70,000 fans . . . it was an awesome atmosphere. Richie Myler had already scored when I got on the pitch, but Leeds had responded and by half-time the scores were locked at 14-14.

None of us were worried. We felt confident in our ability to score tries and defend them, and when Ryan Atkins went over early in the second half we had the perfect chance to put the game to bed. But our ball control was poor and we let them off the hook, which we couldn't afford to do – particularly with Kevin Sinfield pulling the strings for them. I'd played alongside him when he broke into the team at Leeds as a teenager. Sinny was always a special talent, one of those blokes who can do everything well – someone you'd almost hate if he wasn't such a bloody nice bloke!

One attribute of his which often gets overlooked is his toughness, but he proved it in the Grand Final when he played on after being knocked out by Mick Monaghan's tough nut.

Talk tough nuts, of course, and it's hard not to think of Paul Wood, or, more precisely, Woody's nuts! A knee in the balls is not that common in league; if it was, players would wear protective cups. But Woody took a carry early in the second half and caught one right where it hurts. I didn't know anything about it until about 20 minutes later, when he was sat alongside me on the bench.

'Something's not right,' he said. 'It's still hurting.'

The doc had a look at him and sent him to the hospital. By the time he arrived it was the size of a tennis ball, he said. That night, he had his ruptured testicle removed. Woody got some mileage out of his injury – when we met for a post-match review a few days later, we held a minute's silence for his fallen ball!

Sadly, despite Woody working his balls off, it wasn't enough for us. After Atkins's try we never scored again and we lost 26-18. I was gutted. Warrington hadn't won a title in 57 years, and it would have been nice to have been a part of the side which ended that painfully long run, just as we'd done with the Challenge Cup three years earlier.

Inevitably, people will discuss why we lost. They'll ask whether we choked. We didn't. Between two well-matched sides, it's all about executing well for 80 minutes, and Leeds did that better than us.

The pain of losing had subsided a little bit by the time we got back to our hotel in Warrington. I told the boys I was proud of their efforts, and I meant it. Despite the loss we'd had a good year. We did our best to drink the bar dry that night and carried on the next day. I set myself up for a wild old time. But by 8.30pm on the Sunday night, I was back home and tucked up in bed. I am really getting old!

EPILOGUE

Writing my story has given me a chance to reflect on my life.

I'm probably a different player to the one I was earlier in my career. I'm definitely a different person.

When I talk about some of the things I did when I was young, it feels like I'm reading about someone else. By page 65 of this book I've been CS gassed three times. Three times! That's just about as far removed from my life now as it could get. My life now is at home. Taking Leo swimming, playing with Maya, tucking them up and settling down in front of the TV with Clare.

But when you live day-to-day you don't notice yourself growing up, you don't notice how you mature. Recalling my mistakes and achievements has made me feel even more grateful for the life I've had. I've won at Wembley, played in Australia, travelled the world. I've represented my country more than 50 times, won silverware at every club I've been at and made friend-ships that will last a lifetime.

As I finish this chapter now, I've just had a bad day at work – I lost a Grand Final. But I've still played at Old Trafford – the home of my boyhood heroes – in front of 70,000 fans and, tomorrow, I board a flight to South Africa for an England training camp. Business class all the way.

I know I've got it good. I know there'll come a time when I head off to work at 8am and I won't be finished in time to pick the kids up from school. A time when no one will want my autograph or picture. A time when I will have to pay to keep fit, instead of being paid for it.

I know all that.

But I also know that's not what I'll miss the most.

What I'll really miss is that feeling, every week, of taking to the pitch with my mates. Rugby league is a brutal sport, played against opponents who are trying their best to hurt you. And when you've got 12 mates alongside you, all of them hurting, all of them working hard, watching each other's back – it's an incredible feeling which I've never grown tired of. It's probably why I've carried on playing longer than I ever intended and, because of that, I've had experiences and success I could never have dreamed of. Not as a kid, not when I was earning £1.52 an hour as a trainee electrician, and not even when I broke into the Leeds team.

Truly, I am so grateful for the career and life I've had.